Copeau/Decroux, Irving/Craig

In this series of essays, Thomas Leabhart presents a thorough overview and analysis of Etienne Decroux's artistic genealogy.

After four years' apprenticeship with Decroux, Thomas Leabhart began to research and discover how forebears and contemporaries might have influenced Decroux's project. Decades of digging revealed striking correspondences that often led to adjacent fields—art history, philosophy and anthropology—forays wherein Leabhart's appreciation of Decroux and his "kinsfolk," who themselves transgressed traditional frontiers, increased. The following essays, composed over a 30-year period, find a common source in a darkened Prague cinema where people gasped at a wooden doll's sudden reversal of fortune. These essays: investigate the source of that astonishment; continue Leabhart's examination of Decroux's "family tree"; consider how Copeau's and Decroux's keen observation of animal movement influenced their actor training; record the challenging and paradoxical improvisations *chez* Decroux; and recall Decroux's debt to sculpture, poster art, sport and masks.

These essays will be of great interest to students, scholars and practitioners in theatre and performance studies.

Thomas Leabhart, Professor of Theatre at Pomona College, California, worked with Etienne Decroux from 1968–72. He authored *Modern and Post-Modern Mime* (Macmillan, 1989), *Etienne Decroux* (Routledge, 2019) and co-edited (with Franc Chamberlain) *The Decroux Sourcebook* (Routledge, 2008). Leabhart edits *Mime Journal*, and for a decade participated as Artistic Staff at Eugenio Barba's ISTA meetings.

Routledge Advances in Theatre & Performance Studies

This series is our home for cutting-edge, upper-level scholarly studies and edited collections. Considering theatre and performance alongside topics such as religion, politics, gender, race, ecology and the avant-garde, titles are characterized by dynamic interventions into established subjects and innovative studies on emerging topics.

Finland's National Theatre 1974–91
The Two Decades of generational Contests, Cultural Upheavals, and International Cold War Politics
Pirkko Koski

Reading Religion and Spirituality in Jamaican Reggae Dancehall Dance
Spirit Bodies Moving
'H' Patten

Hauntological Dramaturgy
Affects, Archives, Ethics
Glenn D'Cruz

Borderlands Children's Theatre
Historical Developments and Emergence of Mexican American/ Chicana/o Youth Theatre
Cecilia J. Aragon

ASHÉ
Ritual Poetics in African Diasporic
Paul Cater Harrison, Michael D. Harris, Pellom McDaniels

Dancehall In/Securities
Perspectives on Caribbean Expressive Life
Patricia Noxolo, 'H' Patten, and Sonjah Stanley Niaah

For more information about this series, please visit: https://www.routledge.com/Routledge-Advances-in-Theatre–Performance-Studies/book-series/RATPS

Copeau/Decroux, Irving/Craig

A Search for 20th Century Mime, Mask & Marionette

Thomas Leabhart

Routledge
Taylor & Francis Group
LONDON AND NEW YORK

First published 2022
by Routledge
2 Park Square, Milton Park, Abingdon, Oxon OX14 4RN

and by Routledge
605 Third Avenue, New York, NY 10158

Routledge is an imprint of the Taylor & Francis Group, an informa business

© 2022 Thomas Leabhart

The right of Thomas Leabhart to be identified as author of this work has been asserted in accordance with sections 77 and 78 of the Copyright, Designs and Patents Act 1988.

All rights reserved. No part of this book may be reprinted or reproduced or utilised in any form or by any electronic, mechanical, or other means, now known or hereafter invented, including photocopying and recording, or in any information storage or retrieval system, without permission in writing from the publishers.

Trademark notice: Product or corporate names may be trademarks or registered trademarks, and are used only for identification and explanation without intent to infringe.

British Library Cataloguing-in-Publication Data
A catalogue record for this book is available from the British Library

Library of Congress Cataloging-in-Publication Data
A catalog record has been requested for this book

ISBN: 978-1-032-07181-7 (hbk)
ISBN: 978-1-032-07191-6 (pbk)
ISBN: 978-1-003-20585-2 (ebk)

DOI: 10.4324/9781003205852

Typeset in Bembo
by KnowledgeWorks Global Ltd.

Contents

Acknowledgements		vi
Preface		vii
1	Introduction: Lessons from Prague	1
2	Blowing up the palace and hanging up on the Opéra: Dramaturgy in and of the body	7
3	Monkey business and Robin revelations: Animal observation in actor training	17
4	Friday night pearls of wisdom	29
5	E.G. Craig's Übermarionette and E. Decroux's "actor made of wood"	40
6	Triptych: Three aspects/one figure	52
7	Everything weighs: Wrestling with an invisible angel	67
8	From Copeau to Decroux: the mask in actor training: Sculpting new bodies for ancient heads	80
9	The face in corporeal mime: From plaster death mask to living actor's visage	99
10	L'Homme de sport: Sport and statuary in Etienne Decroux's corporeal mime	124
	Index	170

Acknowledgements

Over the years the following colleagues have read these essays and generously shared their suggestions: Eugenio Barba, Professor Frank Camilleri, Professor Franc Chamberlain, Patrick Le Boeuf, Mark Piper, the late Professor Leonard Pronko and Professor Nancy Ruyter. We are equally grateful to Eric Culhane and Megan Marshall who obtained permissions, provided invaluable technical assistance for the illustrations and created the index. The Pomona College Faculty Research fund generously helped with expenses along the way. Our gratitude extends to Harshita Donderia and her team who saw us through multiple page proofs with patience and grace.

First, last, and always, I owe an inestimable debt of gratitude to my wife Sally, to whom these pages are lovingly dedicated, for unflagging support, untold hours of reading, copious editing and substantial additions. Her role in every chapter of this book often crosses into co-authorship.

Preface

After four years' apprenticeship with Etienne Decroux, I began to trace his artistic genealogy to discover how forebears and contemporaries might have influenced his project. Decades of digging revealed correspondences in adjacent fields—art history, philosophy and anthropology, to name a few. In these forays, my appreciation of Decroux and his "kinsfolk" increased. Among those theatre practitioners who themselves transgressed traditional frontiers we find Suzanne Bing, Jacques Copeau, Edward Gordon Craig and Henry Irving.

I also learned more about the man himself. A high school dropout at fifteen, Decroux worked for ten years as a manual laborer, after which his desire to enter politics prompted him to study speech and voice to erase his *accent du faubourg* [working class accent].

As his political engagement intensified, he hid in his home, for a time, a Russian anarchist whom French and Russian authorities were actively pursuing. In the 1930s and 40s, Decroux sublimated his political inclinations into the creation of corporeal mime while he earned his living from commercial theatre and cinema.

In my mind's eye, I see Decroux in 1968 performing with equal ease as scholar and artist: he would leave his book-lined ground floor office and the massive desk over which he devoted part of the day writing about etymology, diction, and his theatrical project. Within seconds, he had effortlessly cut his habitual path across the miniscule kitchen to dash down the steep cellar stairs and plunge into his rehearsal or class. In fact, he was always, simultaneously, both scholar and artist. At his desk, his considerations regarding disappearing sounds in the French language (the "grand *a*," for example) were not the cool observations of a linguist taking inventory. Instead, he expressed his outrage at the failure of French speakers (including public speakers who he deemed should know better) to preserve each performable sound, like so many notes on the piano. Without this advocacy for phonetic "endangered species" the full aesthetic expression of the French language became irretrievably impoverished. Likewise, in the classroom where he dazzled us with his performance skill, he would also share his related observations as a philosopher, an historian, a sociologist, etc.

viii   *Preface*

This vivid image of Theory and Practice dancing together, first one leading and then the other, has guided me for decades. I confirm that the often-bruised toes of Theory and awkwardly tangled limbs of Practice sometimes give way to sublime connectivity. Eric Bentley, another theoretician/practitioner, cites Montague: "If you know a thing theoretically but don't know it practically, then you don't really know its whole theory; and if you know it practically but don't know it theoretically, then you don't really know its whole practice" (cited in Bentley vi).

In these two strands, theory and practice, Decroux foresaw a new theatre evolved in the rehearsal studio through movement improvisation. There, bits were pruned, expanded, altered, timing examined, phrasing and breath honed, until a piece was eventually set into its performable configuration, guided by his particular corporeal technique that includes innumerable restrictions but also limitless possibilities. This theatre piece did not evolve as the interpretation or presentation of an already written text. It had a director and actors, but without a (pre-existing) author per se.

While some may deem these musings (part reminiscence, part research based) unscientific, others—fellow actors, devisers and collective creators, theatre students, corporeal mimes and researchers in laboratory theatres—might find therein reassurance that, despite overwhelming evidence to the contrary, they are not alone. Instead, as adherents of a lost tribe, they share a little-known history that, among other defining characteristics, esteems somatic awareness—embodied knowledge—over written text. These fellow travelers, temporarily engulfed in a sea of "faster is better," and carried into deep waters on the prevalent undercurrents of expediency, gratefully recognize one another despite the tumult. Exchanging timid smiles across the surging waves and vanishing years, they hope to meet soon on some as-yet-uncharted *terra firma*.

One might map this new world by imagining two intersecting realms: one represents the terrain of the live actor becoming more deliberately "wooden," more densely immobile and focused in his search (like Richard Burton in the film *The Spy Who Came in from the Cold* or Alec Guinness in *Smiley's People*); the other represents the world of the wooden statue, tending toward organicity (for example, the peregrinations of a wooden effigy freed from a cathedral niche for an annual procession and borne aloft by village penitents whose swaying forward steps lend to the statue a human quality). Further through this imaginary topography, on the winding road where the lifelike but wooden Bunraku puppet meets the "wooden" yet living noh actor, we find many of our friends, neighbors, kinsfolk and dancing partners, among them Craig's Übermarionette and Decroux's corporeal mime. They and others felt the need to "puppetize" the body, to remove it to some degree from its natural fleshly aspect and coax it toward a less transitory and more "artistic" stuff. The actor, in finding a more stylized and highly visible way of moving, becomes simultaneously a puppet and puppeteer, sculptor and statue.

Preface ix

Little by little the working title of this book, *The Wooden Actor and Other Paradoxes of Theatrical Organicity,* found its referent: from one extreme, the wooden actor seeks life-like organicity; from the other, the living actor desires form, structure and permanence. One may read these essays (literally, these "attempts") in any order, as they inevitably resemble the actors and puppets that evoked them: fluid constructs under continual reconsideration—leaning, lunging, turning, jumping—as they give in to, or resist, the pull of gravity and the gentle or more insistent cues of their dancing partners.

Even though this volume unites essays from a 30-year period, some of which have appeared in earlier forms, the central argument remains the same: the creation myth of corporeal mime maintains its central tenet. Decroux considered his work a reaction against nineteenth-century pantomime's anecdotal play of face and hands, and the supposed lack of mobility and expressivity at its core, the pantomime's trunk. Decroux's project, with its emphasis on abstraction, the inexpressive face and articulations of the trunk, set up a "straw dog," based on one version (probably the only one Decroux had seen) of a complex set of performance possibilities collected loosely under the umbrella of nineteenth-century pantomime. Two publications, Ariane Martinez's *La pantomime, théâtre en mineur* (2008) and Pinok and Matho's *Une saga du mime* (2016) provide a nuanced view of the variety and complexity of these nineteenth-century practices.

With the perfect irony that real life alone provides, Decroux and Barrault created, on one hand, their version of nineteenth-century pantomime for the film *Les enfants du paradis*, unintentionally implanting it into the consciousness of several generations of theatre goers. On the other hand (simultaneously and off the movie set), Decroux and Barrault elaborated a version of modern corporeal mime in sharp opposition to that pantomime they helped recreate and popularize.

In the early 1950s, Decroux explained to Eric Bentley that

the poet's lines follow one another inexorably like the trucks of a freight train. The poor actor can't squeeze himself in between them. You understand, don't you, how in the end, the slave revolts? The cry of the actor against literature is the cry of the native against imperialism, of the Indian against England.

(Bentley 189)

Certainly, the actor's condition cannot even remotely compare to the horrors of slavery and Imperialism, yet we can't dismiss this statement as mere hyperbole as it gives us a glimpse into Decroux's impassioned dedication to his project as much more than entertainment. For him, it became a melding of thought and action, politics, and art. Decroux revolted against the supremacy of the playwright and the towering omnipotence of The Word overshadowing the intuitive and non-verbal. This in no way implies that Decroux x *Preface*

lacked reverence for speech or text. A lover of words, spoken and written, he proposed (as one part of his multifaceted remedy for the ills of the theatre he disdained) banishing the voice from dramatic pieces for a period of 20 years. Its gradual reintroduction could occur over the subsequent decade—first as inarticulate sounds, later as words, but chosen by the actor (Decroux 26–7). This, to undertake as elaborate a study of the process as he had devoted to the body. It was, thus, merely the *subjugation* of the actor's creative process to the pre-existing text, this particular hierarchical relationship, against which he railed, for that subservience of the actor-creator to the written play would extinguish the creative process that constituted for Decroux the new theatre's *sine qua non*.

As recent scholarship has shown, Suzanne Bing's and Jacques Copeau's teaching had no small influence on the development of what we now call verbatim, collective creation, physical theatre, and actor-centered theatre. In these arenas, the "post-colonial" actor, no longer a "slave" to the text, becomes instead a creative center of the theatrical event.

Decades ago, when I first taught collective creation and devising, now standard course offerings at Pomona College but then an innovation, I proposed that students record interviews with their oldest living relative and, after editing and memorizing the account, perform it verbatim. These stories proved moving and instructive. I recognized the importance of giving voice and presence to those who walked up from Mexico; who took cattle boats from Ireland; who abandoned the cane fields of Hawaii; who drove from Mississippi to Chicago to avoid the Ku Klux Klan. Learning by heart every syllable, every pause, every whispered secret of those stories, and then sharing them with an audience, made us better people and better artists, in theory and in practice. In so doing, I claimed for myself and our students a little branch on the vast Bing-Copeau-Decroux family tree.

Works Cited

Bentley, Eric (1975) *In Search of Theater*, New York, NY: Athenaeum.
Decroux, Etienne (1985) *Words on Mime*, Claremont, CA: Mime Journal.
Martinez, Ariane (2008) *La pantomime, théâtre en mineur 1880–1945*, Paris: Presses Sorbonne Nouvelle.
Pinok et Matho (2016) *Une Saga du Mime, Des Origines aux années 1970*, Paris: Riveneuve éditions.

1 Introduction

Lessons from Prague

> The title of this volume serves the reader well in identifying which artists will figure among its pages. Yet the original working title for these collected essays nonetheless hangs in the air: *The Wooden Actor and Other Paradoxes of Theatrical Organicity*. Břetislav Pojar's doll animation, created with rudimentary means and before today's transforming technical advances, raises questions that endure: What is presence? How can a wooden puppet or a wooden mask convey emotion? How could Czech puppeteers and Japanese noh actors arrive at similar techniques without one having appropriated the other's secret teaching? In both cases, they "gave one the impression that the puppet hid more than it showed, and its heart of wood stored even more" (Prague).

An intriguing encounter

In 1975, an International Research and Exchanges Board grant supported our five-month visit to Poland and the former Czechoslovakia, two theatre centers then behind the Iron Curtain. In Poland, Cracow's legendary Stary Theatre and Jerzy Grotowski's Teatr Laboratorium in Wroclaw left profound impressions, whereas Henryk Tomaszewski's glittering and often glitzy Wroclaw Pantomime Theatre failed to capture our imagination even as it dazzled others'. Later, in addition to attending darkly hilarious performances by Czech mime-clowns Boris Hybner, Boleslav Polívka and Ctibor Turba, we happened upon a screening of a 15-minute doll animation film entitled *Jabloňová panna* (*The Apple Maiden*) by the celebrated animator Břetislav Pojar (1923–2012).

This charming story features a prince who sets off on horseback in search of a wife. His perfect match appears miraculously before our eyes from inside an apple fallen from a magical tree. The prince lifts this maiden onto his horse and gallops off. As they proceed along a path suspended over a deep and murky canyon, a flying jealous witch appears from behind and, with lightning speed, pierces the betrothed's heart, appropriates her engagement ring, casts her head first into the abyss and usurps her place behind the unsuspecting

DOI: 10.4324/9781003205852-1

2 *Introduction*

prince. At first sight of this hideous interloper, the terror-stricken audience, strangers in the darkened theatre, responded collectively with a sharp gasp. I imagined classical Greek and commedia dell'arte spectators reacting in unison with similar fervor.

That Czech public's impassioned response has become a focus for reflection over the decades: How did these wooden dolls, from the first moments of the film, induce our suspended disbelief? Why, at the moment of greatest danger to these objectively lifeless characters, did the audience feel viscerally engaged and impelled to respond?

Pojar's inspiration

The film's director wrote of his mentor, the legendary filmmaker Jiří Trnka (1912–1969):

> He always gave his [doll's] eyes a look indefinable. With the simple turn of their heads, or with a change of lighting, rose smiling expressions, or unhappy, or dreamers. This gave one the impression that the puppet hid more than it showed, and its heart of wood stored even more.
>
> (Prague)

Analogous effects from distant forms

Pojar clearly strove for similar effects, as his characters in *The Apple Maiden* had immobile faces and only rudimentarily articulated bodies. By turning and inclining the head, by approaching the light or pulling away from it, the dolls' expressions transformed. Japanese *taiko* drummer/scholar Kunio Komparu (1926–1983) noted equivalent dynamics at work in the world's oldest continuously performed theatre, the noh, founded by Zeami in the fourteenth century.

> [W]hen the [noh] mask is moved and the light changes or when it is seen from a different angle, it can mystically take on an infinite variety of expressions. It has a profound quality that leads to a comparison with the puzzling expression of the Mona Lisa or the intimate yet mystical "archaic smile" of classical Greek sculpture. The basic quality of the Noh mask's expression should be interpreted not as a passive "neutral" but rather as an active "infinite."
>
> (Komparu 229)

Komparu explains the mechanism inherent in this "active infinite": by eliminating the performer's expressively mobile face, "denying raw expression" and by "covering the at best unruly facial expressions of the actor," the mask freely communicates "an unlimited number of expressions in the mind of the viewer. . . " (Komparu 224).

Introduction 3

Body and soul

This technique recalls experiments developed by French theatre revolutionary Jacques Copeau (1879–1949) and his collaborator Suzanne Bing (1885–1967). They covered the actor's face to see what the body alone could express, an exercise which would serve as the inspiration for the corporeal mime that Copeau's student Etienne Decroux (1898–1991) would elaborate over his lifetime. While developing his vast technical repertoire for the whole body, Decroux eventually dropped his early experiments with masks and transformed the face itself into a mask, echoing certain noh plays that also eschew them:

> In such plays [performed without masks] the idea is to fix a still expression like a mask on the "bare wood" of the actor's face—the *hitamen* is a mask that is not a mask. The face is strictly required to function as a mask, so of course makeup is never used and the facial muscles must not be used to make expressions.
>
> (Komparu 230)

Etienne Decroux extolled the sublimely expressive faces of stone Buddha statues at Angkor Wat, citing them as ideal for corporeal mime. Drawing further inspiration from the English designer/theoretician Edward Gordon Craig (1872–1966), Decroux told his students that some human actors developed puppet-like qualities (he especially admired Louis Jouvet in this regard) in order to create the articulation and artifice required of art. I hear Decroux's voice, and perhaps also Artaud's, behind that of French actor and mime Jean-Louis Barrault (1910–1994) in the following quotation:

> Let us not hesitate to say it: *there should be, deep in every actor, an element of the robot.* The function of art is to lead this robot toward the natural; to proceed by artificial means toward an imitation of nature. It is because the violin is a hollow box, like a dead body, that it is so satisfying to furnish it with a soul.
>
> (Barrault 29)

Great events in theatre occur when one possesses the "hollow box" and subsequently finds the soul to furnish it, or when the wandering soul at last finds a body-box in which to live. American stage director Anne Bogart (b. 1951) writes about *kata*:

> The Japanese use the word *kata* to describe a prescribed set of movements that are repeatable. *Katas* can be found in acting, in cooking, in martial arts as well as in flower arranging. The translation for the word *kata* in English is "stamp," "pattern" or "mould." In executing a *kata*, it is essential never to question its meaning but through the endless repetition the

4   *Introduction*

meaning starts to vibrate and acquire substance. . . . If it is true that creativity occurs in the heat of spontaneous interacting with set forms, perhaps what is interesting is the quality of the heat you put under inherited containers, codes and patterns of behavior. . . . Therefore I believe that it is better to set the exterior (the form, the action) and allow the interior (the quality of being, the ever-altering emotional landscape) freedom to move and change in every repetition. . . . To allow for emotional freedom, you pay attention to form. If you embrace the notion of containers or *katas,* then your task is to set a fire, a human fire, inside these containers and start to burn.

(Bogart 101–3)

Ma: the essential ingredient

How to define this "human fire" which enlivens traditional forms? American *kyogen* specialist Jonah Salz (b. 1956) identifies a quality in Japanese art called *ma*, which Komparu translates into English as "space, spacing, interval, gap, blank, room, pause, rest time, timing or opening" (Komparu 70), and which quality, Salz explains, "keeps *kata* from becoming robotic" (Salz). This individual "timing" can manifest in phrasing of set movements in a *kata*, or in complete immobility, as in the *i-guse,*

an important scene that is often the high point in a play. In an *i-guse*, the performer sits at center stage, as still as a rock. To the flow of the choral chanting of the story and the instrumental music he dances only with his heart, going beyond the visual to attain infinite expression.

(Komparu 73)

Wooden: for better or worse?

Barrault, Bogart and Komparu seem to argue for a "wooden actor," words which remind us of Edward Gordon Craig's polemical search for the ideal performer as Übermarionette, one of the most salient arguments in twentieth-century theatre.

The words "wooden actor" also contain a *double entendre*: for most people, "wooden acting" equals stilted, clumsy, non–naturalistic performance. However, Craig and other twentieth-century revolutionaries sought supernatural or "artistic" (artificial, de-familiarized, articulated, marionettized) acting. Therein the absence of "naturalness" and verisimilitude became a virtue, but only when guided by *ma*, or "timing."

Italian director and author Eugenio Barba's (b. 1936) works in the same field, and the research conducted by ISTA (International School of Theatre Anthropology) scientific staff, reveal shared principles illuminating Asian and contemporary European theatre practice. This work reminds us how, in the hands of traditional and contemporary artists, "organicity" (as ISTA scholars

Introduction 5

call it), or *ma* as Komparu defines it, might eradicate mechanical rigidity, allowing art to thrive on artifice and articulation rather than being hampered by it. Hence the paradox: the performance of a wooden puppet (or a human actor with puppet-like articulations) might move an audience to tears.

The artistic body

That Prague audience's con-spiring ("breathing together") in 1975 provided the incentive for a re-reading of my years of study with Decroux and guided me to a more detailed exploration of Decroux's family tree—Copeau, Bing, Craig, Artaud, Jouvet and Dullin. Seen together, for all their differences, they foster an aesthetic that resonates in that animated film audience's decisive intake of air. Beyond the practice and theory of these French theatre practitioners, I have found distant and disparate performances impelled by a similar artistic vision. Indeed, the transfixing power of the wooden actor, who "calls up a wealth of images deep within the heart and mind of the viewer and makes the internal drama possible" (Komparu 230), operates as a unifying principle among various performance modalities. This connective thread reveals techniques developed over generations as in the noh, or ones necessarily created from hard work and persistance over the course of one lifetime, as in the case of British tragedian Henry Irving (1938–1905) or of Etienne Decroux.

In all these forms, ancient or contemporary, the actor's transformed body becomes a meeting place for the artifice (*kata*) of the puppet and the organicity and truth of the rhythms of work and of thought (*ma*). If playing the articulation becomes more important than the music of dynamic variation, robotic rigidity reigns; conversely, when the internal "music" blurs the clear delineations of the articulated body, "overacting" may result. As Decroux's practice revealed, only by holding the two qualities (articulation and musical phrasing, *kata* and *ma*) in a delicate balance, could the actor

> do nothing superfluous. Elegance is born when the ordinary is abbreviated, concentrated and reduced to essentials, and such abbreviating always gives birth to an accompanying symbolism, and this process leads ultimately to *ma*. . . . The interesting part is what is not played, not acted out, not given an apparent reality.
>
> (Komparu 74)

Conclusion

The following essays find a common source in that darkened Prague cinema where we gasped at a wooden doll's sudden reversal of fortune. These essays continue our re-examination of Decroux's "family tree"; sift through evidence arguing for the centrality of animal observation in Copeau's and, later, in Decroux's project; and record the challenging and paradoxical

6   *Introduction*

improvisations *chez* Decroux. Ultimately, they recall Decroux's debt to sculpture, poster art, sport and masks.

Work Cited

Barrault, Jean-Louis (1949) "Child of Silence," trans. Eric Bentley, *Theatre Arts*, October, pp. 28–31.

Bogart, Anne (2001) *A Director Prepares: Seven Essays on Art and Theatre*, New York: Psychology Press.

Komparu, Kunio (1983) *The Noh Theatre: Principles and Perspectives*, trans. Jane Corddry, New York: Weatherhill.

Prague Puppet Museum. Consulted 8 October 2016. Can be viewed at: https://web. archive.org/web/20160422081252/http://www.praguepuppetmuseum.com/about/

Salz, Jonah (2016) Lecture, 22 September, Claremont, CA: Pomona College.

2 Blowing up the palace and hanging up on the Opéra

Dramaturgy in and of the body

> More than 50 years ago, in graduate school at the University of Arkansas, I fell in love with corporeal mime figures and exercises when I first saw them performed by Etienne Decroux in a 16-mm black and white film. Dancer Eleanor King (former Humphrey-Weidman company member) taught the class in which this document left me thunderstruck, altering the course of my impressionable young life. During two years of Covid 19 isolation, the debris of that half century of enchantment and struggle lay piled on my desk and scattered willy-nilly on the floor. From those collected impressions emerge this essay, in which we meet the improbable socialist/anarchist at the start of my quest: Etienne Decroux, who, with a mischievous glint in his eye, told us what he'd do in the unlikely event that the Paris Opera telephoned.
>
> A popular performance choreographed by Swedish dancer/choreographer Mats Ek at the Paris Opera in the summer of 2019 might have surprised Decroux. Ek's father Anders performed with Decroux's company in the 1950s and Ek's mother, Swedish ballet director Birgit Cullberg [Cullberg Ballet], studied with Decroux in Stockholm and in Paris. Mats, consciously or otherwise, embedded Decroux's figures throughout his work in a way that I found exquisite and innovative.
>
> This recalls a story I read somewhere in which an incredulous Samuel Beckett, upon witnessing the acclaim—the passionate response—accorded the Paris premiere of his *Waiting for Godot*, supposedly murmured "I must have somehow, somewhere, made a mistake."

At war with the prevailing paradigm

Searching deeply into my eyes when I returned to his school for a visit after a year's absence, Decroux sonorously and dolefully asked, "*Toujours militant?*" The question "Are you still a militant in the cause?" revealed, through his meticulous word-choice, Decroux's true pedagogical intentions: to train radical actors to overthrow the prevailing theatrical paradigm and replace it with a new one giving actors more authority. Parallel to his long career teaching and performing mime (about 60 years), Decroux successfully infiltrated the enemy lines of commercial theatre. As an actor, his underdog position had taught him well what it meant to lack power; nevertheless, he maintained a

DOI: 10.4324/9781003205852-2

8 *Blowing up the palace*

career as a stage, radio and film actor, operating within an entrenched hierarchy he ultimately wished to upend.

Whereas his teacher Jacques Copeau famously promulgated a bare stage while keeping authors, directors and other members of the text-centric chain of command in their traditional privileged places, Decroux, envisioned exiling the lot, leaving the actor—almost naked and all-powerful—on Copeau's legendary *tréteau nu* [bare stage]. In sum, he proposed overturning the director and playwright-centered theatre of his day in favor of the actor-centered one that he imagined for the future. Could we make a case that Copeau's early twentieth-century experiments are bearing fruit 100 years later in today's penchant for devising and collective creation?

In Decroux's 1931 letters to his former student and co-conspirator Jean-Louis Barrault, he pleads unsuccessfully with Barrault to abandon lucrative stage and film contracts in order to return to mime, to theatre research not governed by commercial values (Decroux/Barrault). Attempting to win back his collaborator, Decroux suggests a compromise: find a way to schedule mime rehearsals in addition to Barrault's other demanding commitments. Finally, for Barrault, commercial success proved more alluring than Decroux's hermetic mime. As we see in other essays in this collection, the pattern repeated as, one by one, his best students left him to join what Decroux considered "the enemy."

Copeau's contribution

Although Copeau's theatre produced plays based on written texts, his school, l'Ecole du Vieux Colombier, gave priority to the body as a dramatic instrument in devised and collectively created experiments. For example, the curriculum featured many movement disciplines: ballet, fencing, acrobatics, noh theatre and masked improvisation. These led to devised performances, Suzanne Bing's *Kantan* figuring among the best examples.

After Copeau had closed the Paris school and moved with his apprentices (including Decroux) to Burgundy, one of France's main wine-producing areas, they began their rehearsals in a space that had earlier been a fermenting room. (One cannot help seeing there a rich analog to their own artistic fermentation.) To prepare the work area, Copeau had an apprentice draw a grid pattern on the floor to divide up the playing space. At the intersections, they drilled holes into which they could insert poles, as needed, or from which they could anchor decor components, as they earlier had done for the stage of the Vieux Colombier Theatre (Gontard 109, 197). Given Copeau's penchant for movement, I conjecture that the grid lines could have also served as blocking guidelines for actors walking, running and moving through the space along clearly defined paths, according to Copeau's specifications. Indeed, Decroux, for whom Copeau (his first teacher) was a major influence, experimented in later years with geometric patterns delineated on his own studio floor (Decroux 2001, 60).

Copeau's poles dropped into the floor grid (like so many fixed points) remind me of Decroux's elaborate technical training that relies on fixed points in the body, as well as outside of it, to which moving parts relate. He understood that movement without fixed points and clear trajectories was diffuse and inarticulate, like trying to speak without consonants. We might say that Decroux took Copeau's horizontal *external* training lines and engraved them *within* his own vertical corporeal mime students' bodies, enabling them to perform scales, segmented movements, triple designs and movement phrases with varied dynamic qualities—slow, fast, sharp, smooth, with or without resistance, broken up by *tocs* (short sudden energetic bursts that punctuate movement) or in *fondu* (slow motion). These internal and external limitations, at their best, created faceted and densely choreographed compositions.

In Decroux's corporeal mime (as in other codified theatre and dance forms), the actor can't do "just anything"; instead, remaining within the fecund limitations of the technique, inspired by predetermined forms and lines of force existing inside and outside the body, he links elements to create movement phrases—*enchaînements*. Within Decroux's system, the arms can arrive at a V-shape above the head, or on the "water level" (parallel to the earth), or on the "house top" (diagonal lines down from the shoulders). If the arms stop elsewhere, they seem "wrong," appearing weak and awkward, "off key." Decroux taught that movements achieve high visibility by following clear geometric paths through space and on the ground, the body passing through geometric shapes and arriving at "logical" destinations, often borrowed from classical ballet, but remaining within the corporeal mime aesthetic. Thus, in Decroux's étude for arms called Sea Horse Tail, we discover a corporeal mime *port de bras*, distinct from classical ballet's but not in aesthetic contradiction to it. As for legs and feet, in corporeal mime they pass through recognizable ballet positions. Any movement that does not successfully thrive within these limitations would provoke from Decroux, thundering in heavily accented English: "Do or not do. No between two!" That said, his students working on their own sometimes intentionally departed from these limitations or grids to make startling contrasts in contradiction to Decroux's choices. For example, parallel or turned in feet were anathema to Decroux— symbols of a moral failing; lifted shoulders, unless figuring as part of a design element within a larger movement phrase, would be considered by Decroux an expression of weakness or fear.

Subverting the hierarchy

In his 1931 article, "My Definition of Theatre," which he called his "first proper piece of writing on art," Decroux outlined his intention to subvert the centuries-old hierarchy that accorded the playwright first place and the actor, last (1985, 27). In a similar vein, he later expressed to Eric Bentley (see also Preface, page vii) his desire to make theatre a place dedicated to "the actor art": "You understand, don't you, how in the end the slave revolts? The cry

10 *Blowing up the palace*

of the actor against literature is the cry of the native against imperialism, of the Indian against England" (Bentley 189).

Decroux not only imagined exiling the playwright: he often railed against mask makers and costumers for failing to understand that actors needed, above all, freedom of movement. Although Decroux strictly forbade students to perform outside the school, I nonetheless sought employment as a parrot (Mr. Blah Blah) in a children's television program. Within seconds of my arrival for a fitting, the costumer placed an oversized *papier maché* parrot head on my shoulders, effectively eliminating any possibility of the segmented bird-like articulations I had naively imagined I might employ. When I voiced my growing concern that I could barely walk, stand and turn in this costume, the designer crisply reminded me that other actors would willingly replace me if I found her body mask inappropriate. Decroux's prophetic voice echoed in my ears: "Actors in the theatre today are mostly models for showing off costumes and for decorating the stage!" Mr. Blah Blah, ironically, taught this lesson well, and I never again broke the school's unwritten law. And, while in subsequent years, I have had the good fortune of collaborating with costumers and mask makers sensitive to the actor's need to move freely in complex patterns, Decroux's observation that actors are "the last hired and the first fired" has remained for the most part true.

To replace it with ...

Decroux possessed both the strength and the imagination required to create a revolutionary actor-centered theatre, inverting the dictum cited above. While training zealous young disciples to perform his repertoire, he also indicated paths that their own creative research might take in future, independent of authors, directors and "alien arts" (Decroux 1985, 27). According to his new theatre paradigm, as he explains in "Creating a Mime Play," movement should take precedence over the written text: "A play should be rehearsed before it is written" (Decroux 2001, 59). As written and spoken text had been theatre's starting point for millennia, how did Decroux envision creating works in this new actor-centered theatre where the "theatre's right hand," the text, had been cut off? (Decroux 1985, 27).

Prior to setting every detail of a mime composition, Decroux's creative process relied on free association of ideas, images and movements guiding the actor as "the theme grew out of the actions, which seemed to happen by chance" (Decroux 2001, 59). In 1969, in creating a duet for me and my classmate Zoe Noyes [Maistre], he asked us to improvise for periods of 10 to 15 minutes while he "fished" for a moment that kindled his imagination. Once found, we would repeat and adapt the sequence according to his tinkering as he coaxed it toward some inner vision. In every rehearsal, we replayed the elements retained from the previous sessions, Decroux arranging and rearranging sections or phrases (like film clips spliced into different sequences). Eventually, he settled on a preferred order, all the while editing, polishing or even entirely discarding certain segments. For Decroux, the

Blowing up the palace 11

dramatic event, born of a montage of movement texts, did not require a playwright, as he never included sung or spoken texts, excepting in his only full-length composition, *Little Soldiers*.

Decroux composed transitional movement phrases to bridge the gaps among the elements he sought to juxtapose—links he culled from his technical studies as well as those discovered in improvisation. For some pieces, he carefully examined "lines of force" latent in daily work movements and subsequently liberated them into expanded gestures. Thus, he created solos ("The Washerwoman," "The Carpenter," "Meditation"), duets ("Love Duet," "The Sculptor," "Ancient Combat"), trios ("The Trees") and works for as many as five (*Little Soldiers*) or six actors ("The City").

As Decroux read omnivorously (almost never books about theatre) and observed life microscopically, theory and practice derived from cinema, literature, statuary, the poster and collage. Additionally, the concept of "art as artifice" nourished his creative process.

Cinema

"I'd rather see a bad film than a good play!" Decroux sometimes quipped. He knew the cinema well, both as actor in a number of important films and also, mostly in his youth, as an audience member. Decroux taught the importance of motion picture camera angles and movements as a point of departure for the stage actor's work: how one might perform, using only the body to achieve cinematic effects in the viewer's imagination. He invented equivalents for the close up (the body immobile and serving as a ground for small moving parts, like eyes, hands and arms) and the long shot (the whole body moving in relation to the background). He also experimented with the "travelling," the zoom, the quick cut, the slow fade and the pan, among others. We explored these concepts in technique class as well as in improvisations. And, in his Friday evening lectures, Decroux often used these concepts as starting points for his ruminations.

For example, "The Washerwoman," Decroux's emblematic 1930s piece, ends as the actor finishes washing a sheet, wringing it out, hanging it up to dry, taking it down and finally ironing it. Now, using a close up, she darns a worn part of the sheet, with precise movements of arms and hands against the background of an immobile trunk. Sharp up-and-down movements of the head coordinate with those of the deft "workers" (arms and hands) drawing in the audience's attention as she takes four stiches in a cross-hatching design to reinforce the worn cloth. For the fifth and last stitch, the washerwoman transitions from close-up to long shot: She slows down and amplifies each articulation, gradually drawing the rest of the body into the sequence. Progressively changing the level and plane of the body, each movement takes her one step further into three-dimensional abstraction of the darning sequence. This transposition creates a faceted full-body version of the "restricted" one (involving only hands, arms and head) already seen in the first four repetitions. The fifth makes the darning gesture still more clearly

12 *Blowing up the palace*

visible, displaying the entire body moving in relation to its background (rather than an immobile trunk serving as backdrop for moving hands and arms) as the audience's camera-eyes pull back to take it in.

Decroux learned not only from acting for the camera but also from observing cinema actors' individual acting styles. Among others, he appreciated stars Michèle Morgan (1920–2016), Raimu (1883–1946) and Jean Gabin (1904–1976), whose qualities—their use of rhythmic phrasing, pauses, immobilities—he appropriated into his mime research. As we have seen in other essays in this collection, mime actor and innovator Jean-Louis Barrault easily made the transition from mime to film acting. Stage actors with whom Decroux worked, like Charles Dullin and Louis Jouvet, also excelled in film work. As Paris was (and remains) the center of theatre as well as cinema in France, the same pool of actors auditioned for roles in both. In looking at French films from the 1930s through the 1950s, we often see traces of earlier styles of stage acting, especially in the acclaimed *Les Enfants du Paradis* in which Decroux played an important role.

In silent films, producers attempted to replace the living presence or "vibrato" of the absent actor, now reduced to a projected image, by using live piano, organ and orchestral music. The first "talkie," *The Jazz Singer* (1927) synchronized words and music with image. In subsequent sound films, increasingly more artful soundtracks attempted to compensate for the living actor's absence.

Many contemporary performances use recorded sound and music to augment the actors' work, just as some nineteenth-century theatres employed orchestras to underscore emotion in dramatic presentations. Decroux sometimes used recorded music with his corporeal mime, always introduced after the piece had been created. This music became a rhythmic grid against which the actor's pre-set movements provided counterpoint, only rarely aligning serendipitously.[1] However, Decroux, Grotowski and other modern reformers, mostly relied on the actor's own vibrations (produced vocally—singing and speaking—and through what Decroux called "muscular respiration") as the main *subject* of a performance.

How something happens (degrees of "vibrato" and other dynamic changes), rather than *what* happens (plot, storyline), has become the subject of some twentieth- and twenty-first-century laboratory theatre research. The "how" sends ripples through the space between actor and audience, becoming more important than story. Traditional texts (ancient songs, poetry) might be seen as pretexts for transportive music and movement, as in flamenco, dervish dancing, or the noh play.

Literature

Decroux's son told me that his father especially appreciated the writing of Francis Ponge (1899–1988), the French prose poet who explored the physicality of language while describing everyday objects—an oyster, blackberries, a pebble, for example. Ponge took pleasure in the "thingness" of words just as

Blowing up the palace 13

Decroux took pleasure in the thingness of movements. In "The Carpenter" (1930s), for example, while depicting a craftsman at work in a previous century, he simultaneously gave free rein to his modernist tendencies to explore movement that otherwise remained latent in realism: continuing a line of force; breaking a line of force; changing the level or plane of his (imaginary) worktable and tools. By articulating movement in cubist ways, Decroux derived sequences of planing, drilling, hammering, etc., which he used as an accurate substructure while at the same time creating stylized portraits rather than realistic imitations. Decroux's modernist way of working had as its literary corollary the twentieth-century pioneers—James Joyce, Gertrude Stein, Virginia Woolf, Marguerite Duras and William Faulkner, among others. They redefined the novel, short story and other forms, moving beyond linear narrative to experiment with a more self-conscious use of language (among other innovations).

Decroux developed corporeal mime dramaturgy along the same lines, separating it from nineteenth-century white-faced pantomime and from reliance on traditional plot. Instead, he explored the musicality of movement and the dramatic elements of pause, weight, resistance, hesitation and surprise, as in "The Trees," "The Factory" and "The Washerwoman." His background as a manual worker and his love of counterweights made resistance (what Laban would call "bound flow") a central element in his compositions. However, two other pieces, "The Mischievous Spirit" (created by Maximilien Decroux and Eliane Guyon, with finishing touches by Etienne Decroux) and "The Statue" (the duet Decroux created for himself and Nel Taylor in the New York years) represent a different current in Decroux's work, showing him in an unaccustomedly light-hearted and entertaining vein, one which perhaps has not aged as well as his more abstract pieces.

Whereas Decroux and associates might define theatre primarily as a symphony of corporeal "music" or a choreography of statues come to life, a bookstore in Toulouse once had inscribed on its wall: "*Tout théâtre est d'abord littérature*" [All theatre is first literature]. Did that message describe all Western theatre? All European theatre of a certain period? Artaud, Decroux, Lecoq and Grotowski tried to liberate theatre from this archaic yet still prevalent perspective.

Posters and statuary

Decroux admired and attempted to emulate the graphic artist's ability, in rendering a human figure's gesture, to distill it (through simplification and amplification) into an abstract line—a kind of shorthand capable of inscribing itself onto the viewer's retina. Decroux's appreciation of advertising posters extended to the skillful workers who paste them onto the walls of the Paris Métro stations. He delighted in the way that these workers' expansive, efficient gestures radiated out from the sacrum like those of a starfish or an octopus. The workmen's organic movement made them a joy to behold in Decroux's

14   *Blowing up the palace*

day, as they still are today, despite inroads in those underground corridors of electronic poster boards which diminish human presence. The bodies of those workers, expertly balanced atop a ladder, brush in hand, display the same practiced specificity of gesture deployed by the poster's graphic artist.

Similarly, Decroux so revered statuary that he named one area of his work Mobile Statuary. He spoke frequently of Rodin, Maillol and ancient Egyptian, Greek and Roman statues, and based mime compositions on specific works of art. For example, the Egyptian statue (in the Louvre collection), "Taharqa offering to Falcon-god Hemen" inspired Decroux's figure (probably created in the 1930s), "Offering the First Grapefruit of the Season to the God." (At that time, scholars had misidentified the spherical objects held by the kneeling suppliant as citrus, whereas now they believe them to be oil jars.) Among others, Decroux also created "Indirect Descent" and "Direct Descent" influenced by Maillol's "The River" and "Air."

Decroux borrowed the aesthetic cores of posters and statuary while inverting the work's position in relation to the audience: the audience walks in front of the immobile poster and around the unmoving statue. The actor, a moving statue, carves the space as the graphic artist inscribes a canvas with a calligraphic gesture. He more accurately resembles the workmen who paste posters on the walls, moving in front of the immobile audience. These artist/workers don't *mean* or *express* anything: they simply work efficiently, expending exact energy and appropriate movement. For Decroux, corporeal mime resembled bridge building or aircraft design, where efficiency+economy = streamlined beauty, the makers' motto: "Nothing in excess."

Collage and artifice

Posters glued one atop another on the walls of the Paris Métro require removal after a number of months before the process can begin again. This procedure reveals a significant aspect of Decroux's dramaturgy, since the same man, whose starfish body smoothed the posters into place with such grace and organic, panther-like agility, must now remove the thick multi-layered accumulation of paper. With a sharp utility knife, he scores the areas just inside the ceramic poster frame. Then with a movement that comes from tail bone and extends the length of the spine to occiput and out to the hand, from an upper corner, he tears diagonally downward with a sweeping movement, removing strata of posters simultaneously and irregularly. A serendipitous collage remains, associating, unexpectedly and randomly: a sliver of beach in Normandy, a gleaming automobile fender, the sinuous curve of a toned nude body, and sections of a large Camembert cheese, *bien fait* [ripe]. The passerby is left to make sense of these surprising collisions of image and unintended meaning, the result of a sort of pictorial automatic writing.

In a similar way, Decroux often began a rehearsal by saying "Make a movement, any movement," and refused to take credit for creating anything, saying that he only moved things from the street (statues, torn posters) into his work. Decroux, the astute observer, took in these accidental juxtapositions so pertinent to his ways of seeing and creating; in fact, so entranced was Decroux with the "poster man" that he created a two-minute étude depicting the laborer's calculated gestures pasting immense wet sheets of paper against the concave Métro station walls. Decroux's own seeing, moving and combining resembled that of collage artists. They created not the thing itself but, instead, the relationships among many diverse already created things, randomly plucked from the streets, or pasted to the side of a building or in a subway station.

In his teaching, Decroux (with a mischievous glimmer in his eye) held up two imaginary roses, one in each hand. He described the one in his left hand as plastic, garishly colored and clumsily modeled. The one in his right hand, a real rose, he characterized as subtly tinted and emitting a delicate perfume. Which rose, he asked, is the more "artistic"? Some students, falling into the trap, said, "Of course, the real rose!"

Decroux countered by offering (despite his avowed atheism) that the real rose, made by God, had therefore none of the artifice usually associated with hand-made things, while the plastic rose, although ugly, demonstrated pure artifice, complete (albeit bad) art. He argued that most theatre directors simply arranged "flowers," actors of certain qualities, employing their voices, bodies and temperaments provided by God, and placing them in logical and coherently pleasant tableaux specified by the playwright. This practice accorded full control to the author and the centuries-old concept of typecasting.

This story sheds light on the difficulty of making art with human beings, and the necessity that Craig, Meyerhold, Decroux and others felt to "puppetize" the body, to remove it somehow, at least by a degree or two, from its natural fleshly self and push it toward a disparate, less transitory and more "artistic" matter. The actor, in finding a more purified and highly visible way of moving, becomes simultaneously a puppet and puppeteer, sculptor and statue.

Inspired by the articulations of the marionette, wearing a mask and moving like an awakened sculpture, the corporeal mime might successfully escape Decroux's criticism of most acting: "Human, too much human!"

Blowing up the palace

Understanding the hierarchical nature of French life in general, and French cultural life in particular, helps us appreciate the significant imaginative leap Decroux's work required. Sectioned into grades, degrees, classifications and orders—from wines and cheeses, lentils and lavender, honey and chicken, butter and lamb, to dancers at the Opéra—everything and everyone in France has a niche, label and pay scale. Decroux created an art, *not* dance, *not* theatre, *not* pantomime, outside the confines of this highly structured system. He lived and functioned outside of it as well, or at least on its fringes, just as he lived on the edges of Paris, far from the Opéra at its center. His grand vision matched his worker's appetite for physical exertion accompanied by an enormous expenditure of energy. Indeed, he felt at home for the last decades of his life in a working-class neighborhood near the Renault automobile factories

16 *Blowing up the palace*

and, for years, taught and rehearsed seven days a week, rarely taking a holiday. High tax rates and stringent control of small businesses or independent workers (fiscal categories Decroux would have fallen into during his years of teaching in his basement) made the practicalities of his research difficult. But a combination of pride and his proletarian origins, which permanently set his internal compass, kept him from trying to get ahead, curry favor or win friends and influence people. Rather, he tended to insult and demean those who didn't understand his work and his monomaniacal devotion to it.

When the telephone rang in his ground-floor study, which it did infrequently, Decroux would project his powerful and well-placed voice up the stairs to Madame from his basement classroom: "If it's the Opéra de Paris, tell them I'm not here!" With a broad smile and a stifled guffaw, he'd resume our work, satisfied with having made a perfect joke. In a country of particularly subtle stratification, the vast Paris Opera and Decroux's cramped suburban studio could not be further apart in every way. In this robin's-egg-blue basement, Decroux founded what Eugenio Barba termed a "little island of freedom" (12). There, with no subsidy and thus no constraints—with only himself to please—he reimagined the human body for the twentieth century.

In an unguarded moment, in thinking of his anarchist youth, Decroux muttered: "I was a coward. I should have blown up the Elysée Palace." Maybe he did, in his own way, blow up some of the grand *idées reçues* of European theatre traditions: the belief that theatre is first of all literature; that the actor's job entails saying the author's words accompanied by appropriate gestures; that you write a play before rehearsing it. If he didn't succeed in blowing them up, he seriously called into question these *lieux communs* by creating a dramaturgy in and of the marionettized body. His dedication to these ideals assured that the Paris Opera would never phone and that, had they done so, he'd have hung up on them summarily, dismissing unwanted interruptions to his all-consuming research.

Note

1. In "The Factory," however, music and rhythm are tightly aligned to the movement.

Works Cited

Barba, Eugenio (1997) "The Hidden Master," *Words on Decroux 2*, Claremont, CA: Mime Journal.

Bentley, Eric (1975) *In Search of Theater*, New York: Athenaeum.

Decroux/Barrault correspondence, Bibliothèque nationale de France, Richelieu-Louvois, arts du spectacle, Paris.

Decroux, Etienne (1985) *Words on Mime*, trans. Mark Piper, Claremont CA: Mime Journal.

——— (2000-2001) "Creating a Mime Play," *An Etienne Decroux Album*, Claremont, CA: Mime Journal.

Gontard, Denis (1974) *Le journal de bord des Copiaus 1924–1929*, Paris: Seghers.

3 Monkey business and Robin revelations

Animal observation in actor training

> Any mention of the Ecole du Vieux Colombier must credit Suzanne Bing (1885–1967) as a primary instigator. "The running of a drama school worthy of the name presupposes the presence of an exceptional being," Decroux wrote, "about whom it would be impossible to say: 'If she hadn't been there, someone else would have taken her place.'" And later, "Without Suzanne Bing there was no one" (Decroux 1985, 1). Bing, a leading actor in the Théâtre du Vieux Colombier, had the desire, the training and the intuition to implement Copeau's grand schemes for a school, bringing to theatrical life his theoretical concepts. Contemporaries especially remember her 1924 production of the noh play *Kantan*, along with subsequent developments in the school's mask making and acting pedagogy—innovations later disseminated internationally by Copeau's nephew, Michel Saint-Denis.
>
> Scholars have recently begun to recognize Bing's heretofore largely ignored contributions to twentieth-century theatre, including in the domain of collective creation and devising. While Copeau's magnetic presence often eclipsed Bing's, recent scholarship brings her out of the shadows. Even though Copeau's contributions constitute the major focus of the following essay, Bing's work underpins it all.

Nénette on film

French director Nicolas Philibert's 2010 documentary, *Nénette*, records, in *cinéma vérité* style, the daily life of a Bornean orangutan who has lived at the Jardin des Plantes in Paris since 1972. While Philibert's lens never leaves Nénette, often joined by her son Tübo, playing, sleeping and eating in her glass enclosure, the soundtrack captures, in real time, comments and conversations of the always off-camera visitors and staff.

Nénette's enigmatic star power draws audiences to the film as it does visitors to her live presence at the zoo; some observers wonder, as Jean-Michel Frondon writes in his blog: "to what extent [what I read in her gaze] . . . is actually there, to what extent is it what I am projecting onto it?" (Frondon). Similarly, Pierre Murat's *Télérama* review notes that Nénette, who favors immobility over the restless meanderings of her younger fellow creatures,

DOI: 10.4324/9781003205852-3

18   *Monkey business and Robin revelations*

"radiates such a calm strength, her gaze evokes such serenity that we can't but ask ourselves countless questions" (Murat).

Philibert remarked, in an interview after the film's release, that when people

> "come into the monkey house, they are overcome, caught by a solemnity, by something that puts them in a reflective state." Consequently he "arranged the film so that the mystery of Nénette would be preserved intact. I filmed her like the Mona Lisa. A strange personality that remains mysterious to the end" (Philibert, Sciences). In another interview Philibert, while underlining her distant, royal presence, echoes Frondon's projection idea: "Behind her glass wall, Nénette is a mirror. A surface on which to project. We attribute to her all sorts of feelings, of intentions, even thoughts."
>
> (Philibert, zoonaute)

Acting improvisations

The film's soundtrack includes visitors' comments like "She's completely depressed . . . maybe her husband's already dead," or "Maybe she misses the country she comes from. I miss mine too." And, in the film's last eight minutes, we hear these words from an unseen visitor:

> The quality of her idleness makes me think of an exercise in an acting class. "The space is yours, just be there." That's the foundation, ladies and gentlemen, that's the foundation. In general, that's a very difficult exercise, for someone put in that situation and watched by others. But she [Nénette] does it with astounding virtuosity. You can follow her inch by inch in her acts that are all linked to each other by idleness and inaction. But she's not going to do anything to amaze us. She won't do anything to cast off that idleness. She is fully there, that's all.
>
> (Ibid.)

The "just being fully there" mentioned by the unidentified voice resonated strongly with me, for my years at Decroux's school (1968–1972) included about 200 lessons in improvisation. These rich, contradictory, frustrating and ultimately rewarding events, brought to mind by Nénette's riveting presence, taught crucial aspects of the actor art. Decroux designed his improvisation assignments to rouse "presence" in those students who seemed not to possess it naturally. As I discuss Decroux's teachings at greater length in other essays in this collection, I limit myself here to a few statements on his special improvisations. First of all he taught us (or rather created conditions in which we could learn): how to empty our minds of quotidian thoughts (to relax) and thus provide room for "God to live there"; how to exist in the space and not disappear; how to remain immobile, yet pulse with contained energy; how to move with asymmetrical rhythm to better portray the movement and sudden interruptions of thought, while allowing the spectator to project onto our screen-like faces and bodies. He taught us a kind of inner vibrato comprised of micro-movements—alternations of muscular tension and relaxation—which bestows a luminosity sometimes seen in children and animals. W.C. Fields cautioned against performing with either, and legendary Russian film-maker Lev Kuleshov similarly noted their "profound innocence, naturalness and simplicity" (Kuleshov 99).

During these improvisation lessons, Decroux spoke admiringly of his first teacher, director Jacques Copeau. Over the years, further research and reflection has increased my appreciation of the extent to which improvisations in Copeau's Vieux Colombier School in the early decades of the twentieth century influenced Decroux's pedagogy. Copeau's love of simplicity and honesty, his preference for the efficient and unaffected movements of manual laborers over an actor's forced and overly expressive ones, Copeau's minimizing of facial expression and subsequent work with inexpressive masks—these meld in Decroux's creation of corporeal mime.

Nénette in person

I first visited the Jardin des Plantes, spurred by Philibert's film, long after my apprenticeship with Decroux. There I watched both Nénette and Tübo busily performing tasks: she sifted through sawdust for bits of food, scraping and scrutinizing while he polished, with a brown paper towel, sections of the glass partition separating observers from the observed. Although absorbed in their respective activities, each embodied distinctive rhythms. Then, without warning, as if hearing a voice or distant music, one would stop to listen, savoring the immobility, then move the eyes or turn the mask-like face as would a marionette, only to get swept up again in the task. Their actions, graceful and unexpected in their shifts of weight, changes of direction and unanticipated stops, captivated the observer. Their immobilities, held just long enough, had (to quote Peter Brook, in his film *The Tightrope*, speaking about successful actors), "a quality of life in which the whole body participates—a connection between head, body, and eyes" (Brook). These orangutans produced movements with qualities of stillness just as their stillness contained inner micro-movements, as if confirming Decroux's frequent assertions that one creates movement with immobilities, and curves with straight lines. In one of his improvisation lessons, Decroux handed a cloth to a student, instructing him to polish a small drop-leaf table, a task not physically difficult to perform but whose art lay in the unconscious selection of dynamo-rhythms (speed, weight and trajectory) required, and the placement of pauses, the manner of stopping, the way of starting again—in short, the whole delicately enchanting "music" of phrasing everyday actions which revealed the actor's inner life.

On my second visit to the Jardin des Plantes in the summer of 2014, Nénette had a different supporting cast, Tübo having moved on. She seemed astonishingly larger, a bit grayer, but had lost none of the smoldering star power derived from her commandingly low center of gravity. I happened to see her at lunch hour, receiving a large globe of lettuce from a deferential human helper, who, like a stagehand in a kabuki play, wore black and averted his eyes in an attempt to remain invisible. Pausing often as she inspected and dismembered the ample vegetable, she thoughtfully chewed each leaf with grace, dignity and an unselfconscious relaxation that I found spellbinding. I joked to my wife "Nénette eating a salad captivates as thoroughly as Baryshnikov dancing!" In fact, they share some rare performance qualities.

Jacques Copeau, Suzanne Bing and Etienne Decroux observe animals

Tracing Copeau's interest in animal observation takes us to a pivotal moment in his career. During his first season (1917–18) as director of the French Theatre in New York, the company produced and presented 21 plays in four and a half months; this sustained hyperactivity so intensified rifts within the group and in Copeau's own thinking about theatre that 11 actors' contracts were not renewed for the following season. On 20 May, with the hope of rest and healing before the second equally challenging New York season, Copeau retreated for the summer with actors and his family to Cedar Court, the Morristown, New Jersey vast country estate of arts patron Otto Kahn.

Copeau's journal provides a reflective record of this anguished moment when he returned, as he had done before in similar circumstances, to an inner research—improvisation without words—to regain his artistic bearings. He hoped, "outside of specifically designated rehearsals, [to] loosen up [*assouplir*] through various exercises [his] disparate troupe" (Copeau 1991, 85). As Copeau noted in his Journal on the first day of work at the Kahn estate (23 May 1918), only two of the actors (Bing and Tessier) demonstrated "quality, an inner will, and *continuity* in expression." He continued:

> there are two sorts of manifestations in the actors' way of playing: discontinuous manifestations which seem intentional, facile, theatrical, and continuous manifestations which give the impression of modesty and interior sincerity, of real life and power. Continuity and slowness [are] conditions of powerful and sincere acting.

In the journal entry of the following day (24 May 1918), he seems to have given up on even his most stalwart supporters and sincere disciples, Bing and Tessier: "none of the actors achieves the prerequisite state of complete relaxation."

The next journal entry—16 June 1918—begins with the heading "Observation of Animals."

> Succession of attitudes. *Hold* each attitude separately. Make sketches of them. Analyze using film.

Monkey business and Robin revelations 21

Complete gymnastic exercises of the body. Comparisons with the use of masks. Example of the marionette. In extreme genres, in tragedy and in farce (I know above all in farce), attitude, expression of the body and of the face must always be pushed to the extreme. None of them should be ordinary. And the *time* between each attitude [should be] well adhered to (muscular engagement as in pure acrobatic exercises). Return to the preceding attitude after each expression of movement. This is what clowns and eccentrics do so well. (Observation of a robin on the lawn of Cedar Court.)

(Copeau 1991, 87)

Copeau, precariously balanced, financially and artistically, while in a foreign country thousands of miles from his homeland (at war with Germany), observed a completely banal event—a robin hopping about a garden. However, Copeau's keen perception, analytical sense and ability to extrapolate led him further than this chance encounter might have done for someone of less vision. This single stimulus of observing the robin's distinctive movement patterns coalesced his thinking and enabled him to sketch out a rich training program for actors including "the example of the marionette," masks, and animal observation as core principles in his mission to cure actors of "ham acting" (*cabotinage*).

Although unable to implement most of this vision immediately, Jacques Copeau and Suzanne Bing founded the Ecole du Vieux Colombier upon returning to Paris from New York in 1920. Decroux studied there during its last year in Paris and for a few months after the school had moved to the country, 1923–24. In that period, Decroux examined living seahorses and carefully drew them. He wrote of "tiny pulsating movements at the base of the seahorse's tail, like the beating of an angel's wings, that propelled the creature through the water" (Decroux 2001, 36). This articulate, bony, marine fish, that served as a perfect model for an "integrated" organic way of moving, influenced Decroux's physical practice: he translated the animal's fluttering micro-movements into human muscular vibrato—quick alternations of tension and relaxation—around the sternum, in biceps and in buttocks.

In their teaching both in Paris and subsequently in Burgundy, Copeau and Bing used, as key elements in their quest for truthful acting: the example of the marionette; improvisation and performance with both neutral (noble) and expressive masks; and animal observation. Later, Michel Saint-Denis (Copeau's nephew and associate for many years), Decroux, Jean Dasté and others (like Jacques Lecoq who joined Copeau's family tree on Jean Dasté's branch) followed this example, with animal observation taking a larger or smaller role in their pedagogy. Michel Saint-Denis went on to found influential drama schools in London, Strasbourg, New York and Montreal, all of which included, to a greater or lesser extent, animal observation in their curricula (Saint-Denis 2009, 167–8).

22 *Monkey business and Robin revelations*

Copeau's observation, then, eventually led to a wide-spread use of animal observation in actor training. For example, in the aforementioned film, *The Tightrope*, documenting Peter Brook's work with actors, Brook, who would have known of Copeau's work from his early training in London, asserts: "if the body is not completely alive—like a cat—the soles of the feet forget." Here we recall Decroux's counsel: "Look at our teacher the cat!" and recognize in Brook's words (also in *The Tightrope*) that "the actor links pure imagination and the body itself." In this we hear echoes of Copeau's quest for sincerity in actually *doing*, and not merely *pretending* to do, in starting first with the body and movement, and only eventually incorporating text. The cat's sequential movement sets a standard of panther-like grace and "connectedness" for performers in every field. Bing and Copeau, corporeal mime's forebears, admired and imitated the cat's low center of gravity and laser-focused stalking. The cat's immobilities (that exhibit a quality described as *sats* in Eugenio Barba's Theatre Anthropology) transform into unexpected, silent and perfectly targeted leaps. The cat, like the manual laborer, makes no unnecessary movements.[1] Copeau observed street sweepers and carpenters; Decroux worked with his hands and his body for ten years before undertaking theatre studies. Both knew instinctively the power and the beauty of efficient, compact and focused movement, and each in his own way encouraged it on stage.

The face, the mask, the marionette, the spine

One might say that a bird visited Copeau in his darkest moments, when he despaired of ever reforming adult actors into selfless servants of drama. His subsequent journal entry on that epiphanic encounter on the lawn informed not only the rest of his own career but also those of many of his disciples. That red-breasted robin, considered by some Native Americans as a sign of spring and renewal, did in fact energize Copeau while helping him define his evolving view of the actor. But how exactly?

Observing video recordings of robins, I noticed explosions of sharp, clear movements followed by almost imperceptible quivering semi-immobilities (different from rigidity). The robin seemed a figure in a flip-book or a pixilated film, moving at irregular intervals from frame to frame (what Copeau refers to as "attitude"—a held position), preserving the element of surprise. Each immobility lasted just long enough, never so long that it weakened, recalling Decroux's saying: "One has the right to kill a movement, but not the right to let it die." The robin's head remains still while the lower body moves, or vice versa. When grooming, the robin produces a quick and complex orchestration of vibratory movements as the bird's beak forages into fluttering wings and feathered body.

Decroux's description of what he discovered in the Bing-Copeau school resembles my own observations of robins and of Nénette. Decroux was struck by the changing dynamics and the non-dancelike qualities in the

Vieux-Colombier's students: he had never before seen this type of slow-motion movement, had never seen prolonged immobilities, or "explosive movements followed by sudden immobility."

> The disadvantage of slowness is that it resembles immobility; it lets you see the verb "to be." People don't like you to see them, they are afraid that you will discover the intimacy of their person, they're afraid of being ridiculous, and this modesty, the intimacy of the verb "to be," is greater than all the others.
>
> (Decroux cited in Leabhart and Chamberlain, 69–70)

While the robin's musculature makes slow motion movements impossible, other birds, cats and primates execute them, as well as explosive movements, easily, even with virtuosity.

Copeau's Journal entries, made in time of crisis, reveal concepts and practices which would renew and revolutionize European and American twentieth-century theatre, distinguishing it from nineteenth-century ways of working. Copeau advocated making sketches of attitudes and analyses of sequences by filming (breaking down into still photos)[2]; teaching gymnastics for the actor; using masks; finding in marionettes inspiration for the living actor; encouraging muscular responsiveness; studying with clowns; appreciating eccentrics; and, last but not least, animal observation. Of eccentrics and clowns, Copeau writes to his wife in 1916:

> I went to the Circus five times to see the same clowns. . . .
>
> An eccentric English juggler interested me greatly. He had remarkable restraint and distinction. Variable enough, depending on the evening, in his humor, in his disposition. His performance: exercises, *lazzi*, walking around the circus ring, entrances and exits strictly established. He always performed them with the same precision, the same conscientiousness.

Copeau goes on to explain how on certain evenings, while everything remained substantially the same, the performer worked with a certain ardor, a special joy.

> I noticed (it) right away by . . . the more incisive quality of his movement, of his voice and by very slight nuances of intonation, by subtle variations, by the way everything, those evenings, obeyed him, even as he sought their difficulty, taking advantage of the slightest accident they offered, improvising discreetly and at the same time with authority, a word, a gesture, an attitude.
>
> (Copeau 1979, 319)

Copeau's admiration for the Fratellini Brothers resulted in his inviting them to teach at his Ecole du Vieux Colombier. In this letter to his wife, Copeau

24 *Monkey business and Robin revelations*

notes that "they are truly a brotherhood, a guild, people who work together and who cannot do without each other, men who practice a difficult métier, artisans of a living tradition" (Ibid., 321).

Just as Copeau's description of the clarity, precision and articulation of the eccentric juggler's movements might describe equally well the movements of an individual bird, his later description of the Fratellini Brothers suggests a well-attuned flock flying in unison, swooping first to one direction and then suddenly to another. Whereas I don't suggest that Copeau expressed these specific analogies (juggler = bird), we observe that his expressed requirements for the actor find a corollary in certain movement qualities of animals.

Copeau's manner of describing confirms his sensitivity to dynamic lines of force, variation in rhythm, negotiation of weight and fine-tuning of transitions. His level of perception includes this varied data that another might overlook. Moreover, he possessed the vision to apply this analyzed "movement information," culled from the world around him, to actor training and performance.

How animal observation became a cornerstone of corporeal mime

In 1931, at the start of their development of corporeal mime, Decroux and Barrault compiled a list of working points (subsequently published in Barrault's *Reflections on the Theatre*) that seem drawn directly from Copeau's "robin revelations," so perfectly do they integrate with the Ecole du Vieux Colombier's pedagogy.

"1. Exercise for total *decontraction* [relaxation], equivalent to a purge."

Barrault and Decroux appropriated Copeau's requirement of relaxation as the foundational principle for improvisation and performance. Decroux named this state "emptying out," or the necessary absence in "presence/absence." (See instructions for putting on the mask in Dorcy 108–9.)

"2. Awareness of *isolated muscles*. Learning particularly how to contract a given muscle while leaving the others relaxed."

The human marionette (marionettized actor) becomes capable of minute isolations or differentiations of one body part from another—a muscular pulsation originating in one area—producing movements beginning in the biceps, the gluteals and others starting around the sternum. Student actors work to achieve these muscle isolations which come so easily and naturally to animals.

"3. Awareness of certain *groups of muscles*."

Monkey business and Robin revelations 25

After learning isolations, the actor must learn to engage muscle groups to achieve movement goals efficiently: performing an effective counterweight, descending to, or ascending from, the ground, etc.

"4. Acquisition of a *muscular tone*—neither contraction nor relaxation."

Decroux wrote:

> There are forces which surge within us. We already know that blood circulates, that air circulates, and so why shouldn't this force circulate—a little like sap which rises in trees; you can't see it but you can sense it. The actor who performs mime with [alternating] tension gives a different performance than one who performs without any [alternating] tension. . . . But there is one who is taut, the other who is not, one who stands there intensely and the other who is there as if he were resting.
>
> (Decroux 2001, 35)

"5. Development of the *abdominal muscles*."

Decroux taught that we might imagine the sacrum in the back of the body and the abdominals in the front as the center of a starfish. Similarly, he once compared the actor's body to a hand: arms and legs represented by the fingers, and the unit of the head and neck represented by the thumb attached to the trunk (the body of the hand). When this "hand" grasps, the abdominal muscles contract.

"6. The [articulated] notes around the spinal column."

Seahorses, orangutans, robins and marionettes move through articulations that relate organically to a center. Perhaps Copeau's mysterious "continuous manifestations which give the impression of modesty and interior sincerity, of real life and power" actually began, at least for humans, with isolations. A study of one discrete body part moving in isolation precedes a more complex study of the body moving with all the other parts. To achieve these isolations, Decroux invented "scales," playing single notes (body parts) in isolation from each other, and then in varied combinations.

"7. Study of the whip represented by the spinal column."

In the late 1960s, 30 years after Decroux and Barrault established this list, Decroux taught me the Whip, an exemplary figure in which one not only mimes a person holding the whip but also becomes the whip—or more exactly, the whole spine, from sacrum to occiput manifests a successive whip-like movement. Although a nineteenth-century pantomime might hold an invisible whip, the twentieth-century corporeal mime embodies it. Music,

26 *Monkey business and Robin revelations*

which Decroux considered the most technical and most abstract of all the arts, provides an appropriate analogy to abstract mime: the power of corporeal mime comprises not what it is (a person using a whip) but rather how it is and what it (the whip) does. It is itself. The movement of the human body, since it can never be "out of context," necessarily evokes or suggests. As Decroux said, "when I see the body rise up, I feel as if it's humanity that's rising up" (Decroux 1978, 10).

> "8. Sincerity of feeling."

While every actor aspires to sincerity, the general lack of it provoked Copeau's grand adventure of the Ecole du Vieux Colombier. Paradoxically, Copeau, Bing and company discovered that one might achieve this sincerity through following what might seem at first circuitous or even counterproductive routes employing "artificial" (articulate) methods suggested by marionettes, masks, film analysis and animal observation to achieve what, to some, might seem their opposites: organicity, a life-like quality. This sincerity had more to do with "doing" than "pretending to do," and with the now almost unknown idea of "authenticity of action" achieved by craftspeople and manual laborers.

> "9. Development of *concentration*. Analytical concentration, respiratory concentration. Shifting points of concentration. Those luminous points, of which we spoke above, that draw the attention."
>
> (Barrault 27)

In later years Decroux called it "presence/absence," "gravitas," "being, not doing," or "listening." Whatever we call it, Nénette unwittingly remains a most adept exponent.

Conclusion

If you see some similarities between the descriptions of Nénette's behavior and my assessments of Decroux's improvisations (and perhaps Copeau's before him), you might find Decroux's letters to Barrault, composed between 1935 and 1945, revealing. In one dated 21 December 1940, Decroux tries unsuccessfully to win Barrault back to corporeal mime, to convince him that their collaborative ascetic research and development counted more than the worldly success of Barrault's lucrative stage and film work. Decroux wrote:

> Do you remember our visit to the Vincennes Zoo and our ecstasy in watching the acrobatic monkeys[3] playing from one tree to another?
> You know why we went there? It wasn't for fun; we should even go regularly, indeed every week.
> What do you say to this proposal: our second outing, in the same spirit, would be to visit the Musée Rodin.
>
> (Decroux/Barrault correspondance)

Thus, Decroux suggested weekly reminders of, on one extreme, the sudden movements, thoughtful rhythms and quivering immobilities of monkeys and, on the other, the heroically spiraling efforts of the eternally fixed human body at the Musée Rodin. Decroux proposed the mysteriously "present" living primate and the inert yet expressively contorted "absent" bronze and marble figures as opposing yet complementary bookends—"in the same spirit," as he wrote—for their nascent corporeal mime.

Copeau's and Bing's scrutiny of animal movements regenerated their own and their disciples' work, eventually giving birth to multiple and diverse manifestations in actor training in many parts of the world, continuing until the present time. Copeau and Bing aimed not at performing clever imitations of animals for their own and others' amusement, but instead discovered how the human animal needed to remember immediacy, a certain state of grace, so evident in Nénette, in children, in the person on a tightrope, and in "our teacher the cat." This "remembering" often had to do with "emptying out" rather than adding on: the actor's ideal state for improvisations and for acting of any kind originated in a letting go of *cabotinage*—of exaggerated facial expressions, of any form of affectation—and a subsequent open embrace of the simplicity and authenticity sometimes known as "presence."

Notes

1. On at least two separate occasions, I heard both Decroux and Jerzy Grotowski say "the actor must be as relaxed as an old peasant."
2. Copeau must have known the work of photographer E. Muybridge and his French disciple Etienne-Jules Marey whose pre-cinema still photographs of animals and people in motion revolutionized the study of movement within and outside the theatre.
3. Decroux's use of the generic "monkeys" leaves to our imagination the specific movement qualities exhibited by the animals they saw.

Works Cited

Barrault, Jean-Louis (1951) *Reflections on the Theatre*, London: Rockliff.

Brook, Peter (2012) *Tightrope*, Film, 2012, dir. Simon Brook.

Copeau, Jacques (1979) *Registres III, Les Registres du Vieux Colombier*, ed. Marie-Hélène Dasté, Paris: Gallimard.

—— (1991). *Journal 1901-1915*, Vol. 1, Journal 1916–1948, Vol. 2, Paris: Seghers.

Decroux, Etienne (1978) *Etienne Decroux 80th Birthday Issue*, Claremont, CA: Mime Journal.

—— (2001) "The Seahorse," in *An Etienne Decroux Album*, Claremont, CA: Mime Journal.

—— (2003) "L'interview Imaginaire," ed. Patrick Pezin, *Etienne Decroux, Mime Corporel*, Saint-Jean-de-Védas: L'Entretemps éditions.

—— (2008) "A New School," ed. Thomas Leabhart and Franc Chamberlain, *The Decroux Sourcebook*, New York: Routledge.

28 *Monkey business and Robin revelations*

Decroux/Barrault correspondence, Bibliothèque nationale de France, Richelieu-Louvois, arts du spectacle, Paris.

Dorcy, Jean (1975) *The Mime*, trans. Robert Speller Jr. and Marcel Marceau, New York: White Lion Publishers Limited.

Frondon, Jean Michel (2010) blog.slate.fr/projection-publique/2010/04/04/nenette/.

Kuleshov, Lev (1974) *Kuleshov on Film*, ed. and trans. Ronald Levaco, Los Angeles: University of California Press.

Leabhart, Thomas and Franc Chamberlain (2008) *The Decroux Sourcebook*, New York: Routledge.

Murat, Pierre. Consulted 21 July 2014. Can be viewed at: www.telerama.fr/cinema/films/nenette,397910,critique.php#9y5dM3GoiRDXEvS.

Philibert, Nicolas. Consulted 21 July 2014. Can be viewed at: www.zoonaute.net/jardindesplantes-nenettelefilm.html.

——— Consulted 21 July 2014. Can be viewed at: www.sciencesetavenir.fr/nature-environnement/20100330.OBS1567/nicolas-philibert-j-ai-filme-nenette-comme-la-joconde.html.

Saint-Denis, Michel (2009) "Acting Guidelines," *Theatre: The Rediscovery of Style and Other Writings*, New York: Routledge.

4 Friday night pearls of wisdom

"It is not necessary to hope in order to undertake, nor to succeed in order to persevere."

William the Silent, often quoted by Etienne Decroux

In Decroux's working-class cottage, a 70-year old master (never at a loss for words) introduced his students to an enriched level of non-verbal learning. Even our few European classmates felt unprepared for this singular educational adventure. We had all landed in unfamiliar territory: we saw the teacher in his home, often in his pajamas and met firsthand a figure from another century and perhaps another world. What a collision—the terre-à-terre, cheek by jowl with late modernist abstraction.

While most of the time he took center stage, we grew to know that Monsieur Decroux's counterpart, Madame Decroux, played an essential role in our uncommon apprenticeship. Our contact with her followed a predictable schedule: we brushed by her table before and after each lesson, crossing her tiny spotless kitchen. Her upbeat, not overly cheerful, can-do attitude grounded the school that otherwise could have self-destructed, whether from an angry explosion of the impassioned teacher or from the students' intoxicated euphoria on discovering new ways of being, on and off stage. Behind and underneath it all, Madame's necessary comings and goings darned the worn places: to the market, to the eye doctor, to the pharmacy, to the health food store, to the newsstand, down into the basement to look at a figure, at her husband's request. Back and forth, back and forth. And finally, toward the end of the evening class, the aromas of Madame's cuisine had wafted down the stairs where famished students were trying to keep body and soul together long enough to make it through the session. When the last student had been ushered out, she and Monsieur shared that fragrant meal.

She was his first collaborator, and his last. Without her, Etienne Decroux could not exist. We begin an essay—mostly about him—by acknowledging this.

During the last two decades of his life, Etienne Decroux taught corporeal mime in his home, a modest brick cottage at the back of a rectangular

DOI: 10.4324/9781003205852-4

30 *Friday night pearls of wisdom*

courtyard garden in a working-class suburb of southwest Paris. When I began classes in October of 1968, Decroux, already 70, seldom ventured out, preferring the world come to him. Students crossed the garden on a gravel path to enter the tiny house through the kitchen. Once inside, they removed their shoes and arranged them in concentric circles around the pot-bellied coal stove while Madame Decroux took roll from her Formica-topped table. (If students arrived while Madame was out shopping, she took roll, upon her return, simply by looking at the circles of shoes around the stove.) Students then proceeded to the upstairs sitting room to change clothes. They returned in single file down the narrow stairs and through the kitchen at the ringing of the brass ship's bell from the basement: it was the captain—Monsieur Decroux—signaling the start of class. Moments before taking his post, he had occupied himself in his study, adjacent to the kitchen, writing notes on etymology with a quill pen while smoking his clay pipe. At the bottom of the steps and before continuing into the workspace, Decroux, now at the helm, acknowledged each student individually with an elaborate ritual: saying the student's name while shaking hands and looking the student in the eye (and not releasing his hold until the student returned his gaze); the bestowing of a rope for the first exercise; addressing each person, sometimes by their real name but routinely by an invented one; and, often, adding a homonymic word play that went over the heads of the non-French speakers.

My four years inside this small and tightly choreographed cottage-world included daily classes and, after the first few months, an additional hour or more daily of one-on-one rehearsal with Decroux. I also attended about 200 eagerly anticipated and fiercely dreaded *séances du vendredi soir* [Friday evening sessions], and required of all students, regardless of their level.

Whereas for most of our lessons we wore tights or gymnastic clothing, during the lecture on Fridays we wore coats or sweaters over our practice clothes since, summer or winter, the basement was cool. We leaned against the damp walls, seated on small folding canvas stools placed around the perimeter of one end of the workroom. Some, grasping the significance of these meetings, held note pads or portable tape recorders in the hope of preserving fragments of the dizzying overview Decroux's spellbinding words provided. While usually solemn in tone, Decroux's remarks also contained flashes of delightful humor, as he often made fun of himself, of the art he had spent decades developing and teaching, and of his modest workspace. "Never forget that the first Christians also met in the catacombs!" he sang out merrily. These quips, which endeared him to us, helped dissipate some of the tension: while savoring our role of student audience, we never forgot that in an hour or less we might have the keen pleasure and terror of improvising for him. If he thought well of our attempt, this buoyed our courage for the next week of work; if he did not, the week-long interval before we might hope to redeem ourselves could seem endless.

Decroux lectured from a white wooden kitchen chair behind a small, varnished drop-leaf table brought out especially for the occasion from the

Friday night pearls of wisdom 31

deuxième cave [second basement]. After 1972, this portion of the basement became a second classroom in order to accommodate the influx of new students. However, during my time there (1968–1972), when our small numbers didn't require the additional teaching space, this depot contained dusty wine bottles, garden tools and small composite boards used by students as a support for practicing hand positions. And don't forget the geranium stems, hung roots-up, to weather the winter months. The pungent odor of those dormant, knobby stems disappeared in spring when Madame repotted them for the little patio in the front garden. Decroux used the geranium pot, like everything tangible around him, as an image to serve his teaching. We had to hold our outstretched arms, no matter what the desired shape, as if supporting geranium-filled clay pots. To make the point a physical one, he pushed on our arms with the approximate weight of these aforementioned pots, while shouting: "Don't move!"

The door to this "backstage"—the secondary basement beyond the basement studio—usually creaked open only once during each class when Decroux hung the ropes, used for the first exercise, back on their nail on the inside of the door. These color-coded cords reflected the rank of the various students: ordinary tan hemp for beginners, green silk for "*les anciens*" [senior students] and gold for the assistant. Decroux ceremonially distributed them at the start of every class and collected them with the same flair for ritual at the end of the first exercise. On other rare occasions, Decroux's imagination led him to rush to the door, fling it open and re-emerge seconds later bearing a rusty plumber's wrench, just the right heft to give a baffled student the sense of imposing weight needed in studying a counterweight.

In the "first basement," the high gloss sky blue paint of the walls merged with the linoleum floor of a similar blue streaked with white, the colors creating an aqueous effect. To Decroux's right, we saw the door leading to that *deuxième cave* along a mirrored wall reflecting his image in profile; to his left, the small and squat ceiling-level windows squinted onto the garden.

Decroux dressed in flannel pajamas, bathrobe and slippers most Friday evenings; he so preferred this costume at any hour of the day, that a journalist interviewer once came away calling him a *poseur en pyjamas*. For technique class, he sometimes dressed in black cotton boxer's shorts (Everlast, then a brand used only by professional boxers), black long-sleeved shirt and black leather gymnastic shoes; but he also happily and comfortably taught some technique classes in his flannel nightclothes. Decroux also demonstrated an unusual sartorial sense on his rare forays outside the house: black tuxedo trousers, white tennis shoes and an ample sky-blue shirt, sewn for him by a student assistant.

The English translator, indispensable, as most students were not French-speakers, sat to his right, facing slightly toward Monsieur. During my tenure in that chair, I wore, over my tights and leotard, a honey-colored velour bathrobe, a gift from Monsieur and Madame. This luxurious garment replaced my well-worn pea coat that doubtless worked against their desired

32 *Friday night pearls of wisdom*

stage picture. Monsieur Decroux requested that my successor as translator, the Englishman Mark Piper, would best perform his task, and most appropriately represent his country, by wearing a dark business suit and tie. While probably appearing incongruous to the other students, Mark's orchestrated attire reflected Decroux's sense of the evening's formality.

For the first hour of this event, Decroux "lectured": in fact, he responded to our questions. Among our other fears, loomed the dread of not knowing what to ask. If no suitable question surfaced, Decroux's mood darkened. Yet the crisis always passed; the questions, no matter how banal, usually opened his prolific imagination. The prelude to his response consisted of a noisily theatrical clearing of the throat, after which he would retrieve from the depths of his bathrobe pocket two hard honey candies. He slid one across the table to the translator and unwrapped the cellophane of the other with exaggerated crackling. He popped the sweet into his mouth and deposited the empty wrapper into his pocket. Thus fortified, he launched into that week's lecture. Throat clearing and candy sucking provided a warm-up of sorts for his beautifully placed voice whose musicality, rich timbre and clarity were not lost on any of us, including the non-native speakers. He remains one of the few people I have known who could truly thunder; when he did, anything or anybody within a certain proximity vibrated. He often pointed out that both speaking and corporeal mime required incisive articulation. One must, he admonished, "ar-ti-cu-late," whether with the voice or the body, as if addressing a hard of hearing person who, moreover, did not speak our language.

His delivery on these occasions could be relaxed and informal but as his enthusiasm rose, he resembled a political orator. At age 25, his interest in oratory led him to Jacques Copeau's, now legendary, Vieux Colombier school, where the study of movement soon replaced his initial desire simply to lose his *accent du faubourg* [an accent of working-class people from the suburbs of Paris]. In his 30s, he frequented large political meetings at the newly constructed Maison de la Mutualité where he became fond of the saying: "For the Orator, the Party is always in danger." Decroux, for whom the Party became corporeal mime, often treated the subjects "Mime does not yet exist" or "The Infirmities of Mime" with something of the same fervor and ardor that had spellbound him years before at those political rallies. Obsessed with the fear that his fledgling art could easily perish, he determined that it would not. He transfixed us with his deep conviction and with all the poetry, passion and eloquence he could muster on topics such as "Vocal Mime," "Mime and Sculpture," "Mime and Animated Film," "Mime and Marionettes," "Mime and Masks" and "Mime and Music." (See Patrick Pezin's "Imaginary Interview.") He returned to the same themes again and again, always cautioning us that he proceeded by free association, that his ideas on these issues were not yet completely set, and that doctrines, political or artistic, could easily become a refuge for the lazy-minded. Thus, his lectures were spoken improvisations, performed in response to our questions in the same way that

Friday night pearls of wisdom 33

we would subsequently perform, every Friday evening, silent improvisations in response to his reflections.[1]

With difficulty, he limited his remarks to an hour, digressing unrestrainedly until the last few moments of skillful synthesis in which he wove together all loose ends, responding to each apparently rejected question to return triumphantly to the original topic that had seemed long forgotten. He would then smile shyly, aware that his eloquent citations from a wide reading of French poetry, socialist and anarchist politics, and art had worked magic in strengthening his argument. As his son Maximilien pointed out, Decroux almost never read books on theatre or mime; he cited Baudelaire and Hugo more readily than the words of Stanislavsky or Brecht. He did, however, frequently mention his work with those theatre practitioners whose ideas he considered indispensable to the formation of corporeal mime, especially and reverentially Jacques Copeau, but also Louis Jouvet, Charles Dullin and Edward Gordon Craig. As an autodidact, who in his youth had implored Copeau's daughter Edi to teach him French grammar, he had little patience for academic scholars who didn't have his physical experience (both as a manual laborer and a mime) and who were, as he disdainfully described them, "sitting down." In his lecture on 8 February 1974, when asked about François Delsarte, Decroux admitted to having read the transcript of one of his lectures, but not having found it of much interest. He considered Delsarte a "sitting down person," not someone, who like himself, preferred to stand. In the next breath—and in perfect Decrouvian fashion—he allowed that he might have judged Delsarte unjustly, and that perhaps he had something to say after all.

Sometimes, due to fatigue or for want of inspiring questions, Decroux's customary eloquence failed, his talk rambled, took several false starts, sputtered and died. On these rare occasions, when unexpectedly defeated by the magnitude of his undertaking, he sighed loudly, casting hands and eyes to heaven while proclaiming that, as there remained so much more to say, he might as well say no more. Invariably, regardless of the relative success or failure of his extemporaneous speech, he generously thanked his listeners by observing that it was they who had accomplished the real work in having to struggle to follow where inspiration led him easily.

Then, while a few of the students dashed upstairs to the WC, he efficiently removed the wooden table, positioned his chair near the staircase to face the part of the studio that now became the stage, perhaps cleared his throat and unwrapped another honey candy (specially purchased by Madame at the health food store, La Vie Claire), in preparation for the grand finale of the *séance* and of the week: improvisations.

Although Decroux taught Saturday morning class during my years there, the formality and tension of Friday evening always made it seem like the climax of the week. Contrastingly, Decroux devoted the Saturday class almost entirely to that part of his research entitled Walks which allowed our eager bodies to devour the space, despite the confining parameters of the basement

34 *Friday night pearls of wisdom*

studio. This unleashing made us giddy after having worked for so many hours during the week standing in one place.

Thus, of Decroux's seven weekly class sessions, Monday through Saturday (with a daytime and evening session on Friday), six were technique classes. And, as I've begun to explain, the Friday session had a different format and different content: unlike the technique classes, Friday evening's two-part session began with that lecture by Decroux on the philosophical under-pinnings of corporeal mime, after which the students improvised. With this two-part structure of the class, Decroux's lecture had prepared the way—provided a context—for the improvisations that followed. With the post-lecture, Friday improvisation practicum, Decroux afforded the students an opportunity to demonstrate how technique, instead of merely a highly articulated form they strove daily to master, could become a servant of their imagination, could function from the "inside out," and could also operate as a basis for dramaturgy in a non-Stanislavskian context.

For the improvisation part of the class, Decroux extinguished the fluorescent lighting and, with a mock-affected wave of his hand, called for the two spotlights that he affectionately termed *lumières artistiques*. Bathed in the cold white beams, we made that transition from theory to practice more or less successfully: the blue linoleum under our feet became either a sky, exalting us, or the ocean's depth drowning us in defeat.

Under Decroux's unblinking regard that filled us so much more with terror than did the opinions of our peers, solo or duet improvisations often began from behind the white curtains that covered the far wall of the rectangular basement. The student–actor waited there in silence for the right moment of appropriate "emptiness" before appearing, gradually or suddenly, through the curtains' center opening: first a hand or an arm, perhaps in slow motion, followed by a sudden unveiling of the face, an immobility followed by the gradual emergence of the rest of the body into the playing space.

In successful improvisations, no matter what the theme, the dynamo-rhythm (speed, weight, itinerary and quality of movement) dominated. While one of the common criticisms of corporeal mime depicts it as lacking breath, the performer a kind of rigid automaton, Decroux's teaching and performance at its best highlighted the contrary: he insisted that we initiate movements internally, originating in the biceps for arm and hand movements; in the buttocks for leg and foot movements; and radiate out from the sternum for movements of the trunk. These internal vibratory movements, thus, began invisibly before the first externally discernable ones. The body's visible movements emanated from "muscular respirators," originating with a "singing within," in order to become "*en-chanté*." Moreover, these micro-movements continued oscillating invisibly even after the apparent movement had ceased. As an example, Decroux reminded us that an automobile's engine turned before the vehicle itself began to move, and also after it had stopped. This idea of a pre-movement, essential in technique classes, was equally crucial to his notion of improvisation.

Friday night pearls of wisdom   35

From among the improvisation themes—at once simple and almost impossible—Decroux frequently selected that of The Thinker (either alone or in a group, and which he sometimes called Meditation). With varying levels of success, we manifested the attitudes and rhythms of thought: perhaps at an auspicious moment, The Thinker became Pure Thought as the actor changed movement styles from *Homme de Salon* (a purely classical and highly articulated vocabulary) to *Homme de Sport* (a more athletic way of moving, engaging the whole body and often taking the actor onto the ground).

One student, Jan Munroe (b. 1952), expressed what so many of us felt during these attempts to reach some level of achievement in this elusive exercise.

Fear of failure at something one couldn't HOPE TO SUCCEED at. His improv goals (unlike his technique) were completely incomprehensible to me. How do you portray the abstract through the concrete? What did that even MEAN? But the few times I actually saw one "work" was a vivid and rare experience: one which indeed did transcend the actor's flesh and personality and portray thought in pure movement. However I also know in the two years I was there, I never accomplished it on my own nor as part of a "love duet." That said, toward the end of my time there, I DID begin to understand what he was talking about and the purity to which he wished all of us to aspire by doing them.

Most Friday nights I looked forward to his lectures, his humor, his grace, his "old school" outlook on life. For most of us Americans of "a certain age" who were burdened with the blade of Viet Nam hanging over our heads, his basement was truly the portal to another dimension. But after the lecture, as time approached for the "improv" section of the evening, I found myself pressing harder and harder against the wall in an attempt to melt through it to the relative safety of the draft board. Communist hordes and getting shot at took on a certain appeal; didn't seem such a bad alternative to standing behind that white curtain waiting for the spotlight to snap on which would signal the improv's beginning.

I remember thinking, "Perhaps if I do not move or breathe, I will NOT be noticed and called upon. I won't be chosen." This trick actually worked quite a few times. But the Friday night finally arrived when I heard my name being called: Ce soir, notre camarade Jan, debout!" [This evening, our friend Jan, on your feet!] Slinking behind the curtain with my partner (at this point of my life, I can't remember which ones I embarrassed by my participation), the light snapped on, I took a deep breath (or maybe I stopped breathing which would account for my not remembering it that well) and parted the curtains.

And then the improv began. The problem was in order to portray "pure thought," one had to quit thinking. And of course, when all you can think about is NOT thinking, your mind becomes a whirl. "Okay, portraying the abstract by the concrete here!" popped into my mind while I desperately tried to "fit the hump into the hollow" in regards to

36 *Friday night pearls of wisdom*

my partner's body position and at the same time, stay BEHIND her so as to avoid being seen FAILING MISERABLY at my attempts to transcend this too, too mortal flesh.

If to portray thought was the goal of the improv (NOT humans thinking but THOUGHT itself–without thinking, mind you, nor ACTIVELY trying to do so), I believe I managed two quite well: terror and confusion.

(Munroe)

Decroux sometimes called these group improvisations of Thinkers "Lunch Break at the Research Lab," imagining individuals gathered in the same space but with each occupying his own mental world, not consciously relating to the others. Often, Decroux started with solo and duet work but, as class time slipped away, moved on to larger groups (sometimes as many as five or six), assuring the participation of all class members. An analogous improvisation, entitled "Waiting," required students, either alone or in groups, to manifest five qualities essential to corporeal mime: pause, weight, resistance, hesitation and surprise.

Frequently, Decroux selected the Love Duet as an improvisation subject contrasting with The Thinker. He warmly praised love as a motor force in human life, and with tears in his eyes, reminded us how Jesus had forgiven Mary Magdalene because she had "loved much." (We soon grew accustomed to seeming contradictions which had in fact deep convergence: although an atheist, Decroux's depth of emotion in quoting Scripture in defense of love seemed coherent within the totality of his teaching.) In the Love Duets, we were encouraged to place convex parts of our body into the partner's concavities: the head fit nicely into the small of the partner's back, or into the cradle of the partner's arm, or between the partner's shoulder and neck (decades before the invention of Contact Improvisation). In all improvisations, he insisted that we develop relationships without looking with the eyes, encouraging us to "look" with other parts of the body. The improvisers should relate to each other as do puppies of same litter or like two or more thoughts in the same mind, but never as person to person in a realistic situation requiring eye contact and speech.

Decroux responded to our unaccustomed efforts to work "from the inside out" variously: mockery, warm praise, anger or compassionate tenderness. Sometimes in the middle of an improvisation, he could be heard breathing loudly in the basement twilight, encouraging in a loud stage whisper *C'est beau, mon petit . . . continue!* [That's nice, son . . . keep going!]. Or he interrupted incisively with a mocking "*C'est beau . . . mais c'est pas ça!*" [That's nice, but that's not it!], signaling an abrupt end to the exploration. Often our efforts were met with a long, cold silence followed by a tentative "*Oui . . . si tu veux*" ["Yes . . . whatever"] as a transition into a lengthy catalogue of our failings on that particular occasion—comments like "You must sing with your muscles," or "You have not found the rhythm of thought," or "Don't try so hard to be interesting, just be," or "When you look directly at your

Friday night pearls of wisdom 37

partner, it is obscene," or "You blind the eyes of the space with your brutally sharp gestures," or, perhaps the worst reprimand, "You are directing yourself!" I remember him asking me to "empty out the apartment so that God can come to live there," and Leonard Pitt (b. 1941), student from the mid-1960s, remembers a similar admonition to a fellow student, this time during a technique class: "You must not want to express yourself. On the contrary, you must empty yourself and fill this space with the soul of God." Decroux immediately countered anything that seemed the least bit self-expressive with a comment like: "Don't show yourself. It is indecent to do so!" All this while, delicious aromas of Madame Decroux's cooking wafted down the staircase and into the studio filled with students whose meager budgets had likely prevented them from having eaten anything substantial that day.

Two mythical goddesses reigned over these unusual subterranean activities. The first, a black-and-white photograph of the *Winged Victory of Samothrace*, hung on the east wall near the staircase. Decroux, always learning from sculpture, admired this statue's forward movement, the aerodynamic swirl of cloth pulling backward against the figure that pushed forward onto one leg. The second goddess-witness, more physically present than her winged sister, but similarly enigmatic and equally black-and-white, was one Madame de Billy, who sometimes attended on Friday evening. A woman of a certain age and amplitude, she usually dressed in black and wore a double-strand necklace of large, perfect white pearls. When she arrived by taxi from her apartment in the elegant 16th arrondissement (adjacent but light-years away from Decroux's working-class Boulogne-Billancourt), either Monsieur or Madame greeted her courteously at the door, at which time the cry rang out: "*Qui va chercher le fauteuil de Madame de Billy?*" ["Who is going to get Madame de Billy's armchair?"] Students scurried, exchanging knowing glances. Finally, some courageous male student obliged, lugging the comfortably padded chair from Decroux's office, backing down the perilously narrow staircase, almost stumbling under the chair's weight. Monsieur Decroux then escorted his guest deferentially to the basement studio, adding with a vocal and gestural flourish, "*Voilà! Le fauteuil de Madame de Billy!*" [There we are! Madame de Billy's armchair!] as he kissed her hand and led her to her perch. From there, as the evening unfolded, she listened with obvious affection and rapt attention, took notes, made drawings, nodded, murmured and peered up with eyes almost lost in the creases of her round face.

Monsieur once explained to me that she was an aristocrat, the wife of a diplomat and a trusted friend of many years standing. Leonard Pitt, given the task of hanging the embossed leather wall covering in Monsieur's study, told me that it had been a gift from Madame de Billy.

In retrospect, Monsieur Decroux must have had Madame de Billy's pearls in mind when telling us the following story. "Imagine," he said, "that I show you a necklace of potatoes (that is, a long performance piece, as yet poorly done, ill conceived, under-rehearsed) and ask you to imagine a necklace of pearls (the transformation of this sloppy work into an exquisitely polished

38   *Friday night pearls of wisdom*

piece, after sufficient rehearsal). It would prove impossible to imagine! But, if I show you one perfect pearl (a brief, perfectly executed figure or improvisation) and ask you to imagine an entire necklace (a whole performance composed of equally beautiful sections) you could do it." Decroux delighted in spending months on creating a treasured pearl and often despaired of ever keeping students long enough to realize his dream of completing a necklace.

The pearl metaphor became important in another way, as Decroux delighted in the way artists create work ("pearls") from small and difficult irritants that come into their experience; such bits of sand must be coated, daily a bit more, with the luminous secretions of technique, imagination, courage and persistence. One might well compare the blue basement to a pool where oyster-artists produced cultured pearls. Under the tutelage of the master oyster-cultivator, who believed in technique and method as much as he did in the beauty of inspiration, we learned that "Patience is a long passion."

The conclusion of the improvisations marked the end of the Friday night session. As Madame de Billy found her taxi back to the 16th, most students proceeded either to the Métro or to Georgette's café next door to celebrate success, drown failure or debate the issues Decroux had raised. And, thus, the little house at the back of the garden at 85, avenue Edouard Vaillant returned to a quieter mode as Decroux retired to his study with Mark Piper. Over a glass or two of Pelforth (a heavy brown ale, brewed in Marseille, that Decroux affectionately called *la faiblesse*), they discussed the "*grand a*" in English and French words. As interested in language as he was in movement, Decroux had lost patience with the tendency of the French to neglect pronouncing the broad or large "a." In this regard, he felt that speakers on the French radio set a poor and "lazy" example. Piper's fluent French and Oxford degree in linguistics made him the perfect companion from whom Decroux eagerly sought English parallels to fortify his argument that the gradual disappearance of this sound in French, like the disappearance of one of the musical notes on a scale, impoverished the language. This linguistic concern, far from being a new one, had occupied his thought for years. Indeed, for the previous generation of students, Decroux had offered weekly diction lessons.

Sometimes, at this point in the evening (provided that she had not already stopped by earlier in the day), Madame Hiturelde would appear with her *petit* scabby dog under her arm. This rheumy-eyed neighbor was wife to the Basque bus driver who occasionally captured bits of Deroux's work with his 8-mm home-movie camera.

Madame Decroux's high pitched squeals of "Oh, my sweet little thing!" alerted Monsieur, who emerged swiftly from the study, all tender solicitation enveloped in agile, efficient movement. Deftly, he took the tin sugar box down from the shelf, placed a cube between his front teeth and, as Madame Hiturelde pushed the wriggling creature forward, the dog's rosy tongue and pointed teeth, well-trained in the ritual, withdrew the sugar from Monsieur's lips. For a fleeting moment, their shining liquid eyes met in mutual and unabashed love.

Any lingering student would have witnessed this exchange after an evening in which an anarchist entertained a royalist and an atheist praised God. These incongruities surprised no one in a small garden cottage in Boulogne-Billancourt. The last exhausted student boarded the Métro at the Marcel Sembat station; after a final commute (his fourth of the day) in the fluorescent harshness of rumbling tunnels beneath the City of Light, he returned to his seventh-floor walk-up maid's room (no heat, shared toilet and cold water spigot in the hall, but a view of the Eiffel Tower out the tiny skylight window), to a dinner of baguette and *gruyère* while balancing on the edge of a narrow bed. Soon, succumbing to the deepest sleep, his dreams plunged him into the sublimity and grandeur of art, and eyes and pearls and lights swimming in a deep-blue pool.

Acknowledgment

Thanks to Mark Piper, Leonard Pitt, Morton Potash and Corinne Soum for allowing me to incorporate some of their memories into this essay. Thanks also to Professor William Fisher for reading and commenting, and to Jan Munroe for his account of improvisations. An earlier version of this article first appeared in *Mime Journal* 1997.

Note

1. In earlier periods, Decroux lectured on other evenings.

Work Cited

Decroux, Etienne (2003) "L'interview Imaginaire," ed. Patrick Pezin, *Etienne Decroux, Mime Corporel*, Saint-Jean-de-Védas: L'Entretemps éditions.
Munroe, Jan. E-mail to author, 29 July 2012.

5 E.G. Craig's Übermarionette and E. Decroux's "actor made of wood"

Co-written with Sally Leabhart

Mention Edward Gordon Craig, even among the well-educated, and brace yourself for mocking words: "Oh, he's the guy who wanted to replace actors with puppets!" If we consider the timeline of Craig's event-filled life, only the tiniest fraction represents the period in which he held the absolute conviction that puppets should replace actors. Craig kept learning, experimenting and growing, looking at theatre, reading about it and pondering it. Trying to pin Craig down on the subject of the Übermarionette, then as now, proves impossible. His visionary work confronted thorny issues in twentieth-century theatre: the role of the director; three dimensional vs. painted scenery; the actor's spatial relationship to the audience; the nature of "acting" itself; lessons from the mask and the marionette and many more.

Curiously, Jacqui Beckford's sign language performance of Prince's "Nothing Compares 2U" (Beckford 2021), sung by the late jazz vocalist Little Jimmy Scott (recorded in 1998), brings to mind Craig's description of the "Art of Showing and of Veiling in the House of Visions." Craig fell under the influence of the Orientalism of his time in imagining the ceremonial and theatrical movements of the fictional Egyptian queen. A century after Craig's description, does Beckford's performance, with origins, this time, in American jazz and British Sign Language, embody Craig's textual example of a spellbinding and transporting presentation?

In search of ancestors

When I studied with Etienne Decroux from 1968 to 1972, he mentioned Edward Gordon Craig less frequently than he did Copeau, Dullin or Jouvet, but often enough that I considered Craig a member of Decroux's inner circle of influences. I read Decroux's comments on Craig in *Words on Mime* and in later years encountered a 1940s photo taken by Etienne Bertrand Weill of Decroux, Craig, Craig's daughter Daphne and Decroux's company at that time: Marcel Marceau, Eliane Guyon, Pierre Verry, Decroux's son Maximilien and others.

I found in Craig's manifesto, "The Actor and the Über-Marionette," similarities to Decroux's statements and practice. For example, Craig writes that

DOI: 10.4324/9781003205852-5

actors "must create for themselves a new form of acting, consisting for the main part of symbolical gesture" (Craig 2009, 300). For Decroux's actor, the "new form" involves a highly articulated body, not as a substitute for a missing text (as in pantomime or a text-driven performance) but as an expressive element in and of itself. I believe we can understand Craig's use of the term "symbolical" in the context of the late nineteenth-century's Symbolist movement where signifiers (words, in the case of poets) self-consciously find their value, their primacy, in their associative or evocative function rather than merely as tools for denotation. In the theatrical realm about which Craig writes, the moving body appropriates this evocative function. The description of "symbolic movements" in the following Orientalist passage, gives priority to the power of gesture to evoke, suggest and coolly express. The following excerpt, in which Craig sets forth "The Art of Showing and Veiling," seems to adumbrate corporeal mime in its discussion of those phrased, articulate, and controlled gestures as embodied by a puppet. Or does he refer to the performance of a fully evolved living actor as Übermarionette? In either case, in underscoring the need to resuscitate the lost high art he vividly evokes, Craig dissembles by attributing the account to an old Greek traveler of 800 BCE.[1] Craig, thus veiled, presents his own suggestive and deliberately paradoxical view of acting—a portrait of and for the ideal future actor:

> Coming into the House of Visions I saw afar off the fair brown Queen seated upon her throne—her tomb—for both it seemed to me. I. . . watched her symbolic movements. With so much ease did her rhythms alter as with her movements they passed from limb to limb; with such a show of calm did she unloose for us the thoughts of her breast; so gravely and so beautifully did she linger on the statement of her sorrow, that with us it seemed as if no sorrow could harm her; no distortion of body or feature allowed us to dream that she was conquered; the passion and the pain were continually being caught by her hands, held gently, and viewed calmly. Her arms and hands seemed at one moment like a thin warm fountain of water which rose, then broke and fell with all those sweet pale fingers like spray into her lap. It would have been a revelation of art to us had I not already seen that the same spirit dwelt in the other examples of the art of these Egyptians. The "Art of Showing and Veiling" plays the larger part in their religion. We may learn from it somewhat of the power and the grace of courage, for it is impossible to witness a performance without a sense of physical and spiritual refreshment.
>
> (Craig 2009, 40)

Does Craig's seated "fair brown Queen" tell a story with her hands and fingers, creating *mudras*, or are her movements what Decroux called "subjective mime," a kind of pure corporeal expression which suggests emotions without plot: "the passion and the pain . . . caught by her hands, held gently, viewed calmly"? Whether we imagine that she moves only arms, hands and fingers

42 E.G. Craig's Übermarionette

or perhaps includes subtle sympathetic movements of head, neck and upper body, her style of playing avoids expressionism in favor of cool classicism.

Craig's "inconsistencies": venturing beyond the "either-or"

The actor's bodily movements—we find no reference to the voice—provoke "a sense of physical and spiritual refreshment" in the audience whose response attests to the performer's artistry. And yet, now in his own voice, Craig's subsequent query as to "whether the puppet shall not once again become the faithful medium for the beautiful thoughts of the artist," raises other questions for us too: was that imaginary performer an inanimate object, controlled, directed or in some way inhabited by a human? Craig leaves no doubt that his actor performed consummately, but was he advocating a wooden marionette or a living actor? How can we know, since during his long career, Craig envisioned many and various permutations of inanimate actors and animate ones.

The question—living actor or marionette—tantalizes theatre practitioners since the human body and the body of the marionette pose dissimilar technical challenges. Patrick Le Boeuf, for example, reveals a host of technical problems facing an actor animating a large puppet from within (2010). Theatre professionals quickly realize that the size, weight and structure of an Übermarionette driven from inside by a living actor would greatly limit movement possibilities, reducing the actor to a supernumerary or a stage-hand assigned to move props but incapable of transferring variations of dynamo-rhythm[2] to his load.

Thus, the compelling musically phrased and articulated performance described by Craig (see above), emerges as a feat far easier to imagine than to realize. For example, the phrase "With so much ease did her rhythms alter as with her movements they passed from limb to limb" highlights two things: the *trajectory* of the movement, *passing from limb to limb*, and the *alternating rhythmic qualities* of the movement. Only a finely articulated instrument can execute such a complex trajectory with ease, and no puppet Craig might have seen in Europe could have pulled off the sophisticated dynamo-rhythm of a performer whose "arms and hands seemed at one moment like a thin warm fountain of water which rose, then broke and fell with all those sweet pale fingers like spray into her lap."

Had Craig travelled to Japan, he could have witnessed Bunraku puppetry that, since the 1600s, has codified and polished an exemplary total theatre form. To each wooden entity, Bunraku assigns three highly skilled puppeteers with decades of training; two musicians, a singer-narrator and a *shamisen* player, accompany the action. Thereby, the Bunraku theatre successfully intertwines human *and* wooden elements, the fruit of centuries of development, allowing complex geometric trajectories along with intricately varied movement qualities of speed, weight and vibrato.

Had Craig been able to look into the future, he might have enjoyed the work of South Africa's Handspring Puppet Company. Adrian Kohler and Basil Jones create finely jointed, lightweight and transportable cane figures, often manipulated by as many as three puppeteers. Their ability to move at once "realistically" and "poetically"—unencumbered, articulate and variously dynamic—rivals the level of complexity attributed to the Egyptian Queen's fluid gestures.

As the ingenious solutions brought to bear by Handspring or the Bunraku were unknown to Craig, his theoretical writings expose valid technical limitations in the European puppetry of his time. However, we might well consider his proposals from another perspective, one that sees "living" or "wooden" as qualifiers designating opposite, yet co-existing, *qualities* for the performing agent (whether living or wooden) worthy of the title Übermarionette. To the question "living or wooden," one could answer living *and* wooden, both at the same time, in the same space and in the same single performer. In other words, if the performer is a wooden puppet, those who move it would have found the means to endow the cool puppet instrument with sufficiently subtle "warm," human-like movement qualities; if the performer is a live actor, he or she would have sufficiently mastered a complex movement vocabulary so as to achieve a highly articulated, extra-quotidian, and puppet-like quality. From this standpoint, Craig's descriptive paragraph provides a treatise on magical performance with its indispensable components and their constantly changing organization. His undeniable ambiguity, then, does not perhaps aim to obfuscate—is not an invitation to a guessing game ("Is he describing a wooden puppet or a live actor?"). Instead, it reads more like a thoughtful delineation of Craig's vision for the modernist actor: a call to reinvent the actor's art. From this reading, instead of Craig attempting to throw us off track, he holds nothing back. Or, as Kohler and Jones stated in their TED Talk, "The [living] actor struggles to die on stage, the [wooden] puppet struggles to live" (Kohler/Jones).

Contraries are complementary

Influenced by the poems and prints of the mystic-Romantic William Blake, to whom he dedicated *On the Art of the Theatre*, Craig's visionary and poetic writings on the Übermarionette sometimes baffle scholars who find them "contradictory" (Le Boeuf 2014, 102). Craig's dedication to Blake—"the ever living genius of the greatest of English artists"—calls to mind that creator's highly theatricalized watercolor rendering of human figures. Often in opposition, lunging, kneeling, leaning, dancing and swooping, struggling with spirits and demons, these vigorously and fluidly committed embodiments seem to illustrate Blake's belief that a "man who never alters his opinion [or in this case, position] is like standing water and breeds reptiles of the mind" (Blake). To guide us further in considering whether the indiscernible (i.e. wooden puppet or actor moving like a puppet) in Craig's

44   E.G. Craig's Übermarionette

writing represents an omission or a gift, we might remember the words that Saint-Exupéry attributes to his Little Prince: "It is only with the heart that one can see rightly; what is essential is invisible to the eye," (Saint-Exupéry) or of F. Scott Fitzgerald's oft-quoted lines: "The test of a first rate intelligence is the ability to hold two opposed ideas in the mind at the same time, and still retain the ability to function" (Fitzgerald). Similarly, some entrepreneurs and scientists cultivate a "tolerance for ambiguity" as a key to success, while physicist Niels Bohr adopted as his motto *"Contraria sunt Complementa,"* later borrowed by Eugenio Barba's International School of Theatre Anthropology (ISTA).

Craig "contradicts" himself only in the same invaluable way that artists frequently juxtapose disparate elements to create Dadaist poems, or to assemble surrealist collages, to edit films, or to write jokes, Zen koans, Christian parables and Sufi stories. For example, in lines near those quoted above, Craig describes the Übermarionette not as "flesh and blood but rather the body in trance—it will aim to clothe itself with a death-like beauty while exhaling a living spirit" (2009, 40). This presence-and-absence, a performer simultaneously alive and dead, conjures up a marionettized actor who, like a dervish dancer or one of Blake's energetic figures, embodies the ambiguity of that double consciousness: the ability to move with stillness, and to stand still while moving within.[3]

In the "Actor and the Über-Marionette," Craig delineates four versions of animate (or living) and inanimate (or wooden) actors. Clearly, Craig seeks to banish the degraded approximation of the living actor, led by personality and ill-equipped to induce "physical and spiritual refreshment" in audience members. Such an actor offers flashiness rather than the flash of genius. This actor remains vulnerable to the pull of the ego, having failed to cultivate the physical and mental resources that would save him or her from distraction; thus, applause or the lack of it guides the performance down a less than noble path. Craig lays out for us what a living actor could learn from the highest manifestation of the art of the marionette (Craig 2009, 39–40).

Yet, in proposing a non-human performer, Craig issues a warning rather than offering a panacea, since even the admirable and noble marionette has a degraded counterpart: comic-looking (and only seeking a laugh); with an expression of blank stupidity instead of gravitas; with a jittery, jiggling body displaying angular deformity instead of calmness (Ibid., 39). Craig found that these demeaned variants of their estimable wooden forbears "have forgotten the counsel of their mother the Sphinx. Their bodies have lost their grave grace, they have become stiff. Their eyes have lost that infinite subtlety of seeming to see; now they only stare (Ibid., 40).

Without presuming to read Craig's mind, his texts invite us to consider the possibility of a performer manifesting "living qualities" (whether in an actor of flesh and blood or in a wooden marionette), along with "puppet qualities" (in an actor of flesh and blood or in a wooden marionette). Every person alive does not possess stage-worthy "living qualities." Craig warned against the failed (human) actor, doomed because subject to personality. Likewise, not every marionette demonstrates stage-worthy "puppet qualities." As we have seen, Craig railed against a banal and comic version of a marionette. The highest actorly "living qualities" exist thus only through their perfect and nearly impossible marriage with the highest artful "puppet qualities" *within the same performer.*[4] They require each other, emerge through a negotiated co-existence of opposites, in the way that a flickering candle flame vacillates between light and darkness: this "intermittency" gives to its light, paradoxically, a fragile vibrancy, a vibrant fragility, while conferring to its darkness an explosive potential that accords vulnerability and therefore more depth to its shadows. The "and-and" transfixes and delights in a way that the "either-or" does not. The "and-and" depends on muscular respiration[5] and the constantly oscillating, flickering candle flame named dynamo-rhythm.

If the wooden actor (like a robot) becomes too humanized, or the human actor becomes too wooden, it falls into Masahiro Mori's "uncanny valley," where the spectator feels at best uncomfortable and at worst threatened. Only delicate alternations and shadings of artifice successfully produce a *portrait* of life.

Thus Craig's text, we speculate, never argues simply for the "either-or," the fleshly vs. the wooden, but presents both failed and noble versions of the marionette as well as the failed and noble versions of the actor. Even if the Greek Traveler's account of "The Art of Showing and Veiling" leaves us to wonder if he chronicles a *puppet* performance, Craig unequivocally identifies a multi-faceted performer embracing commonalities in acting/puppetry/ ritual/performance.

Decroux and Craig

Decroux first encountered Craig's ideas, filtered through Copeau, while a student at the Ecole du Vieux Colombier in 1923. Craig and Decroux began a mutually respectful acquaintanceship in Paris in the 1940s: not only did Craig write perceptively and appreciatively of Decroux's performance in 1945 (Craig 2001, 95–7), he also lent his name as President to Decroux's school the following year; actively undertook a search for an impresario to help book tours for Decroux's troupe (Decroux/Craig); and sent his daughter Daphne and his apprentice Harvey Grossman to study with Decroux. These signs of admiration and affection were perhaps unmatched in Craig's life of single-minded focus on his own work.

In recent years, I have attempted to identify influences leading to various strands of Decroux's work. Although a Darwinian chain, echoing the biblical "begats," fails to explain everything, it associates nonetheless certain personalities and movements. For example, passages in Craig's biography of his godfather, Henry Irving, suggest that Irving's idiosyncratic, hypnotic acting style (Craig 1930, 52–4) served as a partial and indirect source of Craig's and, later, I argue, of Decroux's aesthetic.

46 *E.G. Craig's Übermarionette*

In Craig's subsequent writing about the Übermarionette, he trades the borrowed historical voice for his own and relates what he *saw* rather than only imagined:

> Irving was the nearest thing ever known to what I have called the Übermarionette . . . *an actor who should be all that a marionette is and much more.* But there is a point that I never touched on. It is a human point, and it is related to Irving, for *from Irving the whole notion receives corroboration.*
>
> (Ibid., 32, emphasis added)

"We have done well in choosing him as our leader" (1985, 9), Decroux wrote of Craig in 1947. He deals with the perplexing parts of Craig's text by suggesting that these "contradictions" are unimportant:

> [I]s it really important to know whether Craig declares himself for the marionette or for the human body; for the actor alone or as complemented by the other arts? Does it matter if he contradicts himself *or if I have misunderstood his thinking*? It does not matter that he writes sometimes as a pamphleteer, sometimes as a philosopher, and sometimes as an artist; what counts is the idea suggested by the central current of his thought.
>
> (Decroux 1985, 8)

Decroux's "actor made of wood"

Decroux, as much a pamphleteer, philosopher and artist as his subject, and not to be outdone by Craig, defends the idea of a literal Ubermarionette—a wooden articulated figure—as a *potential* instrument for true drama, for high art. He proclaims, however, that the art of the marionette was not yet sufficiently evolved in that direction. Moreover, corporeal mime, through its continued development, could one day richly inform the art of the marionette, providing a training ground wherein it could reach those dramatic heights. Decroux writes:

> I personally wish for the birth of this actor made of wood. I envision this large-scale marionette arousing, by its appearance and its movements, a feeling of seriousness and not of condescension. The marionette that we desire must not make us laugh or feel moved as does the playing [stage acting] of a young child. It must inspire terror and pity and, from there, rise to the level of the waking dream. . . . Is it not obvious that our way will have been substantially paved when the practice of corporeal mime becomes learned.
>
> (Ibid.)

Whether a marionette-like living actor or an inanimate puppet that seems alive, Craig spoke of (and inspired in Decroux) the notion of an absent-present performer, a dual presence on the stage, showing by veiling, and art as vibration (muscular respiration). These irreducible, non-negotiable, qualities of the new/old actor (whether live or wooden), constitute for Decroux the essence or distilled aspect of Craig's doctrine. As we have seen, Decroux considers the question of whether Craig advocated a living or a wooden Übermarionette irrelevant and perhaps unknowable. More pertinent for him is the fact that theorizing does not suffice. The wooden Übermarionette has yet to be constructed and Craig had yet to elaborate completely his actor art. As for the living Übermarionette, Decroux labored in that field until the end of his life. The construction and performance of a wooden Übermarionette, like Decroux's corporeal mime, would require a detailed study of geometry's possibilities for the body. And geometry sets a high standard.

The field of geometry, which exists in the realm of thought, opens untold possibilities ignored by a gravity-bound body (living or wooden) moving randomly or without undertaking a scientific approach. However, when this living body (of an actor) or this wooden portrait of a living body (a marionette), aspires to geometry's promise of a higher level of craft, the untrained body inevitably encounters limitations. This, unlike the hand that easily traces geometric lines on paper or the hands that move disembodied sticks freely in three dimensions. (Decroux often manipulated sticks to illustrate technical principles). The richness of the actor's art form will lie: (1) in the challenging working out of the untold geometrical possibilities as they confront the limitations of the human form whether of flesh and blood or of wood and (2) in the vibration (muscular respiration and dynamo-rhythm) that the actor brings to the form. The way geometry meets vibration (in the same way that "puppet qualities" meet "living qualities") allows for *internal movement within stillness* and *quietness or stillness within external movement*. In other words, the *immobile* actor can achieve and maintain a state of vibrancy or a shimmering quality and, *while moving through space*, can manifest a level of control, a lack of reactive corporeal agitation, and a kind of internal stillness. These qualities provide an other-worldliness to a living actor as well as a breath, a lifelike *élan*, to a marionette.

As we touched on earlier, the prospect of a wooden Übermarionette, animated from within by an actor, poses perhaps insoluble problems for the marionette and, likewise, the more the living actor wears cumbersome vestments (large costumes, masks) the more severely these burdens limit his range of movement.[6] Whereas Decroux, on occasion, advocated masked and nearly nude performance, Craig sometimes envisioned massive and elaborate body masks that would have restricted an actor's movement and thus thwarted a partnership between geometry on one hand and vibration, muscular respiration and dynamo-rhythm on the other.

Despite the pertinence of Decroux's "actor made of wood" to his studio research, it remains conspicuously absent in the transcriptions of his subsequent lectures and in his other writings. The evocative metaphor of an "actor made of wood," as such, a notion that nourished corporeal mime's essential

48 E.G. Craig's Übermarionette

qualities, retreated from Decroux's vocabulary while remaining the invisible but ever-present guiding metaphor in his teaching. His convictions regarding the development of the actor never wavered; the effect of the image endured.

Connecting the dots

Decroux told three stories to illuminate his thoughts on acting:

> First: Look at the pointillist painters. They place side by side a blob of blue and a blob of yellow paint. From a distance, and in the spectator's eye, this juxtaposition creates the color green. For the viewer, this color-event vibrates.
>
> Second: Examine the Sistine Chapel ceiling. Note that God's finger does not touch Adam's: in this space between the two digits, the spectator's imagination comes alive in striving to complete the circuit.
>
> Third: The actor's job consists of throwing a handful of dots into the sky; the audience, in connecting those dots, sees the Great Bear (of the Ursa Major constellation).

In each story, the artist deliberately leaves a gap that the spectator must fill, constituting true "audience participation." Jerzy Grotowski explained the Principle of Induction, another story about a gap, as illustrative of the actor-audience relationship. We attach to a board two parallel wires only one of which connects to an electrical source. Yet, the current passes through *both* wires, including the disconnected one, albeit with a weaker charge. The electrical power, thus, bridges the gap between the two wires; the disconnected wire appropriates, to some degree, the energy conducted by the live one.

For Grotowski, the actors represent the live wire, connected to the energy source developed through years of training. The audience represents the second wire through which "current" may be induced. In Henry Irving's late Victorian England, one might have described the same situation as the actor hypnotizing the audience.

In Grotowski's story, the audience participates through their openness, their pure receptivity, their "un-blocked-ness," their ability to surrender to the event, to join with it. They fail to receive the "current"—to participate as active receiver in the creation of the drama—as long as they remain "blocked." By this term, Grotowski designated analytical audiences who strive to attribute a literal or even a figurative "meaning" to the drama while viewing it or who wish to "comment" on the dramatic proceedings through applause, laughter or by participating in an intrusive way (i.e. foot tapping to the music or singing along).[7] For Grotowski, the actors are not performing to or for the audience. Rather, the audience witnesses the actors' performance for God.

Through his marionettized body, the corporeal mime suggests, rather than explains, by having the studied movement of one part of the body function as a portrait or emissary for another part, thus replaced. In this way, he amplifies, through transposition, what would otherwise go unseen; he creates an artistic or defamiliarized version of the original. In denying "voice" (in this case, *movement*) to the original "speaker," (in this case, *body part*) and by managing, through study, to regenerate that voice in an unexpected body part (otherwise ill-suited—not "naturally" trained for the task), the voice manages to speak more powerfully. The portrait of the thing touches the receptive audience member more potently than would have the original. For example, if an actor uses his own lungs to present a stylized or exaggerated version of breath by altering the respiratory activity in rhythm or volume, he performs a banal facsimile of breathing instead of creating art (artificiality, transposition). While the human actor must breathe with his lungs or die, his marionettized body (in corporeal mime) depicts breathing in subtle, rapid-fire alternating currents in "muscular respirators": biceps, buttocks, and pectorals. He renders his own natural breathing as invisible as possible while casting a spotlight on the artificial, articulated breathing of the non-lungs. To give another example: for the *act of looking*, Decroux assigns it to parts of the body other than the eyes (in fact, to *any* other part of the body), contending that looking with the eyes lacks poetry, indirection and discretion.

One might describe the cherished and fertile gap between the pointillist's blue and yellow blobs of paint, or the one between the two electric wires on the board, as a metaphor for the dynamic state of mind to which Craig's and Decroux's actor aspires—a version of "emptying out your apartment so that God can come to live there."[8] The space between the two wires—the territory across which the electric charge navigates–constitutes the "empty apartment," Michelangelo's anticipatory space between Adam's finger and God's, the space between the blob of blue paint and the blob of yellow. Electric current jumping from one wire to another, or the vibrating color green (vibrating because in a continual state of becoming), or breathing with the arms (defamiliarizing and therefore presenting an amplified portrait of the respiratory act), is "God's arrival." This advent constitutes the very subject of drama rather than its window dressing. This appearance takes center stage, placing plot and literature in a subservient position to action and presence: *the wooden actor* becomes the only thing we want to see in the theatre. Neither wooden marionette nor living actor, but an amalgam of the two, the wooden actor transports us in the noh, in flamenco dance, in dervish turning, in bunraku and in Craig's imagined "performance" in Egypt.

Theory and practice

Every day, corporeal mime students in Montreal, in Barcelona, in London, in Paris, in Los Angeles, in Sao Paulo and elsewhere, begin their lesson with a conceptually simple, yet difficult to execute, geometric scale. They incline the head, then the hammer (head plus the neck), bust (head through chest), torso (head through waist), trunk (head through pelvis) successively around

50 *E.G. Craig's Übermarionette*

three different axes, finally inclining the whole body as one unit. The class continues as students perform the scales forward and back, in rotation, and in rotation on an inclined plane. They study drama in walks, in figures of style and in repertory created by the founder of their discipline. Slowly and over a period of years, with the help of their teachers, they marionettize and puppetize their bodies through a study of geometric and poetic forms with accompanying dynamo-rhythm. The enormous physical possibilities of this technique created by Decroux under the influence of Copeau and Craig (and certainly through "fertile misunderstandings" of them as well) slowly erodes the paradigm Grotowski mocked: "Is the actor only someone who says the author's words and makes appropriate gestures?" (1996). This family, this tribe, esteems Craig's provocative writing and has chosen him as their grand-father, even if Craig might not have chosen them.

Often invisible to scholars and ordinary theatre practitioners, Decroux's subversive, subterranean work has proceeded day after day, year after year, in an unbroken chain since 1931. Though some may have heard of it, most have never seen these lessons that influence the way some perceive Craig and his *oeuvre*.

Decroux and Craig, different in physiology, political views, class, and education, had two things in common: their lives encompassed both theory and practice, and they moved freely back and forth from one to the other. I recall Decroux curved forward over a desk in the study of his modest home, one hand clasping his clay pipe, the other holding his quill pen or an open book—it might have been one of Craig's. Then, crossing his miniscule kitchen and descending the steep stairs to the basement studio, Decroux greeted students from far and wide to join them in marionettizing the body: head, neck, chest, waist and pelvis.

Craig, like Decroux, read and wrote. Yet when he worked practically, Craig usually employed gauze and muslin, wood-blocks and carving tools, models and diagrams, and only practiced rarely (certainly not every day for 60 years, as did Decroux) with living human beings. In Decroux's daily brief passage—less than a minute from his ground-floor study to his basement studio—he translated theory into practice, his thoughts and visions manifesting directly through him onto the bodies of his expectant students. It's not surprising that his version of the Übermarionette, while having a similar origin, might not resemble Craig's in its realization. Some, however, see a similar root and similar intentions in both men's work: the wooden actor.

Notes

1. Craig, ever the fabulist, doubtless wrote this description himself, as the earliest Greek travel writer, Pausanias, lived in the second century AD.
2. Decroux coined the term dynamo-rhythm to describe the trajectory, speed and weight of movements performed with the human body. For an in-depth analysis, see Alaniz.

E.G. Craig's Übermarionette   51

3. While some dictionaries don't yet contain the verbs "to marionettize" or "to puppetize," they are in use among artists and scholars.
4. For Craig, his godfather Henry Irving achieved this apogée of the art. See Craig 1930.
5. Muscular respiration is Decroux's term for alternating currents of tension and relaxation the actor produces in buttocks, biceps and pectoral muscles.
6. Will Spoor (1927–2014) created a larger-than-life wooden figure inside of which he performed. Photos of this cumbersome construction suggest that this body mask limits the actor's movements considerably.
7. Instructions given to the "witnesses" by a Grotowski associate before a presentation at Grotowski's work center in Pontedera, Italy, June 1996.
8. In improvisation as well as technique class Decroux often described the actor's first job as "emptying out the apartment so God could live there."

Works Cited

Alaniz, Leela (2013) "The Dynamo Rhythm of Etienne Decroux and His Successors." *Mime Journal* 24 (2): 1–50. doi: 10.5642/mimejournal.20132401.01

Beckford, Jacqui (2021) A short film for the London International Mime Festival, filmed at the Barbican during the performance of Michèle Anne de Mey and Jaco van Dormael's *Kiss & Cry*.

Blake, William. *The Marriage of Heaven and Hell*. Consulted 23 September 2021. Can be viewed at: http://genius.com/2360513/William-blake-the-marriage-of-heaven-and-hell/The-man-who-never-alters

Craig, Edward Gordon (1930) *Henry Irving*, London: Longmans, Green and Company.

——— (2001) "At Last a Creator in the Theatre, from the Theatre," *An Etienne Decroux Album*, Claremont CA: Mime Journal.

——— (2009) *On the Art of the Theatre*, ed. Franc Chamberlain, New York: Routledge.

Decroux/Craig correspondence, Bibliothèque nationale de France, Richelieu-Louvois, arts du spectacle, Paris.

Decroux, Etienne (1985) *Words on Mime*, trans. Mark Piper, Claremont, CA: Mime Journal.

Fitzgerald, F. Scott (1936) "The Crack-Up," in *Esquire Magazine*. Consulted 23 September 2021. Can be viewed at: http://www.esquire.com/news-politics/a4310/the-crack-up/

Grotowski, Jerzy. (1996). *Lectures at ISTA (International School of Theatre Anthropology)*, Copenhagen. 3–8 May.

Kohler/Jones TED Talk. Consulted 23 September 2021. Can be viewed at: https://www.youtube.com/watch?v=h7u6N-cSWtY

Le Boeuf, Patrick (2010) "On the Nature of Edward Gordon Craig's Über-Marionette," *New Theatre Quarterly*. doi: 10.1017/S0266464X10000242

——— (2014) "Gordon Craig's Self-Contradictions," *Brazilian Journal on Presence Studies* 4, no. 102. Can be viewed at: http://seer.ufrgs.br/index.php/presenca/article/viewFile/45468/31128

Saint-Exupéry, Antoine de (1940) *The Little Prince*. Can be viewed at: http://srogers.com/books/little_prince/ch21.asp

6 Triptych

Three aspects/one figure

Decroux's love of the Greek statue the *Winged Victory of Samothrace* reveals his taste for the sublime: carvings in stone; the eternal and heroic; upward-lifting against the downward pull. He disdained, then, popular entertainment for its lightweight, fleeting, ironic and comic aspects. Moreover, in his search for the absolute, he questioned popular success of any kind. His aesthetic centered on spinal articulations, including undulations, created from years of disciplined study and from experimentation with particular images as inspiration for this investigation ("a fire in the belly"; a "sunburst between the shoulders"; a vibrato in the occiput). It may seem that Grotowski and Decroux each developed his own individual notion of energy flow along the spine as a metaphor for the actor's project. One might see this cultivated and sequential rising and sinking as a European adaptation of chakras. Grotowski spoke of the coiled serpent at the base of the spine, and Decroux considered the entire spine as that serpent. Additionally, both carefully calibrated the audience's size and location within the room to maximize the possible effect that the actor's internal work might have on the audience members or "witnesses."

This concept of an organic corporeal ebb and flow found resonances in diverse performance projects from many artists or religious practitioners, separated by space and by time: in Martha Graham's "contraction and release"; in the spirals of the dervishes; the trembling of the Shakers; and rhythmic isolations of Gurdjieff movement. Continuing this investigation will prove a rich project for scholars in future.

Hidden victory

On a wall in the basement studio of Etienne Decroux's brick cottage in Boulogne-Billancourt, students encountered a photograph of one of the most celebrated statues in the Louvre Museum, the *Winged Victory of Samothrace*. In this black and white image, displayed alone against the aqueous blue cement, the headless, armless, larger-than-life goddess moves forward on one foot as the other trails behind in a swirl of cloth. French diplomat and amateur archeologist Charles Champoiseau unearthed the *Victory* in 1863 on the Greek

DOI: 10.4324/9781003205852-6

Triptych 53

isle of Samothrace; a century later, her image found its way into Decroux's underground workspace. Her "theatrical stance, vigorous movement, and billowing drapery" (Astier) inspired Decroux's subterranean research, linking his high modernist experiments to ancient Greece.

> The *Winged Victory of Samothrace* . . . one of the masterpieces of Hellenistic sculpture . . . creates a spiraling effect in a composition that opens out in various directions. This is achieved by the oblique angles of the wings and the placement of the left leg, and emphasized by the clothing blowing between the goddess's legs. The nude female body is revealed by the transparency of the wet drapery, much in the manner of classical works from the fifth century BC. . . . In the treatment of the tunic—sometimes brushing against the body, sometimes billowing in the wind—the sculptor has been remarkably skillful in creating visual effects.
>
> (Astier)

British art historian Kenneth Clark described this use of cloth to depict movement as the "wet drapery" technique:

> From archaic times onward, the earliest sculptors seem[ed] to recognize how drapery may render a form both more mysterious and more comprehensible. The section of a limb as it swells and subsides may be delineated precisely or left to the imagination; parts of the body that are plastically satisfying can be emphasized, those less interesting can be concealed; and awkward transitions can be made smooth by the flow of line.
>
> (Clark 119)

Despite the statue's damaged state (Figure 6.1), the *Winged Victory's* graceful movement through the veiled trunk and legs remains highly expressive. Decroux's appreciation of this vibrant artifact derived from the captivating energy and heroic dynamism expressed by the extant stone. Moreover, the absence of head and arms makes the statue a symbolic, if unintentional, representative of Decroux's corporeal mime: Decroux eschewed the primacy given to face and hands in nineteenth-century pantomime, an entertainment he considered outdated and "detestable." The *Winged Victory* expresses fully, despite, or because of, her missing parts and Decroux envisioned an evocative human movement language that could do the same. He liked to cite Michelangelo's well-known preference for statues that might, through their compact form, tumble downhill without losing any of their appendages. Similarly, by covering the face and relegating hands and arms to roles subordinate to the performer's powerfully expressive trunk, Decroux created solid yet dynamic human statuary: "always stronger in a ball," he maintained. In the *Victory's* case, time and accident had pruned away elements that Decroux considered excessive and transgressive.

54 *Triptych*

Figure 6.1 The *Winged Victory of Samothrace*.
Source: Photograph edited by Eric Culhane.

Let's digress for a few paragraphs before returning to the *Victory*. Not much has been written about Decroux's keen interest in the French language. Far from having selected mime as a way of escaping words, he spent hours daily pouring over them. Two clusters of hand-written notes, penned on white paper about 3×3″ square, and butterfly clipped into divisions, battled on his desktop, receding and advancing like armies over its polished surface. One unit recorded categories of mime exercises, the other etymological roots of words that intrigued him. Just as the study of word origins reveals otherwise hidden verities that can alter our reading of a text, Decroux believed that the pantomime's obscured trunk imprisoned truths that his own uncovered body endeavored to bring to light.

Thus, when he labeled the pantomime's face and hands as *superficial* liars, he referenced not only the pejorative modern sense of the term but also its etymology, indicating physical location in relation to other parts: on the surface or exterior as opposed to deep, central and interior. Indeed, just as he emphasized, for example, the link between *art* and *artifice*, or defined *enchanted* as "singing within," so he noticed that face and hands, superficial since they occupy an outlying position, could easily serve as agents of superficiality by diverting attention from the profound—what is deep within the body. The truth-teller (the trunk) occupies the deeper place, quite literally, in relation to the facile surface-communicators (face and hands). The trunk, through its daunting and hard-won articulations, rises to an artistic challenge with which merely gesticulating hands or a facial expression cannot compete in order to portray human drama. It is the trunk, as Decroux said, that must "pay the bill" in a way that finds the face and hands coming up short.

For political and philosophical and not only for aesthetic reasons, Decroux advocated near-nudity in corporeal mime as a reaction against certain amply swathed nineteenth-century pantomimes whose costume enshrouded the trunk and revealed only face and hands. His work harmonized with late nineteenth- and early twentieth-century clothing reform that attempted to free the body from constraints; Isadora's flowing and often revealing Greek tunics; renewed interest in sports; and the revival of the Olympic Games. All of these found inspiration and support in concurrent archeological discoveries at Pompeii and elsewhere.

Decroux, influenced by the compensatory twists and turns embodied in Rodin's figures, named a major category of corporeal mime *statuaire mobile*. Three-dimensional movement through the trunk particularly captured Decroux's imagination as he sought a new mime for the twentieth century. Thus, while American dancer Loie Fuller (1862–1928) and her students created silk spirals that moved dance toward symbolism (Acocella), they apparently did so mostly with their arms. While they did sometimes incorporate the trunk—in an impressive upper backbend, for example—their performance focused principally on the ways in which the arms could cause their voluminous costumes to swirl—massive swaths of cloth that hid the body. The dancers animated the gossamer fabric of their billowing, often tent-shaped, costumes by tracing with their arms sweeping figure eights. Hand-held rods extended the dancers' wing-span by another foot, allowing them to control the flowing costume all the way out to the edge of the fabric. We can contrast Fuller's somewhat limited movement vocabulary to the spinal torsions represented in Rodin's statues and to the highly differentiated curvilinear spines of Decroux's *statuaire mobile*.

Shadows from the dark days of the German Occupation still crept into Decroux's classes in the late 1960s and early 1970s. Then he recalled peering down from his Paris apartment windows at the goose-stepping Nazi troops who thrust out legs mechanically and whose spring-loaded arms swept upward in salute. He asked himself how he might create, through a process of

56   *Triptych*

reversal, a vulnerable Walk of the Poet by repositioning the soldiers' *forward* legs and arms into *backward* diagonals. The Poet's trunk would thus advance in a trusting and unprotected way, the back foot and leg coming to the rescue at the last second to prevent the trunk—head, neck, chest, waist and pelvis—from falling forward. Whereas the Nazis' legs and feet shot out in front and then displaced the trunk, the walking Poet that Decroux imagined moved the trunk first, the foot and leg intervening only when absolutely necessary.

In attempting to define his Walk of the Poet, Decroux, who found inspiration in ancient sculpture like the *Victory*, was mitigating somewhat—at least in his Paris apartment and in his own body—the nightmare of the war. While the Château de Valançay in rural central France sheltered the marble *Victory* during the Occupation, Decroux embodied his versions of it in that Paris apartment. There, the distinction between the Nazis' forward thrusting leg and the Poet's leg, suspended softly behind the gradually advancing trunk, became a crucial point in his pedagogy.

As we have seen, numerous elements of the *Victory*—created from static marble—give the impression that the figure is in the process of advancing her whole trunk onto the most forward plane possible. Since she stands on the prow of a ship (the sculpture's base), the vessel moves forward and moves *her* forward. The *Victory* reflects, appropriates, this powerful advancing surge from below. The prow upon which she alights provides a massive dynamic support.

Her enormous wings, mentioned briefly above, inform Decroux's poetic image of *atterrissage* [landing] that infused his project. The arms in Decroux's figures, études and walks often assume wing-like qualities, moving like a billowing cape or a ship's sail, while the legs, with turned-out knee and foot, suggest a voluminous robe trailing behind the actor. The arms and legs execute continuous, minute adjustments, perhaps invisible to the spectator, but imbuing the figure with vibrancy. The body, no longer a *thing*, has become a gyroscopic *event*, a symphony of micro-movements.

The shared vocabulary (billowing, wing-like, voluminous, etc.) describes aspects of two movement projects (Fuller's and Decroux's) that remain, nonetheless, utterly dissimilar. In Fuller's dance, the fabric takes precedence. She is the operator of her virtuosic costume. Her body, for the most part hidden, performs relatively rudimentary movements. In Decroux's *statuaire mobile*, by contrast, the shared vocabulary mentioned above would describe not an accessory to the body—not a costume—but a highly differentiated body (including the trunk) with a flexible spine in full view of the audience (as Decroux often performed almost nude). Decroux's movements, far from rudimentary, involve complex combinations of articulated designs, the sculptor himself becoming the statue.

The impression of power and forward progression of the *Victory*'s unconcealed and open trunk inspired Decroux to take it further—to the (physically challenging) horizontal translation of the vertical trunk in which both thighs would angle backward from the pelvis. For Decroux, the *Victory* appeared to

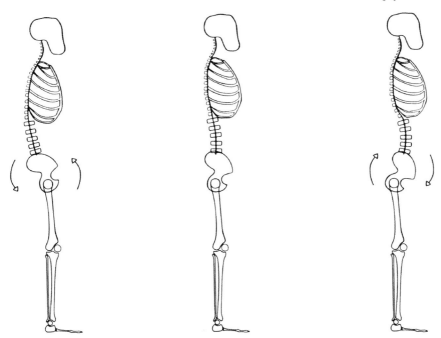

Figure 6.2 Degrees of Inclination for the Pelvis. From left to right: posterior tilt, neutral, anterior tilt.

Source: Drawing by Megan Marshall.

move in that direction, the sculptor immortalizing the moment just before the arrival.

Painting with a broad brush, one might say that Decroux taught three main orientations of the pelvis in relation to the spine and legs (Figure 6.2). In reference to an upright figure, he identified: (1) vertical pelvis (inclined neither forward nor backward); (2) top of pelvis inclined forward and (3) top of pelvis inclined backward. For Decroux, these positions spoke volumes about the person manifesting them since, as he was fond of saying: "Everything is a symbol for those who know how to see."

Even though every possible orientation of the pelvis appears in one or another of Decroux's classroom *études*, he held aesthetic biases: he disdained the forwardly inclined pelvis (with increased arching of the low back) when taken as a habitual posture. In that forward tilt of the pelvis ("nostalgia for the chair"), Decroux divined the "limp cowardice" of certain nineteenth-century pantomimes who often took it as their default position. In the period that preceded overhead stage lighting, some pantomimes (see *Children of Paradise*) played to the footlights. In order to achieve maximum visibility, these performers wore white make-up and reached face and chest forward while crouching toward the light source. Decroux, however, often insisted

58   *Triptych*

upon the moral necessity (and the symbolic value) of standing up, of resisting. From Jacques Copeau, he learned that in the Golden Ages of Theatre—Greek, commedia, noh, Elizabethan—the actor, performing outdoors, usually assumed an upright stance in relation to his natural lighting source, the sun.

Decroux said that a vertical pelvis or one with a slight posterior tilt corresponded to the classical ideal, based on the Greek and Roman sculpture he admired. He joked with his students that photographers visiting his class always, regrettably, snapped the shutter the moment the pelvis tilted forward. He found that a pelvis tilted gently *backward* helped to lead the whole spine into a smooth C-curve which guided the body into a strong work position; such a curve more readily allowed for the full engagement of the actor's weight in pushing, pulling or manipulation of real or of "phantom" (metaphysical) counterweights. This open C could, admittedly, also describe the spine of a person relaxing in a deck chair or a hammock. But when the energetic spine of a person on two feet assumed the shape of a parabolic receiving dish, that body was best positioned to displace, most efficiently and in any direction, a cumbersome and weighty object. The curve increased in proportion to the weight of the object to be displaced.

The vertical or neutral orientation of the pelvis creates an effective support for less challenging counterweights (pushing or pulling lighter weights) and noble displacements of the body (most of Decroux's walks). In technical *enchaînements* (movement phrases) such as undulations, the vertebrae and pelvis weave sequentially along a particular curvilinear path, thus changing, with each movement, the relationship among the parts. In this wave-like succession, the pelvis (as if it were the last vertebra in the line), follows the path that the previous bone has just traced. In Decroux's vast technical repertory—scales, figures, walks, counterweights, études—the moving body passes necessarily through various positions of the pelvis and this, with no stigma attached to this or that "frame of the film." (Indeed, his joke about the visiting photographer testifies to the fact that, for Decroux, the forwardly tilted pelvis can function as a crucial element within an aesthetically pleasing movement design and yet fail—offend—when divorced from the other components constituting the sequence: a film vs a photo.) For the movement pedagogue and for the student, all relationships between the parts must be available as needed, just as notes on a keyboard or sounds constituting a language.

Decroux, when describing the *Winged Victory*'s arrival onto the prow of a ship, used the word "promontory" to describe her risky cliff-like destination as well as the orientation of her pelvis. Many of Decroux's *études* use this "promontory" of the pelvis as a site of daring forward engagement of weight, a sign of courage. For students, the challenge in this position, legs back behind a vertical trunk, consists in maintaining the vertical orientation of the pelvis. An inadequate level of technical control causes the pelvis' position to degrade into a forward inclination at its top, with the resulting display of what Decroux described as an unfortunate eagerness to sit even before finding an appropriate place to do so. For Decroux, this technical malfunction reverses an evocation of courage into one of laziness and even cowardice.

Sometimes he described the relationship of upper (the trunk) to lower parts (the legs) as that of rider to horse or identified the corporeal mime's typical stance as that of a wind-swept figure on the prow of a vessel. For Decroux, occupying this "promontory" (pelvis vertical with thighs angled backwards) denoted nobility, a calm dominion, gravitas and rootedness, as seen in a classical marble frieze. The promontory also denoted risk and uprising, as seen in statues that commemorate the French Revolution.

Decroux's now almost century-old analysis of the body's articulations and its displacements through space may seem, today, functionally naïve, dated. But while complementary movement studies may inform the actor's practice, Decroux's vision of the actor's body, trained to move according to these geometric constraints, remains an essential discipline for students of corporeal mime.

A religion of failure: King Kong meets Mallarmé

In Decroux's writings, and in texts by colleagues and former students, one perceives a *leitmotif*: for fear of being misunderstood, Decroux sometimes delivered a preemptive strike, insulting his audience and his students before they could reject him.

Jean-Louis Barrault writes of his association with Decroux at Charles Dullin's school at the Atelier Theatre in Montmartre, a northern Parisian quarter. Decroux's premier disciple and collaborator remembers their earliest encounters.

> The first time he [Decroux] deigned to speak to me he wounded me to the quick. I have forgotten his exact words but I know they were highly unpleasant, if not cruel.
>
> Some days later he asked me, in a discouraged and not-daring-to-hope tone of voice, if by any chance "bodily expression" interested me. I suppose he expected me to shy off, like the others. He had already caused many to flee!
>
> (Barrault 21)

Decades later, I experienced a similar scenario. After some weeks at his school in October of 1968, Decroux asked if I wanted to work with him outside of class to reconstruct "The Carpenter," a solo piece he first mounted in the early 1930s. With my limited French I responded inappropriately: intending to express my eagerness and gratitude, and imagining that "Oui, Monsieur, je veux *bien*" meant "Yes, sir, I would *really* like that," I didn't know that the addition of "bien," in this instance, could diminish rather than increase the power of the verb (depending on the intonation). It could translate as a

60 *Triptych*

lukewarm: "Yes, sir, I guess so." He took offense and stormed away with a "Dans ce cas, on verra bien!" [In that case, we'll see about it, eventually.] For weeks, I worked to repair my gaffe and demonstrate heartfelt interest; he finally relented and asked: "Veux-tu *maintenant* travailler 'Le Menusier'?" [*Now* would you like to work on "The Carpenter"?] I inclined my head forward in submission and said eagerly: "Oui, Monsieur!" I had learned an important lesson in levels of language, as well as what it meant to work with someone for whom everything mattered, and deeply.

Contradictory strains coexisted within Decroux: on the one hand, he longed to convert his audience and his students to an absolute way of working in theatre. On the other, he, the cynically and perpetually disappointed artist/reformer, wanted to limit the number of audience members or eliminate them altogether. One student saw only the Decroux who was

> hostile to those he was supposed to win over; he disliked his public, and worse still he had no respect for it. It often seemed he took malicious pleasure in antagonizing the audience.
>
> (Dorcy 49)

Another saw the overachiever with an insatiable appetite for rehearsal. His untold hours in the studio—his remarkable work ethic—never sufficed in allaying his fear of inadequate preparation. Moreover, he was known to interrupt his performance abruptly to start it over in order to correct even the slightest mistake. Welcome to Decroux's hall of distorting mirrors, site of self-defensive behavior based on fear of rejection, where commercial success guarantees artistic failure and commercial failure seems a requisite for artistic success.

We can identify, within the anecdotes recounted in this essay, the coping mechanism that Decroux employed in order to continue his work in an environment hostile to his values and with collaborators who could not share his rigorous approach. When talented students left his school prematurely, he might show his vulnerability and frustration: they were "wax in his hands"—just as the material became pliable, he lamented, it slipped from between his fingers. Alternatively, Decroux might simply shrug and mutter, "Ce n'est pas pour nous que la marmite bout" [French expression translated literally as "It's not for us that the soup pot is boiling," which means "We are not meant to be the recipients of this resource"].

When, inevitably, Barrault began his own experiments, rehearsing and performing his initial creations, Decroux attempted to persuade his young acolyte to resist the lure of the Devil: the fame and fortune promised by commercial theatre and film. Their correspondence over the course of a few years exposes the intensity of dissimilar longings: Barrault's, for the freedom to explore and create; Decroux's, to elaborate corporeal mime unimpeded and with the undivided energies of Barrault as second-in-command.

American actor and Decroux's student Alvin Epstein noted that in October 1942,

> just as the long-awaited recognition of Decroux and his company seemed imminent the actors dispersed in every direction to bag personal success in the theatre and films more quickly than the fostering of a new, still unpublicized theatrical art could do for them.
>
> (Epstein 133)

This assessment from an empathetic student leaves out Decroux's displays of temper, pre-performance nerves and ill humor which might have figured just as powerfully in the actors' desire to abandon the company, according to his son, Maximilien.

An off-stage drama replayed itself over the years with different disciples (Marcel Marceau; Decroux's son Maximilien; Yves Lebreton, and others). Each craved breathing space far from the intransigent High Priest and each wanted to avoid the subsequent clash of wills, the sadly inevitable rupture of artistic and personal relationships. Thus, while Decroux sometimes considered his students deserters, opportunistic cowards spurred on by mad ambition, others could interpret their actions in a different light.

Decroux's translator in New York, Mark Epstein (Alvin's brother), remembered that Decroux was "truly indifferent to commercial or public notice. He would say 'Success is the death of creativity.'" Even an ally as close as Decroux's wife Suzanne could ask, only half-jokingly, following one of her husband's tirades: "But Etienne, maybe just a *little* success would be alright?" (Loui 106).

We see from this accumulation of evidence that Decroux did not conceal his disdain for the audience. In 1970, by which time he almost never left his little house and studio, he and I gave a rare public presentation in a cultural center about an hour's drive from Paris. Before the performance, we warmed up by walking back and forth, arm in arm, behind the closed theatre curtain while he muttered: "Don't worry, son, it doesn't matter if you perform well or poorly. They (indicating the murmuring mass on the other side of the drawn curtain) won't know the difference. They're imbeciles, all imbeciles!"

In *Words on Mime*, he writes of the audience:

> And you, mighty shadow of the public, whose dark eye watches us, like the thousand-celled eye of the fly; you whose vigorous mouths have the power to boo us, and whose flexible throats have the power to acclaim us, do not be offended at being our bull.
>
> Your sharp horns are the critical spirit; your furry shadow, our doubt; your gaze, our problem.
>
> Our task is to plunge the sword into the tendon of irony.[1]
>
> (Decroux 1985, 117)

62 *Triptych*

During this same period (1951), Decroux wrote to Edward Gordon Craig from Liège, Belgium where he was performing with his troupe. His postcard depicted the sculptor Leon Mignon's *Bull Tamer* which figured a nude man restraining a beast many times his weight and size. The message read: "Corporeal Mime has triumphed in Liège. The Walloons are conquered. Our heart is satisfied" (Craig/Decroux Correspondence). In Decroux's remarks cited above, the matador/actor seeks, while dreading it, the bullfight/performance. The "Matador" (from "matar," "to kill"), usually conquers the bull with a thrust of his sword. However, a bull that has nobly fought might be granted life, just as a matador might be gouged, or even killed, in provoking an angry, wounded beast. Reading the evidence, it seems that, for Decroux, the performance, while not a matter of life or death, had very high stakes, as his colleagues over the years have testified in this essay and others in the volume. His best acting, in my estimation, happened in the classroom, where he was completely at ease while literally and figuratively *chez lui* [at home].

His life-long confrontation with the audience led him to declare: "the real revolution is to do away with [them]. . . . We must continually insult the audience" (Decroux 2001, 31). To inoculate his students against the virus of wanting to be liked in the short term, he often administered strong doses of his "religion of failure" in the form of philosophical reminders of the virtues of a long apprenticeship: "Patience is a long passion" (or alternately, "Passion is a long patience"), he reminded us frequently. And to compensate for our professional obscurity: "All great art is anonymous. Who designed the pyramids or the cathedrals?"

After a first year of study supported by a Fulbright Grant, I turned to English teaching to subsidize my continuing mime apprenticeship. Decroux beamed approval. "Mallarmé also taught English; he never earned his living from poetry," he insisted. "You must never earn yours from the theatre!"

Jessica Lange's 1976 film success, *King Kong,* provoked a flurry of publicity worldwide, even winning a full-page color photograph on the cover of a popular French weekly depicting her in the clutches of a gorilla run amok. Once the neighborhood shopkeepers read that the megastar had earlier studied with Etienne Decroux, they began showing greater respect for Madame—the butcher, for example, saving her the best cuts of meat. After all, her now-famous-by-association husband was but one embrace removed from King Kong and cinema immortality. Ironically, the shopkeepers' belated deference stemmed not from the ascetic doctrine that Monsieur taught in his blue basement, but from its contrary—his student's cinematic fame and fortune that he disdained and against whose passionate and constricting gorilla-like embrace he vehemently warned his students.

For decades, Decroux subsidized his mime creation by working in theatre, film and radio. As his reputation as a mime increased, his work as a commercial actor diminished, leaving most of his time for teaching. As one who often taught mime while still dressed in a bathrobe and slippers, he once bemusedly confided to me: "I don't have to get dressed and I don't have to go out or take the Métro. They come to me and we go into the basement and move around a bit. It's not work, really; it's rather good for my health."

In the blue basement, Decroux escaped the "thousand-celled eye" of the audience and thereby restrained the bull (Decroux's redoubtable audience). Only his "converted" students, precious few, persisted long enough to witness their own and their teacher's alchemical transformations through movement studies; to discern the difference between commercial entertainment and three-dimensional prayer; to recognize the unfathomable gulf between King Kong and Mallarmé.

Decroux's religion of failure had one sustaining mantra, William the Silent's lines that Decroux intoned from time to time while gazing dreamily upward, as if reviewing his long and largely unrecompensed career:

> Il n'est pas nécessaire d'espérer pour entreprendre
> Ni de réussir pour persévérer.
> [One need not hope in order to undertake,
> Nor succeed in order to persevere.]

This chant, delivered with half-closed eyes and resonant voice, magically removed any discouragement from himself or his students. Class then continued with redoubled energy.

Decroux and verticality

At one of his Friday lectures, Decroux asked rhetorically: "What is man? You see a person on the horizon. Before we can discern a man or a woman, a Chinese or a Norwegian, we first detect a stick, like a Giacometti sculpture." A stick, he argued, best represents man: not a sphere, not a cube, not a pyramid, but rather a stick, a vertical and not a horizontal element.

Part of his decades-long project consisted of articulating that stick, creating the maximum number of distinctly moving parts while reimagining, from the living material of his own and his students' bodies, a new actor-marionette for the twentieth century.

Decroux's teaching enabled me to understand that waltzes, classical ballets and dances in Broadway musicals mostly consume space horizontally, while corporeal mime, the noh theatre, the dervishes and the Shakers, explore the vertical axis that drills down into the earth and builds spiral staircases to heaven. When sacred dancers leave the floor, they do so only fleetingly before being caught again by the tragic inevitability of gravity. One performs flamenco on small surfaces, sometimes literally on table-tops, and Decroux posited that you could perform mime on a barrel head.

Commercial tourism also consumes space horizontally: "If it's Tuesday, this must be Belgium." While the tourist flies over the mountain, the sacred dancer carves a tunnel through it or walks a pilgrimage path precariously across; academic book-based learning "covers" wide areas of study, while

64 *Triptych*

traditional body-based teachings "dis-cover" the whole in a part, the macrocosm in the microcosm.

Decroux worked for decades in one small room, where he preferred vertical movement along the spine's *axis mundi*, never displacing the figure at the expense of the primary subject of his study: research on the raising and lowering of "energy" along the spine, what Grotowski identified as climbing and descending Jacob's Ladder (Richards 125). Both Decroux and his distinguished predecessor François Delsarte (1811–1871) worked in small spaces. Elevated Parisian real estate prices certainly affected their research in concentrating their movements (Leabhart 2005, 15).

Decroux's work usually followed a three-part rule: (1) pre-movement (internal vibration) causing (2) intra-corporeal movement (changing the body's shape) and inciting (3) inter-spatial displacement. Describing pre-movement, he said "Mime is movement in place. It is movement inside external stasis, as if man were a shell, within which things were happening that one could sense but not see" (Decroux 2001, 35). He once inscribed a book for me, part of which reads as follows: "Un tunnel se fait lentement. Lui seul va vers l'autre jour." [A tunnel is made slowly. It alone goes toward a new day.] Digging a tunnel, like most human activities, requires a delicate balance between vertical and horizontal movement along what American modern dance pioneer Doris Humphrey called the "arc between two deaths." Along that arc, Decroux preferred the weighted, resistant, carving and struggling movements, sometimes displacing the body but more often staging the sheer failure of one's attempt to overcome the obstacles that hold us back.

As he had an innate fear of his students' spreading themselves too thin, or of becoming dilettantes, Decroux discouraged us from undertaking performance outside the school, of getting drawn into what he considered the immoral and unhealthy world of professional theatre.

Like his contemporary Jerzy Grotowski, Decroux believed in working on fixed scores or *kata* that allowed for exploration along the vertical axis. Grotowski wrote:

> One cannot work on oneself . . . if one is not inside something which is structured and can be repeated, which has a beginning, a middle and an end, something in which every element has its logical place, technically necessary. All this determined from the point of view of that verticality toward the subtle and of its (the subtle) descent toward the density of the body.
>
> (Grotowski cited in Richards, 130)

Grotowski's and Decroux's research techniques and outcomes differed considerably. To quote one in order to support the other easily invites misunderstanding and yet, their focus on verticality unites them.

François Delsarte, another researcher on the vertical axis, may have anticipated Decroux by 100 years in saying that the actor must first "empty" himself:

> Delsarte aimed for something higher and more important than the mere presentation to the public of the actor's personality. He sought to make the actor an artist to allow him to empty himself of his own personality, so that he could assume as faithfully as possible the personalities of his diverse roles.
>
> (Mackaye cited in Porte 41)

And, in 1954, Decroux wrote a few lines that one might expect to find, a century earlier, in Delsarte's discussion of successions:

> If there is any emotion, the movement starts in the trunk and reverberates more or less in the arms.
>
> If there is only an explanation of pure intelligence, stripped of any emotion, the movements can start in the arms to move only the arms, or to involve the trunk.
>
> (Decroux 1985, 40)

Depending on how you read the evidence, Decroux's advancing years and increasing absolutism seem to have led him to more vertical explorations (what Eugenio Barba calls "pre-expressivity"), his real occupation, while corporeal mime became an indispensable pretext.

Note

1. In French, as in English, the word "irony" ("ironie") can also connote "cynicism," "sarcasm" and even "mockery."

Works Cited

Acocella, Joan (2017) "Variety Lights," *The New Yorker Magazine*, 11 December.
Astier, Marie-Bénédicte (2014) www.louvre.fr/en/oeuvre-notices/winged-victory-samothrace
Barrault, Jean-Louis (1951) *Reflections on the Theatre*, London: Rockliff.
Clark, Kenneth (1972) *The Nude: A Study in Ideal Form*, Princeton, NJ: Princeton University Press.
Craig/Decroux Correspondence, Bibliothèque nationale de France, Richelieu-Louvois, arts du spectacle, Paris.
Decroux/Barrault correspondence, Bibliothèque nationale de France, Richelieu-Louvois, arts du spectacle, Paris.
Decroux, Etienne (1985) *Words on Mime*, trans. Mark Piper, Claremont, CA: Mime Journal.

66   *Triptych*

———— (2001) "Insulting the Audience," *An Etienne Decroux Album*, Claremont, CA: Mime Journal.

———— (2001) "The Seahorse," *An Etienne Decroux Album*, Claremont, CA: Mime Journal.

Dorcy, Jean (1975) *The Mime*, trans. Robert Speller Jr. and Marcel Marceau, New York, NY: White Lion Publishers Limited.

Epstein, Alvin (2001) "The Mime Theatre of Etienne Decroux," *Chrysalis - The Pocket Revue of the Arts*, Vol. XI, num. 1–2, 1958. Reprinted in *An Etienne Decroux Album*, Claremont, CA: Mime Journal.

Leabhart, Thomas (2005) "Misunderstanding Delsarte (and Preserving the Cherries)," *Essays on François Delsarte*, Claremont, CA: Mime Journal.

Loui, Annie (2001) "Interview with Mark Epstein," *An Etienne Decroux Album*, Claremont CA: Mime Journal.

Mackaye, Steele in Porte, Alain (2005) "Four Reflections on François Delsarte," *Essays on François Delsarte*, Claremont CA: Mime Journal.

Richards, Thomas (1995) *At Work with Grotowski on Physical Actions*, New York, NY: Routledge.

7 Everything weighs

Wrestling with an invisible angel

> When students asked the difference between corporeal mime and dance, Decroux answered variously, depending on the day and his mood. As he adored the discipline of dance, giving himself a ballet barre almost every day for 50 years, he had what one might call a love-hate relationship with its airborne quality. Most frequently, he remarked that whereas dancers usually concern themselves with moving their own (and sometimes a partner's) weight efficiently from place to place, the mime struggles to make his way through an imaginary landscape where the atmosphere and the gravitational pull are constantly changing, as is the floor (as if covered in silk, water, tar or all of the above at different moments). The mime pushes or pulls ideas or objects, the body responding accordingly. Or, as Decroux liked to say, with a smile: "Dance makes difficult things look easy and mime makes easy things look difficult."
>
> The actor's cultivation of this image-rich state affects the "witnesses" (to use Grotowski's term for the audience). In the same way, the noh actor or a dervish dancer each uses his own traditional techniques. He touches the audience members, not by focusing on them, but often by not doing so. Instead, these "wooden actors,"[1] through years of disciplined study, pay attention to something other. But no matter the specifics (different in each culture), performers implicate observers through the quality of their being, and as a result of their training, by the How rather than the What.

Creating a human marionette, a living keyboard

To discover the greatest possible number of articulations within the living human body, Etienne Decroux reimagined it sometimes as a keyboard, other times as a marionette. In his attempt to create art (artifice) with the most familiar thing in life, he had to defamiliarize, puppetize/marionettize the body, breaking it apart, deconstructing and then reconstructing it. By arranging elements into new combinations, he fashioned portraits, or transpositions, of actions rather than merely reproducing them as they occur in daily life. Decroux named this research "corporeal mime" after the improvisation class of the same name given by his teachers Suzanne Bing and Jacques

68   *Everything weighs*

Copeau at their school, l'Ecole du Vieux Colombier, in Paris, just after the First World War. In Decroux's subsequent decades of independent research, when he said "move the head without moving the neck," he developed his project of art-as-articulation. (He went on to divide the head and the neck from the chest; the head-neck-chest from the waist; etc.) The corporeal mime could then rearrange his newly delineated segments into different structures, phrases or études. In his daily teaching, and in the Friday lectures[2], Decroux designated five qualities—pause, weight, resistance, hesitation and surprise—as essential in overcoming mechanical rigidity and achieving organicity[3] in the "playing" of this corporeal instrument.

Unlike sounds, which themselves have no physical weight (although playing or singing them entails weight shifts, however slight, in the musician's body), all articulations and displacements of the human body require a negotiation or "dance" with gravity. The counterweight of a human body accommodates a constant pull of gravity. While articulated movement makes the body highly visible, like light refracted through a prism, counterweights give it force, resistance, *gravitas* and drama. Thus, the actor's transformed body becomes a meeting place for, on the one hand, the artifice of the highly visible puppet-like movement, and on the other, the organicity, musicality and truth of the rhythms of work and of thought. As was discussed in Chapter 5, when the execution of these articulations proves more important to the actor than performing the "music" of dynamic variation, robotic rigidity reigns; when the "music" overtakes the clear delineations of the articulated body, excess, blurriness or over-the-top acting might result. Only by holding the two extremes in delicate balance could the actor perform corporeal mime as Decroux originally conceived it.

For more than half a century, Decroux crafted scales, walks, figures of style, movement studies and performance pieces with this corporeal vocabulary. Along the way, he identified three kinds of movements: (1) pre-movement, a kind of purring vibrato usually invisible to the eye, preceding and enabling subsequent articulated movements; (2) intra-corporeal articulated movement (body parts moving in relation to other parts of the body and (3) inter-spatial movement or displacements to another place on the stage. The first two may seem to entail less negotiation with gravity. In fact, all three require an ongoing and considerable struggle with the earth force.

"Dancing" with gravity

In order to survive, animals on planet Earth "dance" as they respond to the gravitational pull. We have only to stand briefly on one leg to discover the constancy of these micro-readjustments. The human body, even in repose or asleep, perpetually plays with gravity, reeling itself in, letting itself out, resisting or giving in, never completely adjusting. The actor's project entails transforming this sometimes invisible, small-scale play into a more visible

Everything weighs   69

and coherent one for the spectator, all the while preserving the movements' organicity and "truthfulness" (actual engagement of weight rather than pretending). Both Decroux and his contemporary Jacques Lecoq identified the essence of acting as pushing and pulling—a constant Promethean struggle, whether on a larger or smaller scale. One could push or pull with the whole weight of the body (in commedia dell'arte or corporeal mime) or distill that effort to a small area as in cinema acting where a gaze or a barely moving hand or sternum could push or pull. An actor might expend the same energy in breaking open a door or pointing his finger.

Director and theoretician Eugenio Barba calls this unceasing bodily endeavor *pre-expressivity*, the somewhat veiled evidence of a counterweight. This counterweight signals the presence of drama even before—and even without—the existence of a specific situation, a relationship or a text. Pre-expressivity continually escalates or diminishes this act of resistance, this basic drama of humans within a gravitational sphere, and Barba recognized that "[Decroux's] knowledge of the actor's pre-expressive level, how to build up *presence*, and how to articulate the transformation of energy, is unequaled in Western theatre history" (Barba 12).

Four physical counterweights

From ten years' experience as a manual laborer (ages 15 through 25), Decroux defined four counterweights: (1) Re-establishment of two elements on the oblique; (2) Jumping to fall on the head; (3) Wool carding machine and (4) Eliminate the support.

Re-establishment of two elements on the oblique

The evolution toward a bipedal state diminished humans' contact with the earth by 50% and doubled their difficulty in negotiating with gravity. Since becoming upright, human bodies have continued adapting to movement through space by using a re-establishment of two elements (thigh and lower leg) on the oblique. One might identify this locomotion in bipeds (sometimes called walking) as falling and recovering, displacing the body mass (the trunk) along a line *perpendicular* to the horizon. In swimming, however, the human body orients itself *parallel* to the horizon, while the re-establishment of two elements occurs in both arms and legs, as it would in a four-footed creature. Straightening arm and forearm, and thigh and lower leg, the swimmer propels her body through the water.

To give a further example of body mass moving *parallel* to the earth, imagine a team of huskies pulling a sled. Their paws engage the earth. They push against it, their knees straightening somewhat as they lunge forward. They then reposition the paws and repeat. As their legs straighten on an oblique line, the dogs' bodies, like the sled they pull, remains parallel to the earth.

70   *Everything weighs*

Now imagine a two-legged creature walking by gently falling forward (pushed by the ball of the back foot) and recovering, falling forward and recovering again, the trunk remaining more or less perpendicular to the earth. When moving the body's own weight exclusively, the free leg bends as it passes from behind to progress forward. This occurs even as the trunk continues to travel forward, supported by the new back foot and leg that guide us to the top of that new—now straight—supporting leg. Concurrently, what was formerly the supporting leg now comes *forward*, to straighten in front of us.

However, to walk while either pushing or pulling a weight, the whole body mass inclines *toward* the weight to be pushed, or inclines *away* from the object to be pulled. If a vertical biped pulls a heavy weight situated behind him or pushes a heavy object in front of his body mass (the trunk), he is supported in part by the pushed or pulled weight. The two elements of the arm (arm and forearm) and the two elements of the leg (thigh and lower leg) re-establish on the same diagonal.[4]

While a corporeal mime moves to carry, push or pull an object (in the case of a physical counterweight) or a thought (in a metaphysical one), a ballet dancer may move for the sheer pleasure of doing so, often repeating movements or combinations of them which brings exhilaration and pleasure to the dancer and, by a kind of kinetic contagion, energizes observers. Dancers can make the arduous look easy (multiple pirouettes, or deftly executed *tours en l'air* finishing on the knee, etc.), while a mime for dramatic effect often gives resistance to an easy gesture (raising the arm, rotating the head). Hence, Decroux's formula: "Dance makes difficult things look easy; mime makes easy things look difficult." While a ballet dancer can appear god-like by toying with gravity in a superhuman way, the corporeal mime, like the tragic actor, constantly struggles to resist the all-too-human earthbound condition. Corporeal mimes, like noh actors, might continue to perform long after the appeal of youth fades, when their human vulnerability becomes more apparent.

A brief examination of steps in ballet technique and their corollary in corporeal mime technique illustrates some fundamental differences between those two art forms. In ballet, the *dis-establishment* of two elements is called a *plié* (knees bending, trunk moving downward); the *re-establishment* follows when the knees straighten). In a *sissonne* (from a closed position, a jump from two feet launches the opening and straightening legs onto an inclined plane, to land first on one foot and then the other, returning to a closed foot position). In a simple jump, the dancer moves upward maintaining a vertical axis in the body.

In mime, a sudden dis-establishment followed by re-establishment is named *départ brusque* [sudden start] and comes about from a precipitous *dropping* of the body weight and simultaneous bending of the knees, as if the floor itself had suddenly disappeared. Then the mime, having reached basement level, rebounds by imploding, keeping the central axis vertical and moving up and down, or inclining it on the oblique, resulting in a horizontal displacement.

Everything weighs 71

The ballet dancer's jumps resist gravity and manifest buoyancy. Contrastingly, the corporeal mime's jump is more about implosion than explosion—more about the sudden landing, highlighting the unavoidable pull of gravity. Likewise, the dancer's "lifted" *plié* is fundamentally different from the mime's split-second drop. With his movement's abrupt dynamic, the mime performs the moment that he no longer equally partners gravity, demonstrating his incapacity to maintain a cushioning counterforce. The mime does not pretend to defy gravity—he fully enacts its unrelenting pull.

Jumping to fall on the head (up and over)

How might I unscrew a jam jar's tightly closed lid? Holding it at sternum height, I try to turn the lid with my right hand while holding the jar still with my left. When the lid fails to yield, I increase my effort by turning the left hand slightly to the right (decreasing the angle of the left wrist as the right hand attempts to turn the lid in the opposite direction, to the left). Still no effect. I now tighten my stomach, contort my face slightly, and while making a sound by pushing breath through clenched teeth, I try once more—still no movement of the sealed metal lid. I now lower my hands holding the jar at stomach level, just below the navel. Then, turning left hand to right and right hand to left while contorting the face and tightening the stomach, I execute a small compact, panther-like jump into the air. The landing of my body (along with simultaneous expulsion of air through clenched teeth) constitutes the counterweight that gives additional strength to my hands as they twist the jar. The jar lid cedes, at first reluctantly, and then with acceleration. The small jump and subsequent landing (up and over) focused the effort of the body onto one point just below the navel, while the two wrists channeled the accumulated gravitational force of landing in order to accomplish the work.

This description illustrates two of Decroux's counterweight principles:

First: The human body works most efficiently in a compacted, spherical shape. This forward curve focuses effort on the work at hand: something requiring great concentration but not much physical strength (writing, watch repair); or something requiring both (i.e., carpentry, blacksmithing).

Second: When the body's weight, thrown into the air, lands, the weight increases. The action of arms and hands at the moment of landing, converts the body weight from a vertical and rectilinear falling energy into a horizontal and, in the case of the jar lid, circular one.

Other examples of Jumping for Falling on the Head counterweights include: rubbing a stubborn spot from the surface of a table; sanding wood; ironing clothes; sawing wood and other work movements that require first lifting the body weight and then guiding and focusing that weight in a useful way as it falls downward and forward.

72 Everything weighs

A classically trained dancer jumps to conceal or deny gravity's effect on the body; the mime jumps to *increase* the ultimate effect, producing a heavy and accelerating fall enabling the body to perform an otherwise impossible counterweight.

Wool carding machine (down and under)

The nineteenth-century wool carding machine (Figure 7.1) that Decroux saw fulfills its task through the down-and-under arc traced by a "card clothing" (a sturdy backing embedded with wire pins). This swinging part, suspended from an axel, untangles and aligns fibers via its J-shaped trajectory. Decroux named one of his counterweight categories "wool carder" to describe the similar curved path of the head-trunk-thighs, as seen in his: pulling a rope towards one; tossing hay from a pitchfork, etc. In these examples, the "worker" brings all of himself to the task, integrating arms and legs into a strong trunk. This consolidation bestows a power to the arms that they would otherwise fail to summon. Likewise, the forward line of the thighs (knees bent, trunk

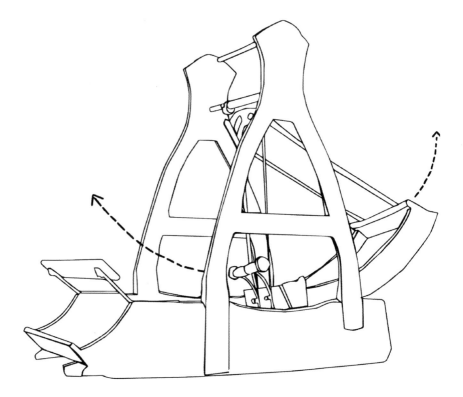

Figure 7.1 Nineteenth-century wool carder.

Source: Drawing by Megan Marshall.

Everything weighs 73

lowered) makes them part of the swinging "J": extensions of the spine and vice versa, structurally separate but functionally unified, stabilized, fortified. To break the inertia of the object (rope, pitchfork, etc.), Decroux's mime pounces with an "ah-ha" of the legs and feet. This landing--grounding-- allows him to pull the object toward the center of his curved body. Decroux observed that counterweights were for those not strong enough to lift, push or pull without them. By wedding the object to the trunk, one allows the unified "trunk-legs" to bear much of the displaced object's weight. Whereas in the previous counterweight, Jumping for Falling on the Head, the arc of the movement followed an "up and over" path, here, the arc is traced from the other end of this integrated structure (See also Figure 10.2).

Removing the support

Imagine that you wish to close a door whose rusty hinges function imperfectly. You could lean into the door with your upper body (from a fixed point where your feet touch the ground). Or, beginning with your feet apart, you could remove the weight-bearing foot nearest the door to project your upper body forcefully against it. As in the previous attempt, also inclining from a fixed point, the worker now adds the increased falling energy of the upper body. Using gravity to project the trunk suddenly toward the door proves efficacious. By removing the support or prop—by lifting the foot from the floor—you make use of gravity's ever-operative pull to incite a sudden acceleration of the unsupported trunk into the object you wish to displace (in this case, the door).

The same principle operates for pulling, but with the weight to be displaced situated behind the body instead of in front. In real life, the weight of the object pushed (a heavy door) or pulled (a wagon full of stones) keeps the sharply leaning body from falling to the ground. In corporeal mime, without a door, or a rope attached to a wagon that would prevent one from falling, the retracted foot finds a place on the ground to support the body while it inclines "truthfully."

A reader unfamiliar with the differences between pantomime and corporeal mime might now imagine an actor, usually alone on stage performing illusions, i.e. walking a dog, cutting a tree, brushing his teeth. The pantomime encounters invisible people and things. Caught in a struggle, he might bare his teeth, grimace, frown. The face tells much of the story.

In Decroux's corporeal mime, on the contrary, counterweights (and not facial expressions) assume full responsibility in depicting the never-ending, mostly tragic, Promethean effort of an Everyman. Indeed, Decroux's corporeal mime students performed with an inexpressive or veiled face. This exclusion of facial expression amplified the Everyman's universal aspect and also confirmed the primacy of the trunk. The performance then became a corporeal hieroglyph of human suffering or struggle rather than a light-hearted

74   *Everything weighs*

guessing game or enacted anecdote. The corporeal mime "wrestles" with gravity, all the while knowing which one will prevail.

How work shapes the worker and thought shapes the thinker

For his students, Decroux artfully described a laborer who had long since disappeared from Paris: the Turtle Man of the late nineteenth and early twentieth century. Decroux named him thusly because of the convex curve of his back, deformed by years of carrying heavy hemp sacks of coal or wood from a *café-charbon* (an enterprise which sold drinks but also heating and cooking fuel) to clients in the neighborhood. The customer places an order, the barman gives the address to the Turtle Man who carries these burdens through streets and up a spiral service staircase, finally dropping his delivery in the customer's kitchen. Accepting a *pourboire* [tip] in his calloused hand, he descends the staircase and, recrossing busy streets, returns to his *café-charbon*. There, while smoking a hand rolled corn-paper, black tobacco cigarette and awaiting the next order, he slides that tip across the scarred zinc bar and orders a *café-calva*—an espresso coffee, accompanied by a small tulip-shaped glass containing an explosive side-shot of calvados [apple jack distilled in Brittany]. As he leans heavily against the bar, his back retains the same forward "turtle" curve into which his daily ponderous burdens have pressed him.

As a child and young adult, Decroux moved through the teeming gaslit streets of Parisian working class neighborhoods. There he keenly observed the Turtle Man and others similarly deformed by manual labor—men and women he respected and admired, but whose subjection to a difficult life he wanted to escape. In that oppressive world, Decroux imagined man as a worm, half smashed onto the sidewalk, the other half reaching toward the sky. This, for Decroux at his most pessimistic, comprised the human condition: aspirations, hard work and intellect reaching toward the stars as his all too miserable human flesh, and the working class into which he was born, kept him firmly anchored to the earth. The theatre enabled Decroux to escape from his own decade-long career as a laborer while imagining a new life, one nonetheless enriched and informed by a worker's values.

In corporeal mime, mastering these four principal *physical* counterweights, ultimately enabled an actor to perform *metaphysical* (or phantom) counterweights, in which the actor's battle with emotional or intellectual weights, rather than with sacks of coal or wood, manifested itself in the body in much the same way as had the physical ones.

While nineteenth-century pantomime might sometimes, through storytelling, depict the human condition with similar pessimism and poignancy, Decroux observed that the pantomime's body played in a lighter dynamic range, usually uninformed by strong pushing and pulling. In corporeal mime, man's relationship to gravity becomes the first and perhaps only subject of drama. Decroux wanted to take the drama (pause, weight, resistance,

Everything weighs 75

hesitation and surprise) out of the narrative story line and put it into the actor's muscles. The corporeal mime finds no relief in the springing leaps of dance or the cavorting of pantomime.

Stages of consciousness: "energy" rising and falling along the spine

Many of Decroux's classroom études reconfigure the rising and falling of the body in much the same way that mercury rises and falls in a thermometer. One in particular, Stages of Consciousness, derives from Decroux's having seen, once in his youth, a man in a semi-wakeful state, seated on the ground, while leaning against a wall. Decroux remembered that person's passage through five states of consciousness and eventually created his étude based on his observations.

1 *Sleeping with the eyes closed.* The actor begins sitting on the edge of a chair, one foot forward, the other under or to the side of the chair seat. Back rounded, face and jaw slack, the "sleeper" relaxes almost to the point of drooling, the head inclining to one side (but not rotated downward, which would make the subsequent movements less visible to the audience).

2 *Sleeping with the eyes open.* As the eyelids flutter, and the actor carefully maintains the forward slouching spine, the head moves slowly toward the vertical, at which time the fluttering eyelids open suddenly to reveal out-of-focus eyes. The eyelids open to a maximum while the eyes themselves are revealed to be profoundly relaxed, usually resulting in crossed eyes.

3 *Seeing but not understanding.* The chest still collapsed, and while keeping the face completely relaxed and the eyelids lifted, the eyes snap into clear focus, creating a compelling contrast between complete relaxation of face and alert tension of eyes.

4 *Seeing and understanding.* Slowly, scalp tightening and neck lengthening, the gaping mouth closes (but not too firmly) and the face gradually reflects the same intelligence as the eyes. The head and neck pull the whole body (like a marionette) up from the chair to standing. Ideally, the body rises straight up, instead of bobbing forward and back as it rises.

5 *Seeing, understanding and acting upon what one understands.* The actor now takes two or three steps forward, supported by the successfully lengthened spine. Coming to a stop with feet widely apart, he savors, for a few moments, his arrival at a vertical stance, before responding to gravity's incessant pull, when the spine relaxes back and downward, retracing the above steps in reverse order.[5]

This sequence epitomizes Decroux's preoccupation with the constant reeling in and letting out of "energy," tension, attention and consciousness. Stages 1 and 3 describe pre-movement; stages 2 and 4 describe intra-corporeal

76 *Everything weighs*

movement and stage 5 describes inter-spatial displacements of the feet in relation to fixed points in the landscape.

Jacob's ladder/the Atmos actor

Imaginative actors, as well as performers of every stripe, including sports practitioners, have had the experience of entering, while in the throes of their specific activity, what I might describe as an altered, or waking-dream state. Some, more colloquially, nowadays call it "the zone." All agree that in the zone, one loses track of time and the self as we usually experience them. Jean Dorcy described this transition to another level of awareness in reference to his preparation for putting on a mask, an act that had for him something of the sacred (Dorcy 108–9). As a matter of fact, every essay in this volume at least grazes this topic that at first sounds otherworldly and exceptional but which turns out to be an integral part of daily life for some, and not at all mysterious, once understood.

Dancers or actors might describe activity in this poetic plane as moving prayer, connecting heaven and earth. Some might read biblical stories, such as Jacob's dream at Peniel, through such a poetic lens: they might interpret angels, ascending and descending the ladder, as the rising and falling of "impulses" or "energy" along the spine. This *état second* [altered state of mind; trance-like state], in relation to the performing arts, has nothing to do with literature or stories per se, but rather implies a shift in the actor's consciousness toward quietness and receptivity.

As we remember from Grotowski's description of induction in Chapter 5, the actor's internal state can find a response in audience members, carrying them to a place of heightened experience, awareness and appreciation of the event. To that extent, they become participants. In this state, they might hear, for example, with new ears, the qualities of vibrato coming from the actor's voice; they might keenly perceive the actor's stage presence.

In describing this "awakening" of the audience members, I am not implying some attempt at mental telepathy or transmission of a specific image or idea from one person to another. It is rather that the actor's "inner work" has an effect on audience members, each one affected in a different way.

We might compare these actors to the Atmos clock, manufactured by the prestigious Swiss clock and watchmaker Jaeger-LeCoultre. This mantle ornament of glass and metal does not require, in principle, manual winding. Instead, it derives energy from slight changes in temperature and atmospheric pressure, and might ideally function for years without human intervention. The Atmos actor, like the Atmos clock, acutely sensitive to the most minute changes in the environment, "listens" intently, "hears" the slight shifts in his surroundings, be they fictional or the actual space in which the actor is working. The actor must first of all attain a quiet mental state, a level of receptivity to his or her environment, and then become one big "ear." Years of training as well as rehearsal prepared the

Everything weighs 77

actor who now cannot *not* hear, cannot *not* respond, first subtly (breathing, "accordion spine," then with some movements of the trunk, and finally with movements of the limbs in interspatial displacement). Actors, becoming all ears, listen to the creaking empty rehearsal hall or theatre (like a wooden ship turned upside down) or to the sounds of an audience unsuccessfully suppressing coughs or discretely unwrapping candies. Imaginative actors constantly knit random sounds into a perpetually evolving fabric of performance. While a less adept actor pushes blithely forward, ignoring an emergency vehicle passing the theatre, sirens blaring, a more alert one listens intently and integrates this chance occurrence into his subtle internal musical score, thereby making every performance an improvisation on the micro level.

Similarly, while sharing a bed, you might suddenly awaken and say, "What is it?" "Nothing, I was just listening," your companion responds. The person listened with such intensity—to an animal moving in the woods outside the window; to exploding fireworks at a state fair some miles away; to the shudder of the motor in an old refrigerator in the kitchen downstairs—that the intensity of the listening awakened you. Imaginative actors listen keenly to their scene partners, to the room, to inner music, all at the same time. They listen so carefully that they abruptly rouse a dozing audience who seems to wonder, in unison, "What is it?"

While Decroux didn't speak of *chakras*, as such, he often said that the actor must have a fire in the belly; that a sunburst might shine between his shoulders; that the occiput could vibrate; that sap must rise in the "tree" of the actor's spine. His stories about acting led his students to believe that if everything had weight, whether sack of coal or human suffering, the actor's primary job was pushing and pulling, "dancing" with that weight as it moved up and down the spine. Analogously, Peter Brook lifted his hand from navel to chest as he demonstrated how the actor constantly moved "millisecond by millisecond up through a scale of qualities" (Brook).

While we usually associate this movement of energy along the spine with meditation and martial arts, a notable Christian example exists in the Cathedral of Notre Dame de Paris. Along the edges of the spine-like spire, one sees protuberances, resembling spinous processes. Below, on the spire's supports (the sacrum), we find statues of the 12 Apostles figured as if descending. Only Thomas looks up as if to get one last glimpse of the heights from which they have come. A brass rooster (whose hollow body once contained relics of Saint Denis, Sainte Geneviève, and a piece of Jesus' crown of thorns) capped the spire.[6] In Hindu traditions, the last *chakra*, often named the "crown," similarly finishes the spine/spire.

Expressions like: "I walked on air," "She felt the weight of the world on her shoulders," and "He held his head high," remind us that, as bipeds on planet Earth (whose evolutionary outcome is uprightness), we are nonetheless continuously subjected to weight, the challenge of gravity's constant pull. We mostly take for granted the welcome aspect of that force that assures our

78 *Everything weighs*

ability to "keep our feet on the ground." Yet, our plight remains gravity's sometimes unmanageable, and always unrelenting, pull. We read its effect on the human body not only in a purely physical context but also in a moral, emotional or metaphysical one. Decroux invites us to notice, for example, how the body takes the same shapes and makes the same effort whether performing a physical counterweight or what he termed a "phantom" one: the shape of the Turtle Man carrying his sack of coal—simply doing his job—resembles that of someone suffering from a broken heart.

Moving efficiently, like an athlete displacing her own weight, does not constitute "acting." When she performs with an unchanging dynamic quality in her voice and movement (jerky, mechanical movements throughout or, instead, sleek, slow-motion movements, or a forced "nobility" everywhere), she acts unimaginatively. Like one performing an aquatic ballet, the presence of the water conditions her every movement. The more creative actor fulfills her expressive potential only when she phrases movement variously, changing weight, speed and qualities as desired, moving through imaginative landscapes or substances: at times through water; other times through air; sometimes through molasses; perhaps through swirling snow or among cherry blossoms; sometimes on Peter Brook's tightrope [see Ch. 3]. Perpetually remaining in one movement dynamic—the equivalent of speaking with the same intensity, volume and speed no matter the circumstances—lulls an audience to sleep.

Decroux's study of physical and phantom (or metaphysical) counterweights provides insight into the variations of dynamism possible in any actor's movements. Able actors' voices howl and whisper; Decroux gives us the equivalent possibility in bodily movement. The corporeal mime's marionettized body, using a full range of dynamics, wrestles with gravity compellingly, as Jacob wrestled with an angel. Struggling with this invisible yet powerful divine messenger becomes the only subject of the play, no matter its title. Although this primary theme may appear in myriad permutations, just as Jacob's heavenly visitors may appear in innumerable guises, the only accurate title for every dramatic production remains: "Everything Weighs."

Notes

1. For discussion of the "wooden actor," see Chapters 1 and 5.
2. Whereas I heard these lectures on Fridays, they occurred on Mondays for some other generations of students.
3. "Organicity," a term Jerzy Grotowski borrowed from Stanislavsky, having to do with the seamless interaction of mind-body, as demonstrated, for example, by the unselfconsciousness of a cat (Richards 66–8) or that of a child (Grotowski 1991).
4. To re-establish: to straighten two elements (i.e. forearm and arm) along a predetermined line (i.e. horizontal, diagonal, etc.).
5. A slightly differently elaborated version of this exercise exists in Leabhart 2019, 146–48.
6. Viollet-Le-Duc made this historically correct addition to the cathedral in the nineteenth century. Although destroyed in the fire of 2019, the restoration plans include an exact replica of the original spire.

Everything weighs 79

Works Cited

Barba, Eugenio (1997) "The Hidden Master," in *Words on Decroux 2*, Claremont, CA: Mime Journal.

Brook, Peter (2012) *Tightrope*, film, Simon Brook, director.

Dorcy, Jean (1975) *The Mime*, trans. Robert Speller Jr. and Marcel Marceau. New York, NY: White Lion Publishers Limited.

Grotowski, Jerzy (1991) "A Kind of Volcano," interview by Michel de Salzmann. www.gurdjieffdance.com/pages/documents/A%20Kind%20Of%20Volcano.pdf

Leabhart, Thomas (2019) *Etienne Decroux*, 2nd edition, New York, NY: Routledge.

Richards, Thomas (1995) *At Work with Grotowski on Physical Actions*, New York, NY: Routledge.

8 From Copeau to Decroux: the mask in actor training

Sculpting new bodies for ancient heads[1]

> "I love a play where you say something and the water beneath you is fathoms deep," Judi Dench once said (Wolfe). As she was then performing in a Chekhov play with no real water anywhere in sight, she must have been speaking metaphorically. Do actors, including those from diverse ethnic and cultural backgrounds, use whatever imaginative techniques they might possess to improve their performances? In this way, do actors with dissimilar backgrounds and training share similar techniques? Did Grotowski's actors truly feel the awakening of something like a coiled serpent at the base of the spine, or did this metaphor simply free their creativity generally? I came upon David Cole's way of understanding the actor's imaginative work across cultures and centuries and realized that this paradigm matched what I had found in researching my roots—an explanation for Dench's conjuring, and then responding to, that deep water. Almost a century before Dench's poetic and intuitive comment, Copeau, Bing and their colleagues considered themselves explorers of rare substances and invisible worlds.

Perplexed in Boulogne–Billancourt

During my four-year study with Etienne Decroux, in the basement studio of his brick workman's cottage in Boulogne-Billancourt (a near suburb southwest of Paris), the curriculum consisted of daily technique classes as well as his Friday evening lectures followed by student improvisations.

For the first three years, I failed to understand these stressful and intimidating improvisations for which Decroux asked individuals or groups of two, three or more, to move to the designated stage area of his small classroom and stand in a pool of light. His only instructions were more enigmatic than helpful: "Portray a thinker. After a while, you will become Thought. Emotion would lead to [undesired] motion, whereas thought begets [the desired] immobility. Begin!" These confusing prompts intensified rather than dispelled the uneasiness surrounding the conundrum of movement/ immobility: damned if we moved and damned if we didn't. We did understand that our improvisations were to involve immobility *and* movement, but how?

DOI: 10.4324/9781003205852- 8

From Copeau to Decroux   81

With Decroux's guidance, we sought an elusive state of being, vibrating on the razor's edge between movement and stillness. Until we finally succeeded, neither our movements nor our immobilities possessed enough of their opposite qualities. While we struggled, Decroux slowly and percussively delivered his most damning criticism, in heavily accented English: "Human, too much human!" He beseeched us to "evict the tenants from the apartment so that God could come to live there." These startling words came from an avowed atheist and "*anticlérical de père en fils*," [anticlerical, like his father before him] encouraging us to banish the voices lodged in thought, the self-consciousness, the concerns. This prerequisite *emptying out* prepared us for the crucial moment of being "struck with a thought," upon which one became a Thinker. Further into the improvisation, sufficient experience and cultivated relaxation led to the embodiment of what Decroux called Pure Thought. All this sounds bewildering enough, but one had to do the above without actual premeditation. The empty and serene mind became the site of what Decroux called "music" but what others might describe as total attentiveness within tranquility, or "the alpha state."

While perhaps seeming esoteric, this manifestation happens, to a greater or lesser degree, in every soccer match and musical performance in all parts of the world, in those moments when the performer forgets him/herself and enters into what psychologist Mihaly Csikszentmihalyi (1934–2021) called "flow," referred to in everyday language as "in the zone" or "in the groove." This state has always existed in traditional arts; for example, Japanese noh actor Michishige Udaka (1947–2020) said that an actor might "experience a shining instance of serendipity—that amazing and fresh light that is the true beauty of Noh" (Udaka). And, nowadays, this psychophysical body-mind has become the subject of study by neuroscientists and anthropologists as well as actors.

Though we improvised without masks, Decroux asked us to emulate the mask-like faces of Angkor Wat's Buddha statues. He encouraged us to visit these haunting stone faces at the Musée Guimet,[2] where their otherworldly expressions (created by a gently tightened scalp that lifted the visage) looked subtly inward. While the process of achieving a present-yet-absent state proved difficult or impossible to describe, the condition itself was unmistakable: in these improvisations we knew which of our colleagues had succeeded and which had not. The successful ones appeared larger than life, radiant, almost possessed, while those less so looked uncomfortably diminished, petty, and even embarrassed by a kind of psychic nakedness. While some "crossed over" into a different world, others, due in part to their excessive effort, remained embedded in this one.

Decroux spoke often enough of his first teacher, the legendary Jacques Copeau, that he became for us a beloved and long-lost grandfather. Years later, I perceived possible origins of Decroux's curious improvisation exercises in studying the writings of Copeau and his associates and disciples. Perhaps Decroux taught us what Copeau had impressed upon him: a method

82 *From Copeau to Decroux*

of achieving theatrical presence through absence. One must experience this optimum performance state to understand it, since words seldom describe satisfactorily non-verbal states and stages of consciousness.

Copeau's readings as interior journeys: absence allows presence

While considering links between Copeau's teachings and Decroux's, I remembered that while neither had achieved unequivocal success as an actor, both had excelled as presenters of dramatic readings. Copeau often spell-bound audiences in public readings of plays or short stories while Decroux favored presentations of poems by Victor Hugo, Charles Baudelaire and Emile Verhaeren. Joseph Sampson (1888–1957), provides an account of Copeau's powers in this domain, describing a reading he attended with a few others in Copeau's Pernand-Vergelesses study in the 1940s. Sampson chronicles different phases of performance as Copeau gradually "disappears" and is slowly taken over by the characters he incarnates:

> He leafed through [the book] as if by chance. We became quiet. Words began to come to us again from the large armchair where he was sitting, back to the window. These words were at first like the continuation of our conversation. Then, there was something a little new; the sentences took a more organized form, the syllables seemed to be measured, the accents became more intensified, the voice began to be modulated. Furtively, Philippe Chabro and and I looked at each other, like people similarly moved: the reading had begun. Reading? Yes. It was still Copeau. But already it was not Copeau anymore; Péguy, author of "The Legend of Three Ducats," had borrowed his voice. Little by little, the tone became more elevated, certain inflections occurred that belonged to song and to the most authentic speech, the most spontaneous delivery. Copeau was still immobile in his large armchair. Only his face, directly across from us, never stopped moving the eyes, the mouth. . . . Aside from that, not a gesture, unless it was a light movement of the hand that raised or lowered. Immobile, yet each of the fable's characters came to us with their vital tone, their accent, their personality. They responded to one another. It was like a string quartet when the violin dialogues with its associates. And as for us, we were caught up in the net of the adventure. Tangled up in it. These dire straits, we felt their anguish. They captivated us. We were obsessed by them. As for Copeau, we've forgotten him. We don't know if he's still there. There remains only the poor man who is going to be hanged, and a queen who wants to shield him from torture. This was the virtue of the symphonic incantation that unfolded its magic through the September Sunday twilight. When the music stopped, we stood up. Philippe stammered a thank you and we left.

(Sampson 5–6)

In the twilight of his career, Copeau, as a medium for a "symphonic incantation," knew how to visit the world of the text and bring it back alive to his listeners. Sampson's nostalgic and romantic formulation, reflective of the time in which he wrote it, pinpoints physical transformations in "Copeau the actor" that characterized Copeau's physical work in actor training.

Copeau and his colleagues use a similar vocabulary to describe an actor's ideal state

Elsewhere in the writings of Copeau and his disciples—among them Charles Dullin (1885–1949), Michel Saint-Denis (1897–1971), Jean Dorcy (1898–1978), Etienne Decroux (1898–1991) and Jean Dasté (1904–1994)—one finds similar recurrent metaphors to describe the actor's ideal mental and physical state. Their words bring to mind precisely what Decroux's students strove to embody during those harrowing Friday night improvisation assignments.

Let us read anew, more than half a century later, the terms these actors frequently used to detail their inner work. Now received terminology, these words have lost somewhat their original strength: Jean Dasté declares that he was "possessed" and that he experienced "moments of frenzy." Dullin writes of an "altered state of consciousness." Jean Dorcy uses the word "trance." And Copeau writes of a character that "comes from outside, takes hold of him, and replaces him." An actor under Copeau's direction in *The Brothers Karamazov* used Dullin's vocabulary—"altered state of consciousness"—to describe how he continued to act despite having been seriously injured on stage. And Decroux often said that the actor should be "inhabited by a god."

Copeau's desire to create a sacred theatre, as a reaction against the commercial approach of Parisian theatres of his day, led him to found not only his own theatre but eventually a school, thereby attempting to restore to this sacrosanct tradition its original vitality, its physical truth. He rediscovered the mask's centrality in actor training, remembering it as a *sine qua non* of most Asian, African and First Peoples' ritual and theatre. By using masks, Copeau imposed a strong countermeasure to divest the commercial actor of his most precious asset—the expressively mobile, personal face—and to require a deeper exploration into heretofore underused parts of the body and the psyche.

Masked exercises in actor training, now as commonplace (or even banal) to us as they were exceptional in the early days of the twentieth century, became for Copeau the key to a new theatre and a new way of acting. (Copeau often reminds us that his "new" ways in fact resurrect previous practice during what he calls theatre's Golden Ages: Greek drama, the noh theatre, Elizabethan theatre, and commedia dell'arte.) His masked exercises altered the course of Decroux's artistic life as well as that of many other disciples who in turn taught young actors around the world.

One might expect that Copeau and his associates, who lived and worked in the country of Descartes with its trust in reason and clarity, might follow an artistic path that eschewed the primeval, the hidden, the extra-rational.

84 *From Copeau to Decroux*

On the contrary, like Artaud, Rimbaud and Jarry, they sought access to this intuitive state of mind. Copeau's masks helped actors develop sincerity and presence through anti-intellectual self-abnegation; even without a deep knowledge of Asian, African or First Peoples' systems and approaches, Copeau and his circle intuitively chose the mask as a tool to spiritualize theatre. Although not professional scholars or anthropologists, they wrote and spoke about this choice using (and sometimes misusing) the specialized vocabulary of spiritual practice and ritual.

David Cole's paradigm: an optic through which to view the work of Copeau and his associates

In his book *The Theatrical Event* (1975), David Cole invites us to view theatrical activity using a paradigm consisting of three parts. In the first, the actor embarks on a shamanic quest or voyage—a psychic journey—to the *illud tempus* or world of the play. Second, the actor surrenders to a psychic takeover (called rounding or possession) by the script character. Finally, the actor returns to the everyday world, possessed by the Image (personage, text, world of the play), yet still in control of himself. Cole calls this third phase a "hunganic return," alluding to aspects of Haitian rituals. An attentive audience can then witness the inspired performance of the possessed actor.

While he does not claim a religious function for drama as Copeau ultimately did, Cole finds in ritual practices useful analogies for theatrical ones. Cole's optic proves a tantalizing one through which to view Copeau's mask work and also reconsider student improvisations at Decroux's school.

> Shamanic activity and possession behavior frequently resemble theatre, while contemporary rehearsal and actor-training methods often recall the practices of shamans and possession specialists. In the moment of an actor's passing from shamanic voyager to possessed vehicle, the theatre, as an event, is born.
>
> (Cole v)[3]

After my initial enthusiasm for Cole's text, a more critical examination ultimately shifted the question from whether or not Cole is "right" to whether or not his perspective is useful in helping one understand the actor's inner work as Copeau and his associates saw it. While neither Cole nor Copeau was a professional anthropologist or religious studies scholar, each came upon a similar paradigm which functions effectively as a metaphor for the actor's inner activity.

Why the mask?

After the splendid reception of Copeau's 1913–1914 inaugural season at the Vieux-Colombier, the First World War interrupted his work. During this hiatus he visited Adolphe Appia, Emile Jaques-Dalcroze and, most significantly and despite their language difficulties, Edward Gordon Craig at his Florence

From Copeau to Decroux 85

headquarters, the Arena Goldoni. In a 1915 journal entry, Copeau describes Craig's "glass cases containing masks" (Copeau 1991, 718) and records Craig's assertion that "[o]ne can do nothing artistic with the human face" (Ibid. 719). Whereas Craig wrote extensively about masks but used them very little, Copeau came to employ them as tools to revitalize the moribund theatre of his time.

Craig's dictum that "the mask is the only right medium of portraying the expressions of the soul as shown through the expressions of the face" (Craig 2009, 7) later became a central tenet in Copeau's philosophy. He and his disciples reacted against what Craig called the "spasmodic and ridiculous expression of the human face" (Craig 2009, 6) in a number of ways: some performed with a mask or cloth covering the face, others adopted a noble or mask-like face thus limiting its expression. Either choice immediately rendered the effect of the full body's performance more potent.

In diagnosing student work in 1915, Copeau remarked that

> from the moment the student conjures up a human feeling (fatigue, joy, sadness, etc.) to motivate a specific movement, a mime bit, immediately and perhaps unconsciously from necessity, he allows the intellectual element to predominate in his action, the play of facial expression. It is the open door to literature and ham acting.
>
> (Copeau 2000, 101)

Copeau experimented with placing a handkerchief over an actor's face, and later a stocking on a student's head, in order to block this "open door" to intellectualism, this invitation to facial play. Without recourse to the face, the student followed more complex, more challenging and ultimately more satisfying routes that Cole described as "[i]nterior journeys in search of psychic components that correspond to external realities [and] are the specialty of a class of religious practitioners called 'shamans'" (Cole 11). Acting exercises, sense memory and meditation can unveil to actors elements of their own personality that correspond to those within a character.

One of the students with whom Copeau and Bing first worked on mask exercises, Jean Dasté, describes it this way:

> With the mask, it is impossible to cheat. When we try to express a feeling or an emotion, if we do not feel impelled by an interior force, we know that we're not "with it." Every contrived gesture was a false note; wearing masks taught us also to be sincere.
>
> (Dasté 1987, 88)

Copeau believed his students could learn from making masks as well as by acting through them: the process of mask making enriched the actor's process. Jacques Prénat wrote of a visit to the school in Burgundy:

> Since they wore masks in their exercises, why wouldn't they make them themselves? This could only refine their knowledge of the laws that

86   *From Copeau to Decroux*

governed facial expression. Their experiments, the trial and error of their fingers in the clay, must also ripen and deepen their knowledge of man as revealed in the face. And these fringe benefits were not negligible. But it remains to be explained why, harking back to the commedia dell'arte and to ancient Greek theatre, Copeau revived the use of the mask.

(Prénat 377–400)

The mask: a tool for actor training

In *The Mime*, Jean Dorcy gives detailed instructions on how to put on (*chausser*) the mask. Note the flavor of the language, the resonance of Dorcy's words to describe his embarking on a kind of shamanic quest and how easily his words fall into Cole's paradigm.

Here are the rites I followed so as to be ready to perform masked:

a Well seated in the middle of the chair, not leaning against the back of the seat. Legs spaced to ensure perfect balance. Feet flat on the ground.

The actor's vertical spine becomes Cole's *axis mundi*.

b Stretch the right arm horizontally forward, shoulder high; it holds the mask, hanging by its elastic. The left hand, also stretched out, helps to shoe the mask, thumb holding the chin, index and second finger seizing the opening of the mouth.
c Simultaneously, inhale, close the eyes and shoe the mask.

In b), Dorcy provides a practical and regulated way to put on the mask. In c), the shaman/actor must close his eyes to block out this world as the mask that he dons transports him to a different one.

d Simultaneously, breathe and place the forearms and the hands on the thighs. The arms, as well as the elbows, touch the torso, fingers not quite reaching the knees.
e Open the eyes, inhale, and then, simultaneously close the eyes, exhale and bend the head forward. While bending the head, the back becomes slightly rounded. In this phase, arms, hands, torso and head are completely relaxed.

What Dorcy here describes as a prelude to total relaxation, Dasté called "creating the void" and Decroux called "evicting the tenant," evident in this next step which could read as a technique for entering into a state of meditation or trance:

f It is here, in this position, that the *clearing of the mind* [my emphasis] occurs. Repeat mentally or utter, if this helps, during the necessary time

From Copeau to Decroux 87

(2, 5, 10, 25 seconds): "I am not thinking of anything. I am not thinking of anything. . . ."

If, through nervousness, or because the heart was beating too strongly, the "I am not thinking of anything" was ineffective, concentrate on the blackish, grey, steel, saffron, blue or other shade found inside the eye and extend it indefinitely in thought: almost always, this shade blots out conscious thought.

g Simultaneously inhale, sit upright, and then breathe out and open the eyes.

Now the masked actor, sufficiently recollected [collected, axis mundi maximally vertical] can be inhabited by characters, objects and thoughts: he is ready to perform dramatically.

(1975, 108–9)

In reading these instructions, I remembered the successful improvisations at Decroux's, which always began with a kind of "waking up," and recognized that the process just described had occurred there, in a reduced form, without the mask (see Sklar 116).

Saül and masked acting

Although Decroux spoke of both noble and character masks, in corporeal mime he wanted faces to resemble the former, never the latter. Copeau, however, experimented with both; by the 1921–22 season, his mask experiments at the Ecole du Vieux-Colombier had progressed far beyond simply placing a stocking over the head. For example, in *Saül*, André Gide's reworking of the biblical story (directed by Copeau), the members of the chorus wore their own hand-made masks.

As preparation to making masks and devising appropriate choreography, students studied animal movements. In the *mise-en-scène,* as described by Copeau, the chorus members appear head first from behind curtains, followed by the rest of the body: "cautiously, like mice in an empty apartment, making quick steps, turning the head from left and right to the middle at the moment that two other demons entered, etc." (Copeau Notes). One critic wrote: "Demons appeared on stage in flesh and blood, with their bestial forms, their insidious murmurs, their lacerating and burning words" (Saül, *Paris Journal*). Another critic noted "the scenes where Saül is visited by the demons are fiercely hallucinatory, savagely grand, as is the scene in the cave with the Witch of Endor" (Saül, *Excelsior*). A third critic, however, found that "[t]his appearance of frowning masks which exchanged their immature chitchat, seemed ingenious the first time; as the fantasy repeated itself in each act, it finally became tiring" (Saül, *Le Gaulois*). While the results may have been uneven, Copeau's use of the mask strengthens a play rife with sorcerers, predictions, fate and adumbrations. The demons' parting of the curtain to appear head-first recalls the actor's appearance from Cole's *illud tempus* (the world of the play, Heaven, or in this case, the Underworld), and their gradual

88 *From Copeau to Decroux*

manifestation in this world; the actors' shamanic quests (rehearsal, observation of animals, making of masks) allow the "rounding" to occur.

Emptying out the apartment

In a 29 January 1994 letter to me, Jean Dasté writes of using the mask:

> Before each exercise, we had to prepare, to create in ourselves a kind of void in order to allow another self to live. I discovered, in changing faces, that I was no longer my usual self, my everyday self; it was as if I were possessed by another, and that other existed in a dimension that was not mine, and that the exercise that I was trying to express commanded my body to perform other gestures, different attitudes.

Dasté's description confirms Cole's model: in preparation for acting, as for most shamanic ritual, the performer relaxes and gives up the conscious self, creating a void that Dasté identifies as the site of possession or "being taken over"—what Cole calls rounding. The mask then commands his body to perform gestures and attitudes belonging to the mask, rather than to him personally.

Dasté's language echoes Jean Dorcy's, who wrote:

> When one puts on the mask, what happens? He removes himself from the external world. The night he imposes on himself permits him first to reject everything cumbersome. Then, by an effort of concentration, he attains the void. From that moment on he can relive and act, but dramatically this time.
>
> (1958, 30)

Elsewhere Dorcy writes: "The mime, from the moment he puts on a mask, no matter what its nature, empties himself out and fills up with another substance" (1962, 91). While this may seem to some readers esoteric and unscientific, almost any actor will attest to having similar experiences, as their daily work involves embodying images rather than writing them.

Jean Dorcy noted that one of his fellow students in Burgundy, Yvonne Galli, succeeded more than the other students with her "clearing of the mind, this preliminary state, better and more rapidly." He goes on to ask: "Had she another Sesame? I have never asked for her technique" (Dorcy 1975, 109). Galli also expressed the most religious fervor when students were asked to write the Ten Commandments of the Ecole du Vieux-Colombier (Leigh, 164–5). Is it a coincidence that she could easily enter the trance state and that she was also devoutly, and perhaps to an unhealthy extent, dedicated to Copeau? A psychologist might call her suggestible or unbalanced, while an anthropologist or religious studies scholar might call her a shaman, reminding us that suggestibility is an ideal trait for this activity (Cole 21). At any rate, the special vocabulary Copeau and friends used, while perfectly clear to them, may seem peculiar to readers not accustomed to performing images (moving as if walking on sand, or on ice, for example), or allowing themselves otherwise to enter an imaginary landscape.

Copeau wrote: "I think that there is, as a point of departure [for acting], a kind of purity, a wholeness of the individual, a state of calm, of naturalness, of relaxation" (Leigh 73). Similarly, Marie-Hélène Dasté recorded in her notebooks from 1921–22 that meditation or contemplation was the act of taking time to put on the mask and collect one's thought, to free oneself for the influence of the mask (Leigh 117). Copeau encouraged his mature actors as well as the apprentices, to empty out, in performance, the daily self in favor of the character.

... Then, God takes possession

Copeau, in his introduction to Diderot's *Paradoxe sur le comédien*, describes "rounding" precisely:

> You say that an actor enters into a role, that he puts himself into the skin of the character. That is not correct, as it is the character who approaches the actor, who demands of him everything he needs to exist at [the actor's] expense, and who bit by bit replaces him inside his skin. It is not enough really to see a character, or to understand a character well, to be able to become him. It is not even enough to possess him well to give him life. One must be possessed by the character.
>
> (13–14)

Copeau describes here what Cole names the hunganic return or "rounding," when his character inhabits or possesses him. Cole writes that

> [f]or the actor, as for actual shamans and hungans, the "journeying toward" and the "possession by" are inner experiences; but also as with actual shamans and hungans, these inner experiences serve a public function. The actor-as-shaman is the audience's envoy to the *illud tempus* of the script: he draws near that the audience may draw near. The actor-as-hungan is the script's envoy to the audience: he consents to possession so that the audience may have figures from the script *illud tempus* present in the flesh.
>
> (Cole 14–15)

Charles Dullin describes his rehearsals with Copeau for *Les Frères Karamazov* thusly:

> Once, some stage business suggested by the director made me suddenly enter forcefully into an altered state of consciousness necessary to the

90   *From Copeau to Decroux*

actor. . . . Copeau's intelligent critique reinforced my own efforts admirably. Day by day, I felt more possessed by my character.

(Dullin 39–40)

Dullin's use of the words "altered state of consciousness" and "possessed" indicates that he remained keenly aware of the actor's process. Stage business, in this case, was one of the doorways into what Cole called the *illud tempus* (Great Time). Dullin goes on to say that this

> manifestation, at the same time animal and spiritual, where the body and the soul feel the need to merge in order to exteriorize a character, gave me that possession of the character and dictated to me at the same time, in a more general way, one of the great laws of the art of acting.

(Dullin 40–41)

Another actor in *Les Frères Karamazov*, Paul Œttly, said of complete concentration: "This kind of unconsciousness is only possible, I believe . . . when one is in an altered state of consciousness, which is a grace infinitely rarer than some actors claim" (Cézan). When Mr. Œttly accidently cut his hand on stage and began to bleed profusely, neither he nor his acting partner, Valentine Tessier, noticed anything until the audience insisted they stop and bind the wound (Copeau 1979, 181).

Jean Dasté describes this process in another way:

> I have always remembered my first discovery of going beyond myself. . . . I was a twenty-two-year-old hothead; I wanted to do so well that I never did well. Always tense, never self-possessed, with a throaty voice, I articulated poorly and spoke too fast, thinking I was sincerely living the situation. . . . One fine evening, on tour . . . during my big love scene, without having prepared more than usual, I suddenly felt in possession of my voice, of my elocution, of my gestures, in control despite myself; I could prolong a movement, a silence, an intonation. I found myself in a different time, a different space, in another dimension. When the scene was over, filled with an immense joy, I entered the wings, glowing; Jacques Copeau was waiting for me, he took me in his arms, hugged me and said: "Tonight, you acted."

(Dasté 1987, 82)

These accounts suggest that Copeau encouraged this kind of imaginary voyage—discovery and return, with or without a mask—in all who worked with him. In this case, Dasté succeeded in making what Cole calls "imaginative truth" present on the stage, relaxation playing a major role in Daste's transformation, as it does in performance of any sport or art. We might begin to see Copeau and his associates as forebears of Grotowski, Eugenio Barba,

From Copeau to Decroux 91

Phillip Zarilli, Richard Schechner and others who have developed beyond a purely Stanislavskian perspective.

"Dédoublement" [dual personality]—present yet absent

As noted above, Jean Dasté held that in the most effective acting, one feels carried away while also maintaining control. Cole calls this a "doubled consciousness which we have found to be characteristic of possession experience" (Cole 50). A student in the Ecole du Vieux Colombier recounted her experience of "an unknown strength and security—a kind of balance and consciousness of each gesture and of myself" (Leigh 117). In these descriptions, we recognize that state toward which Decroux coaxed his students, a state of presence-yet-absence apparent in the expression of those Cambodian statues that Decroux suggested could serve as our teachers.

Dorcy gives us a good notion of this "doubled consciousness" in masked improvisation when he cautions: "above all, even in the depths of the trance he experiences, he must not lose sight of the general structure of the improvisation" (1962, 92). Copeau writes:

> The actor who works with a mask gets from this paper object the reality of his character. He is ordered by it, and he obeys it irresistibly. He has barely put it on when he feels pouring into himself a being he was empty of, which he never even suspected. It is not only his face which is changed, it is his entire person, even the nature of his reflexes where feelings are already forming which he was incapable of experiencing or pretending to have with an unmasked face. If he is a dancer, the entire style of his dance, if he is an actor, even the accent of his voice, will be dictated by his mask—in Latin, persona—that is to say his personage or character, without life unless he embraces it, which life comes from without and takes hold, substituting itself for the actor.
>
> (1929, 14–15)

The flower of the noh

Drawn instinctively to a restrained theatre based in spirituality, Copeau and his colleague Suzanne Bing, researched an ancient masked shamanic theatre, rich in chant, dance, trance and gesture: the Japanese noh play. This theatrical form defined an aesthetic that Copeau and Bing passed on to Decroux and others.

Bing and Copeau lacked first-hand exposure to the noh play in performance; moreover, they had not so much as even spoken to anyone who had seen it. Working solely from literary sources, their notions of the noh theatre, incomplete at best, gave them courage to continue the artistic vision they had conceived and nurtured in the theatre and in the school. Copeau and Bing's

92   *From Copeau to Decroux*

noh research sought qualities that did not yet exist in French (and perhaps European) theatre, at least outside the Vieux Colombier. They looked to Japan for the authority to establish in the West what they found lacking in the theatre of their time. Bing's notes continue to explain the noh project, by pointing out that in French there was no word to designate this new form. "Lyrical drama" or "dramatic poem" didn't account for the harmony, discretion and communication with the audience, among numerous elements: poetry, drama and music as well as dance, song, declamation, colors and forms, costumes, beautiful movement (Bing).

Bing's notes show that during the summer of 1923, their continuing study of the noh revealed to them that:

> dramatic laws [the Noh] obeyed were closely related to the laws that Copeau had developed for the school of the Vieux-Colombier. The Noh was an application of musical, dramatic and movement studies which they had given their students for three years, so much so that the students' improvisations in this style were more related to Noh than to any contemporary style.
>
> (Bing)

During this period, while Copeau finished writing and began producing his play *La Maison natale*, Bing prepared the noh play *Kantan* for the apprentices. The 5 November 1923 entry in the *Livre de Bord* of the Ecole du Vieux-Colombler documents the first lesson on this play that would be directed by Bing (Copeau 2000, 387). Unbeknownst to Copeau and Bing, the theatrical season for which they were preparing would be the last for the now world-famous Théâtre du Vieux Colombier. Copeau's semi-autobiographical play, honed for 20 years, ultimately failed in production, effectively closing the door to his aspirations as a playwright. Bing's workshop project, *Kantan*, however, was more successful, though never performed for the general public.

These hinge events mark an end to Copeau's preference for secular drama and the beginning of his turn toward religious plays and pageants. Hereafter, he developed an even higher estimation for what we now know as devising, collective creation and actor-centered performance.

Because one of the performers sprained his knee, the apprentices gave only one preview performance, 13 May 1924, of *Kantan*, witnessed by students of the school, by Copeau's friend, the author André Gide, as well as by the British director Harley Granville-Barker who praised the work effusively. Gide found it disappointing. Copeau's own reflection was that it "remains for me one of the crown jewels, one of the secret riches of the productions of the Vieux Colombier." Decroux told Barbara Kusler Leigh that it was "the only time in my life I felt the art of Diction" (Leigh 47–8).

Remarks made by Decroux's son years later underline the importance of this performance in Etienne Decroux's thinking. Maximilien said that his

From Copeau to Decroux 93

father's work was not based on European models like *commedia dell' arte*, but rather on Japanese theatre.

> A turning point has been made without it being realized or inspired by this model (continuity with the commedia dell'arte) but by the contrary model of the Japanese nô and new means of expression which came from and were inspired by this pole, this source.
>
> (Maximilien Decroux cited in Wylie-Marques 110)

Jean Dasté and Marie-Hélène Dasté, still indelibly marked by this performance 20 years later, created and performed two adapted noh plays in the first years of the Comédie de Saint-Etienne. Jean Dasté describes his experience as an actor in these plays:

> Supported by the chorus, accompanied by the drum, punctuated by the flute [the actor] speaks and mimes. . . . In playing . . . I experienced moments of frenzy. In Japan, during the performance of Noh plays, this frenzy occurs in the actor at certain moments in the play; unexpected, unique, the audience anticipates it as does the actor; it never happens in the same way; it is called "the flower of Noh."
>
> (1987, 82)

Two days after the presentation of *Kantan*, Copeau closed his theatre and retired to the country with a small group, hoping to dedicate full attention to his apprentices, undistracted by the all-consuming demands of Paris and a theatre troupe.

The macrocosm of the microcosm

In addition to Cole's paradigm furnishing the basis of a re-reading of a single theatrical event, it could also serve in the examination of a period in an artist's career or a whole life in the arts. Might we compare Copeau's artistic life, up to the production of *Kantan*, to a shamanic quest? Could we consider the performance of *Kantan* as the shamanic possession or rounding during which the actors approached the "flower of noh," or what Dasté called "frenzy"? Did Copeau's subsequent career, considered by many as a failure—on the margins of theatrical activity—become the hunganic phase, making present the *illud tempus* through the staging of overtly religious drama?

In this last period, Copeau gave many public readings (including the one described at the start of this chapter), as well as lectures throughout Europe and America. He directed a few plays to keep busy, but his true interest lay in religious drama. For the Florence Festival in May 1933, Copeau adapted and directed the fifteenth-century Tuscan mystery play *Santa Uliva*, and in 1935 in the same venue, he directed *Savonarola* by Rino Alessi. In 1943, he wrote and directed *Le Miracle du pain doré* ["The Miracle of the Golden Bread"],

94   *From Copeau to Decroux*

staged at the Hospices de Beaune. The following year, he published his play about Saint Francis of Assisi, *Le Petit Pauvre* [*The Poor Little One*], never produced in his lifetime (Rudlin 114–18).

Were Copeau's seemingly quiet years, when seen from a different perspective, in fact his most productive? Having drawn the full lesson from the mask—having "rounded"—he no longer relied upon his theatre company or his students for explorations and research. However, overcoming his reluctance to let them go entirely took a few more years.

An unidentified writer opined that "In a few years of struggle, Jacques Copeau renewed French theatre. However, when the creative period was over, the *"Patron"* lived a secret life, silent and more fertile than one might imagine, united with God" (Sampson 15).

Copeau's theatrical process that I have figured in terms of shamanic search, rounding and possession, might be summed up with words Copeau provided for his Saint Francis in *Le Petit Pauvre*: "If you have the gift of silence and immobility, if you don't move, if you unite yourself with the silent waiting glade, with the sweetness of the air and of the branches, you will see all creation come to you" (1946, 28–9).

Saint Francis' cleared space of "silence and immobility" finds a corollary in Copeau's famous prescription for a sick theatre—an empty stage (*"un tréteau nu"*) on which courageous actors could stand, immobile, and "be." Likewise, this stripping away of ornament (in decor and in the actor's approach) creates the conditions for what Copeau deemed of the greatest importance in a dramatic presentation: the "mysterious correspondence of relationships" between the characters (Copeau 1913, 350).

In 1959, ten years after Copeau's death, France's leading daily newspaper of record published an article interrogating his legacy. We note that a decade had done nothing to erase his legend, his hold on people's imagination: He was remembered as a man

> devoted to the theatre as others are to the Virgin, a Jansenist apostle, burning with faith, abandoning the world at the height of his success to go from village to village in Burgundy, pilgrim stick in hand. A legend is always fertile, above all in the superstitious world of the theatre. Copeau left that world forever, having become through his efforts, the object of a most demanding, and almost religious, cult.
>
> (Touchard)

Return to Boulogne-Billancourt

Sometimes "secret" teachings go underground and continue on in basement schools of "minor" arts, preserved by "heretical" practitioners. Like seeds in hibernation, they await a more receptive climate while gathering strength. We could argue that mime schools have kept alive Copeau's teaching of actor presence as much as have theatre schools.

In a basement in the proletarian outskirts of Paris, Decroux invoked the name of Copeau practically daily; likewise, Decroux gave it a prominent place in his book *Paroles sur le mime* [*Words on Mime*]. Above ground, however, during many of the years of Copeau's retreat from full-time company directorship and after the demise of his research group, he was less than a central figure—all but forgotten. Decroux based both the technical and the improvisational parts of his teaching on Bing's and Copeau's techniques for building the actor's scenic presence through a process of emptying out in order to fill up. Non-religious spirituality shines through titles of many of Decroux's études: "Awakening consciousness"; "God fishes man"; "The Prayer"; "Life begins at the bottom"; "Life begins at the top."

Today, in the studio and on the stage, we often see aspects of theatre practice against which Copeau rebelled: the star system, elaborate scenery, overwhelming special effects, *cabotinage* [ham acting], the cult of the personality. The mime schools and certain other theatre laboratories have preserved the empty stage, the well-schooled body, the intelligent use of mask, a respect for craft, and the text in an honored (but not superior) place.[4]

In October 1994, Eugenio Barba gave a lecture in Paris at the Théâtre Renauld-Barrault in which he declared himself an *homme de la périphérie*— [person on the margins, on the periphery]. He spoke of the importance of remaining on the outskirts, even if geographically in the center, and cited the names of theatre workers with whom he felt an affinity: Jacques Copeau and Etienne Decroux, both of whom created and nurtured, from their position as influential outsiders, a strong tradition of cultivating actor presence through the mask.

Is it shamanic?

Can we use the qualifier "shamanic" to characterize the mask used by these French practitioners? While remaining separate from the diverse traditions of shamanism as practiced by First Peoples, certainly Decroux and Copeau wanted students and apprentices to touch the sacred in their work. The *livre de bord* [log book] of Copeau's school gives us an idea of the spiritual structures that guided Copeau, and that he recommended not only for training actors from childhood but also for "renormalizing" adult actors already tainted.

Decroux, in his teaching, changed students' spines, their movement and articulation patterns and possibilities, their breathing and, through improvisations, initiated them into states of mind favorable to performance. In some cases Decroux gave students special names and handed them different colored ropes used in training once they became "initiated"—*anciens* [advanced students]. He invited only a small selected public of "believers" to watch improvisations or works-in-progress. And since the majority of his students were not French, apprenticeship involved a radical change of language and of culture. While this required level of commitment may seem daunting, the rigor and inclusiveness of Decroux's work matched that of other serious theatre, dance

96 *From Copeau to Decroux*

or martial arts training schools. Or, as Deidre Sklar wrote: "Students who remain with Decroux long enough to master the system have undergone a deconstruction and reconstruction process that more closely resembles ritual initiation than theatre" (Sklar 120).

When dancers in the Alvin Ailey company speak of "crossing over" (entering a trance state) during performance, as Anna Deavere Smith reported to me in conversation, they simply describe what they do rather than presenting an anthropological point of view or an exegesis of what Copeau described as their *"commerce étrange."* Between King David's dance before the Ark of the Covenant and Molière's burial in unconsecrated ground, a break—the secularization of performance—occurred. Our understanding of the actor/dancer's sacred role shifted. Some contemporary performers, however, speak readily of the shamanic component of their work. Parisian dancer-teacher Elsa Wolliaston and the late Brazilian Luis-Otavio Bunier acknowledged trance and possession elements similar to those described earlier in the century by Copeau and his associates. And Grotowski's last phase, Art as Vehicle, focused on Performer who "must develop . . . an organism-channel through which the energies circulate, the energies transform, the subtle is touched" (Grotowski 376). Peter Brook wrote: "Grotowski is showing us something which existed in the past but has been forgotten over the centuries; that is that one of the vehicles which allows man to have access to another level of perception is to be found in the art of performance" (Brook 381).

In the chapter "Masks and Trance," from his classic text *Impro*, Keith Johnstone records what his mentors passed on to him. His description resembles the teachings of Michel Saint-Denis, Copeau's nephew and disciple, who established Bing and Copeau's tradition of mask and trance within British actor training.

> [A]n actor can wear a Mask casually, and just pretend to be another person, but [we] were absolutely clear that we were trying to induce *trance* states. . . . To understand the Mask it's also necessary to understand the nature of trance itself.
>
> (Johnstone 143–44)

Although Copeau, Decroux, Johnstone and Grotowski did not belong to traditional ritual cultures, they found shamanic elements essential to their work. Or perhaps they discovered within a shamanic vocabulary a convenient and practical way to think about and communicate their actor training.

Many years after my first encounter with Decroux, I realized that his project involved the construction of idealized bodies that could support neutral or noble masks. Decroux also encouraged certain attitudes of thought to correspond to those faces from the temples at Angkor, those sculpted heads at the Musée Guimet. The ever-changing articulated planes of the corporeal mime's body became the equivalent of facets and rounded surfaces of noble masks, refracting light in alternating sudden bursts and slow unfoldings. The mask exercises at the Vieux-Colombier taught Decroux how the nearly nude body—a starkness equivalent to Copeau's bare stage—could move to achieve maximum presence. The architectural lines that Decroux then constructed within the body heightened its visibility, creating a moving surface on which to splash colorfully varied dynamic qualities. Finally, the unadorned body on a bare stage glowed with an inner light when the actor succeeded in "emptying out the apartment" for "God to come to live there."

The history is circular: In the early days of his apprenticeship at Copeau's Ecole du Vieux Colombier, the novice Decroux observed masked improvisations and mask-making in the class called "*mime corporel*." That specialized exercise, in contrast to nineteenth-century pantomime, covered the face and exposed the body. In this small portion of Bing's and Copeau's extensive curriculum, Decroux recognized the seeds of a new theatrical paradigm which he called corporeal mime, a heightened total-body version of Copeau's mask, and one that privileged the actor rather than the text.

Copeau's mask work required but also facilitated the actor's altered consciousness. Decroux bestowed on that inner work the emblem of an ancient dreaming Cambodian face, uniting it with that extra-quotidian articulated body, the whole then functioning as a kind of head-to-toe living mask. This marriage of elements constituted the cornerstone of a new-old actor-centered theatre.

Notes

1. An earlier version of this article appeared in *New Theatre Quarterly* Vol XX, Part 4, November 2004.
2. The Musée Guimet, now a beautifully appointed Parisian cultural commodity, was, in the late 1960s and early 1970s, more a colonial attic than a museum. Leaking roofs created stained walls, floors wobbled and squeaked, and glass display cases contained unimaginable treasures littered with desiccated insects. Almost non-existent lighting fought unsuccessfully with grey winter afternoons and huge stone statues loomed in the shadows, where (as a retired embassy worker once divulged to me) spies could easily meet to pass information. The infrequence of identifying labels allowed the few visitors to imagine mythic origins for the surprisingly juxtaposed Korean celadon pots, Tibetan masks and Indian jewels.
3. Cole's use of the word "vehicle" to describe the actor's work seems to predate Grotowski's Art as Vehicle.
4. See sections of *Words on Mime* (pages 26–27) where Decroux writes that theatre should be silent for a limited time—just long enough for the actor to reclaim control of the terrain.

Works Cited

Bing, Suzanne (n.d.) Notes, Fonds Copeau, Bibliothèque nationale de France, Richelieu-Louvois, arts du spectacle, Paris.

Brook, Peter (1997) "Grotowski, Art as Vehicle," *The Grotowski Sourcebook*, eds. Richard Schechner and Lisa Wolford, New York, NY: Routledge.

98 *From Copeau to Decroux*

Cézan, Claude (1953) "Les Fondateurs du Vieux-Colombier nous parlent," *Les Nouvelles Littéraires*, 15 October.

Chaplin, Charlie (2012) *My Autobiography*, Brooklyn, NY: Melville House.

Cole, David (1975) *The Theatrical Event*, Middletown, CN: Wesleyan University Press.

Copeau, Jacques (n.d.) Notes, Fonds Copeau, Bibliothèque nationale de France, Richelieu-Louvois, arts du spectacle, Paris.

———— (1913) "Un essai de rénovation dramatique," *Nouvelle Revue Française*.

———— (1929) Intro. *Paradoxe sur le comédien*, Denis Diderot, Paris: Librairie Plon.

———— (1946) *Le Petit Pauvre (François D'Assise)*. Paris: Gallimard, 3ème édition.

———— (1979) *Registres III, Les Registres du Vieux Colombier 1*, Paris: Gallimard.

———— (1991) *Journal 1901–1915, Vol. 1, Journal 1916–1948. Vol. 2,* Paris: Seghers.

———— (2000) *Registres VI*, L'Ecole du Vieux Colombier, Paris: Gallimard.

Craig, Edward Gordon (2009) *On the Art of the Theatre*, ed. Franc Chamberlain. New York, NY: Routledge.

Dasté, Jean (1987) *Qui êtes-vous?*, Lyon: la Manufacture.

———— (1994) Letter to the author, 29 January.

Dorcy, Jean (1958) *A la rencontre de la mime*. Neuilly-sur-Seine: Cahiers de la Danse et Culture.

———— (1962) *J'aime la mime*. Lausanne: Editions Rencontre.

———— (1975) *The Mime*, trans. Robert Speller Jr. and Marcel Marceau, New York, NY: White Lion Publishers Limited.

Dullin, Charles (1946) *Souvenirs et notes de travail d'un acteur*, Paris: Odette Lieutier.

Fournier, Christiane (2001) "For Love of Human Statuary, A Man Decides to be Silent," *An Etienne Decroux Album*, Claremont, CA: Mime Journal.

Grotowski, Jerzy (1997) *The Grotowski Sourcebook*, eds. Richard Schechner and Lisa Wolford, New York, NY: Routledge.

Johnstone, Keith (1982) *Impro: Improvisation and the Theatre*, London: Methuen.

Leigh, Barbara Kusler (1979) *Jacques Copeau's School for Actors*, Allendale, MI: Mime Journal.

Prénat, Jacques (1930) "*Visite à Jacques Copeau*," Paris: Latinité.

Rudlin, John (1986) *Jacques Copeau*, Cambridge University Press.

Sampson, Joseph (1960) *Hommage à Jacques Copeau*, Dijon: Société des amis du musée de Dijon.

Saül (1922) *Paris Journal*, 25 June. Fonds Copeau, Bibliothèque nationale de France, Richelieu-Louvois, arts du spectacle, Paris.

———— (1922) *Excelsior*, 17 June, Fonds Copeau.

———— (1922) *Le Gaulois*, 18 June, Fonds Copeau.

Sklar, Deidre (1995) "Etienne Decroux's Promethean Mime," *Acting (Re)Considered*, ed. Phillip B. Zarrilli, London: Routledge.

Touchard, Pierre-Aimé (1959) "Où en est L'Héritage de Copeau?," *Le Monde*, 15–21 October.

Udaka, Michishige. www.nationalgeographic.com/video/shorts/behind-the-mask-of-the-worlds-oldest-suriving-dramatic-art/

Wolfe, Matt (1990). "If The Role Is At All Unlikely, Call Judi Dench," *New York Times*, 28 January, section 2, page 5.

Wylie-Marques, Katherine (1998) "Zeami Motokiyo and Etienne Decroux: Twin Reformers of the Art of Mime," *Zeami and the No Theatre in the World*, eds. Benito Ortolani and Samuel L. Leiter, New York, NY: Center for Advanced Studies in Theatre Art.

9 The face in corporeal mime

From plaster death mask to living actor's visage

> Twentieth-century practitioners left a bounteous repository of evidence documenting their ventures into theatre-making. Phrasing silence as well as speech, these "wooden actors" [See chapters 1 and 5], in all their various approaches, found internal coherence and theatrical life in fixed movement sequences—in the conscious musical articulations of time and space.
>
> In Decroux's segmented actor, the entire body, when covered with a veil or mask, became a face. And, while Henry Irving had to "enunciate" and polish his own face into a (metaphorical) mask, Decroux's corporeal mime (often interchangeably referred to in the early days as "The Mask") would require the same detailed segmentation, but for the body. In Decroux's fashioning of a new actor for his revolutionary theatrical paradigm, the actor's face became a mask and her body a marionette.
>
> The transformation of face into mask and of body into marionette took place in a world colored by Henry Irving's magnetic acting and Edward Gordon Craig's mysticism. These influences travelled through Irving and Craig, culminating in Decroux's corporeal mime where they distilled into "muscular respiration."

Face to mask = body to marionette

In the biography *Henry Irving*, Edward Gordon Craig traces the origin of his own interest in masks and marionettes to his godfather Henry Irving's idiosyncratic acting style. In the following pages, I link Irving's creation of a mask-like face (as seen by Craig) to the one conceived of by Etienne Decroux for corporeal mime. Both countenances, open to multiple readings, "could be a hundred faces in one." Most importantly, we see in Decroux's corporeal mime the imprint of Craig's Übermarionette, "the whole notion [of which] receives corroboration" from Irving (Craig 1930, 32).

Henry Irving (1838–1905)

When the parents of John Henry Brodribb (the little boy who later became Henry Irving) fell upon hard times, they sent their four-year old son to live with a superstitious, Calvinistic aunt and uncle in Cornwall, then a legendary

DOI: 10.4324/9781003205852-9

100 *The face in corporeal mime*

and untamed region of the British Isles. There, where he encountered a pre-Christian Celtic culture that included masked dancing, ghost stories and magic sites, he also participated in amateur theatricals and saw performances given by touring theatre troupes. One Christmas, John Henry attended a party where children paraded festively at one end of a dimly lighted room while their parents watched from the other. Suddenly, a specter "from another world" intruded from behind a curtain, paralyzing both groups with fear. The terror-stricken Irving described it as "an awful deathly face with heavy eyelids and a drooping face . . . the whole room gave a low long wail" (Holroyd 92). Later one of the children was punished for removing a death mask[1] from his father's office and using it to frighten their guests. Irving cherished this pivotal incident as a "rehearsal for my professional life" (Ibid.). Did this frightful apparition, which determined his future, move from Irving, first to Craig, then to Copeau, and subsequently to others, including Decroux?

After his uncle's death, the 11-year-old Irving reunited with his parents, now residents of London. After finishing his studies, he worked as a clerk while studying theatre in his off-hours. He left London at 18 for an arduous 10-year apprenticeship as a touring actor in the provinces, playing hundreds of parts and slowly, but never entirely, overcoming a stammer and ungainly movements. Making his way from the smallest walk-ons to leading roles, this unlikely genius transformed himself, with great effort, from the awkwardly shy John Henry Brodribb into the most accomplished and celebrated actor of his time, Henry Irving.

Through acute observation, from hours spent practicing vocal and move-ment skills, and from constant reading, Irving learned his métier, earn-ing a reputation as "the greatest stage mesmerist of the late Victorian era" (Goodall 31). While touring in the provinces, Irving met his early mentor, the comic actor J.L. Toole, who possessed a "method of work and mes-meric control [that] taught Irving more about how to hold the stage than any number of visiting hams" (Read 13). I surmise, thus, that Toole prac-ticed mesmerism—prevalent at the time—to excite his own and his audi-ence's imagination, quite different from the "spiritualism" of the touring charlatans who were deceiving gullible audiences throughout America and Europe. For example, the Davenport Brothers, American performers whom Irving saw during their English tour, achieved notoriety with their "Spirit Cabinet." Audience members tied them up before closing them into their wooden cabinet containing musical instruments. Soon afterward, the amazed spectators heard music and saw the instruments floating in space. The doors of the cabinet then reopened to reveal the brothers still tied, sit-ting exactly as before.

After careful scrutiny and reflection, Irving replicated their "impossi-ble" feats, exposing the Davenport Brothers as charlatans. Irving and col-leagues created and produced this crowd-pleasing exposé in Manchester on two or three occasions in February 1865 (Read 15). After these successful recreations, Irving envisioned incorporating Davenport-like qualities into his own acting. Craig imagines Irving considering aspects of mesmerism in order to capture this performance magic:

> perceiving that he possessed something of these powers too—[Irving] made up his mind, and the Rubicon was passed.
>
> These powers of mesmerism he developed in himself to an astonishing degree.
>
> (Craig 1930, 106)

Thus, while Irving disdained much in the Davenports' performance, he perceived that its charismatic ingredient could transform his own acting—"Irving, being fond of the mysterious, had not watched the Davenport Brothers mystifying England for nothing" (Craig 1930, 104). After Irving's 10 years of grueling and often uninspired touring in the provinces, something changed. Within six months of his contact with the Davenports, Irving achieved a renewed confidence in himself as a tragedian, making a highly acclaimed London debut (Batchelder 27–29).

Far from the presentations of the Davenports or other spiritualist entertainers, neither Irving nor his mentor Toole attempted to perform extraordinary feats like flying through the air or dematerializing and rematerializing (except in the exposé described above). Instead, they fine-tuned the dynamic qualities of *ordinary* speaking and moving, performing them in an extraordinary way. They used weighty pauses, clearly articulated puppet-like movements, frequently changing dynamic qualities and, above all, expressive eyes. Through scrupulous attention to these details, Irving awakened the imaginative powers of his audience, thereby eliciting from them an equivalent of the "long low wail" he had heard as a youth in Cornwall when the death mask intruded from "another world."

One account describes Irving, as he performed Thomas Hood's poem "The Dream of Aram," as "motionless and with a haunted gaze [that] brought everyone under his power" and moved "the audience to their feet in a storm of horror and pleasure" (Read 17). The poor or average literary quality of this poem made it an ideal vehicle for an actor of Irving's stature, allowing him to complete in performance what it lacked on the page.

One could consider Irving's acting as "channeling" or acting as a medium or conduit for dead characters or authors; or one might identify it as self-hypnosis and subsequent hypnosis of his audience by contagion.[2] Craig believed that, in addition to the Davenport experience, Irving had developed during his apprenticeship an innate understanding of Voltaire's concept of "*le diable au corps* [the devil in the flesh] which gives the tragic actor the ability to blaze" (Craig 1930, 20).

Toole sponsored his mentee Irving for membership in the Jerusalem Masonic Lodge No 197 in 1877 (Read 19) and, although Irving joined, his busy career left scant time for masonic activities. Yet Dutch freemason Wim

102   *The face in corporeal mime*

Frackers' description of masonic rituals invites comparison to many of the principles embodied by Irving's later theatrical productions:

> Masonic Ritual, rightly performed and understood, emanates this inner strength, wisdom, and beauty—this spirituality. Only a firm oneness—a close-knit unity between spoken word, dramatic acting, music and the silences occasionally required during a ritual performance—is the prerequisite for our Masonic ritual to produce such spiritual emanation. When we create such an atmosphere, then we can say "the Great Architect of the Universe is with us and in us."
>
> (Frackers)

Victorian-era masonic lodges, often sumptuously decorated and equipped with stage scenery, provided richly jeweled costumes and elaborate accessories for the rituals Henry Irving attended, and in which he occasionally participated with his freemason friends and colleagues. Concurrently, he selected, commissioned, adapted and enacted leading roles in plays with strong "spiritual" content, like *The Bells, Faust, Charles I* and others. Eric Bentley observed: "Once we see the hypnotic character of melodramatic theatre, we see in a new light the fact that this theatre often actually presents cases of hypnotic and kindred states of mind" (Bentley 176).

According to enthusiastic audience members and theatre critics, Irving possessed an exceptional presence; even a quick perusal of first-hand responses to Irving's prowess in *We Saw Him Act* confirm his almost universal appeal. Contemporary scholar Jane Goodall describes this rare quality in actors as a "radiating power that transcends the natural." Because of scientific innovations of the Victorian era, "radiation, electricity, magnetism, mesmerism and chemistry provide the keywords around which discourses on presence become organized from the mid-eighteenth century" (Goodall 11–12).

Irving was not alone in recognizing electric aspects of acting: the tragic actor William Charles Macready (1793–1873) writes in his journal of a failed performance in which the audience was "from the construction of the theatre, not within the reach of my electric contact, to coin an expression" (Macready 278). In this entry, he might have been thinking of Michael Faraday, with whose electrical experiments he was familiar. Additionally, Macready's good friend Charles Dickens took an especially active interest in Mesmerism, influencing many in his circle, although Macready strongly resisted.

At the height of his long career, Irving usually performed on stages crowded with painted scenery and ornate furniture, and often peopled with tens and sometimes hundreds of assiduously deployed supernumeraries. His productions used spectacular scenic and lighting effects, the most advanced in Europe at the time. For example, in Irving's 1885 production of *Faust*, Irving's manager Bram Stoker remarked upon the "wonderful scene of imagination,

The face in corporeal mime   103

of lighting, of action, and all the rush and whirl and triumphant cataclysm of unfettered demonical possession" (Stoker vol. 1, 146). Yet Craig saw this possession in Irving's unusual acting itself, quite apart from all the bluster and thunder of the staging around him. Craig divined, in Irving's silences and immobilities, in his clearly choreographed movements and strangely phrased speech, a marionettized (and magnetic) actor. This super-marionette might perform—and in fact become even more visible—on a much different stage. The uncluttered one that Craig later championed contained "mystical symbols . . . scattered all over . . . [providing] that indispensable link between the audience and the supernatural world that performances are meant to unveil" (Le Boeuf).

Craig and a few of his contemporaries emphasized the importance of the actor's "relation to light and space rather than [the Victorian theatre's] pictorial and environmental replication of the ancient or modern world" (Booth 82). And Craig imagined that this might facilitate and highlight future actors who aspired to Irving's "almost mystical level of concentration" (Salter 174).

Irving in *The Bells*

In Craig's writings about Irving, certain turns of phrase, and indeed entire pages, strike the reader as unique: only Craig could have written so cogently about what only Irving could have done. In Irving's oft-performed melodramatic tour-de-force, *The Bells*, Craig perceived (after witnessing some 30 performances) a love of craftsmanship "in every gesture, every half move, in the play of his shoulders, legs, head and arms, mesmeric in the highest degree" (Craig 1930, 56).

In that description of Irving's meticulously phrased movement score during his first minutes on stage in *The Bells*, Craig's use of the term "mesmeric" suggests that Irving's words and movements, like so many mesmeric passes, not only hypnotized the actor himself but also the audience members, inviting them to follow him into the labyrinth of murderer Mathais's guilt-stricken mind.

In the last act of the same melodrama, Mathias dreams that: (1) he is on trial for his crime; (2) a mesmerist brought into the courtroom hypnotizes the accused and (3) the mesmerist lulls the accused with words and movements until the murderer—the accused—confesses. Irving, the actor—mesmerized and mesmerizing even out of the context of this role about hypnosis— embodies a character who reveals the "truth" (his guilt) while dreaming that he is in a courtroom and under hypnosis. The still-dreaming criminal—at home in his bedroom—emerges from the (dreamed) court-ordered hypnotic spell only to hear his sentence of death by hanging. The character, still at home, awakens from his tortured sleep in the midst of his dreamed execution, and promptly dies. The dreamed execution, thus, proves fatal to both the dreamed and the dreamer.

104   *The face in corporeal mime*

In Irving's *mise en abyme*, a dreamed mesmerist extracts the truth from a dreaming *and hypnotized* criminal. Irving, in summary, impersonates a murderer who: feigns innocence until hypnotized (within his dream); reveals the truth while under (a dreamed) hypnosis; and expires as the result of an imagined execution. The play ends with the character Mathais's waking up from the dream and promptly dying. The actor, Irving, steps out of the play as he emerges from behind the curtain to take his bows to tumultuous applause, having moved only a few feet from deep within the darkened soul of a murderer into the blinding footlights of a Victorian playhouse. His dual consciousness (Stoker 21) and the audience's mesmerized state diminish as Irving's stylized movements and sung speech recede and his more quotidian manner returns the audience to the everyday. Irving has led them (and himself) on what one might call a shamanic voyage. They venture, in this case, to a multi-layered fictional world and back, like Russian nesting dolls disassembled and reassembled: from actor to fictional character, to fictional character dreaming, to fictional character dreaming that he was hypnotized, and so on.

At the start of *The Bells*, as Irving buckles his shoe, we

> suddenly saw these fingers stop their work; the crown of the head suddenly seemed to glitter and become frozen—and then, at the pace of the slowest and most terrified snail, the two hands, still motionless and dead, were seen to be coming up the side of the leg . . . the whole torso of the man, also seeming frozen, was gradually, and by an almost imperceptible movement, seen to be drawing up and back, as it would straighten a little, and to lean a little against the back of the chair on which he was seated. Once in that position—motionless—eyes fixed ahead of him and fixed on us all—there he sat for the space of ten to twelve seconds which, I can assure you, seemed to us all like a lifetime.
>
> (Craig 1930, 57)

Henry Irving apparently created a detailed movement score and phrased it like an accomplished musician. Note Craig's evocative choice of words: "to glitter and become frozen"; "at the pace of the slowest and most terrified snail"; "motionless and dead"; "almost imperceptible movement." Irving did not, as the Davenports purported to do, fly through the air or play musical instruments while his arms were tied. He did the most ordinary thing in the world—took off his shoes. The *way* that he removed them resonates more in theatre history than all the Davenports' charlatanism. Did he bring the audience more deeply into his trance world as he sat unmoving, eyes fixed on the audience, for that eternity of ten to twelve seconds? His *enchaînements* [movement sequences] of satisfyingly varied dynamo-rhythms extended throughout the play, "figure after figure of exquisite pattern and purpose is unfolded, and then closed, and ever a new one unfolded in its wake" (Craig 1930, 58).

The face in corporeal mime   105

Having performed *The Bells* more than 800 times during a 35-year period (Stoker vol. 1, 144), Irving must have polished those figures to a high sheen. Each performance enhanced their effectiveness in opening Irving's imagination and that of his audience.

Mesmerism in the Victorian era

Interest in trance, hypnotism, animal magnetism and Mesmerism was not unusual in Victorian times. At venues throughout England, France and the US, professional hypnotists and mediums essayed mesmeric feats, sometimes under assumed names, some wearing costumes and employing stagecraft, although not nearly as elaborate as Irving's. A monthly newspaper, *The Spiritualist*, founded in 1869 by William H. Harrison, published articles and advertisements for the flourishing movement (Noakes).

Mesmerism derived from the teachings of the Austrian Franz Anton Mesmer (1734–1815), who visited Paris and London in the late eighteenth and early nineteenth centuries, disseminating his doctrine and leaving converts in his wake. He first used magnets in treating patients, but later worked only with his hands, guided by his charismatic personality, purportedly to "channel the ebb and flow of astral current" from head to toe through the subject's body (Riskin).

In Paris, thorough investigations by a government-appointed committee failed to confirm the existence of animal magnetic fluid, discrediting Mesmer who spent the rest of his life quietly in Switzerland. His ideas, however, continued to propagate: while Mesmer's experiments may have failed on one level, on another, his invention of hypnotism as a therapeutic tool informs the history of psychology through the work of Jean-Martin Charcot (1825–1893) and Sigmund Freud (1856–1939).

> It was not Mesmer, then, but his investigators who made mesmerism into the source of a new psychology, a nascent theory of the unconscious that credited the mind with startling powers over the body. Writing on the eve of the Revolution, the commissioners cautioned that the imagination could be manipulated to intoxicate crowds, provoke riots, spur fanaticism. . . . Mesmer's astral fluid paled in comparison with what his inquisitors conjured from it.
>
> (Riskin)

Mesmer bequeathed a nuanced legacy to the theatre world. If a Royal Commission (Ben Franklin among the distinguished participants) could not prove the existence of a *material* fluid or electrical connection between hypnotist and subject (or actor and audience), they did not try to disprove the existence of *imaginary* connections which set both actor and audience dreaming, enabling them to "see" heretofore invisible characters, landscapes and

106 *The face in corporeal mime*

objects and, traversing time and space, to enter past and future epochs and inhabit fantastic worlds as palpable as "real" ones.

Irving and mesmerism

Edward Gordon Craig saw Henry Irving's movement score, an *open sesame* to an alternative world, as both "measured dance" and mesmeric trance, "all massively artificial—yet all flashing with the light and the pulse of nature" (Craig 1930, 74).

These phrased gestures and movements impressed the young Edward Gordon Craig and set him dreaming of a theatre in which inspired acting might become even more visible when freed from surrounding visual clutter, a scenography that allowed the imagination to soar and the so-called mesmeric (imaginative) fluids to vibrate. Edward Gordon Craig's scenography, like Henry Irving's mask, open to multiple readings, would prove a more appropriate screen for these imaginative projections of thoroughly engaged or even hypnotized audiences. In his new scenography, Edward Gordon Craig, a partisan for the mask, saw Irving's face: "clean-cut, expressionless till he let it speak, and when it spoke it said one thing at a time,[3] clearly" (Craig 1930, 76).

Irving's clarity and precision of body and voice, as well as his eyes shining "like cinders of glowing red from out the marble face," (Stoker vol. 1, 56) resulted in the hypnotic effect referred to time and again by critics and attested to by the thunderous "coming down of the house" after many of Irving's performances. Ellen Terry, his long-time partner on and off stage, writes in her *Memoirs* that Irving, in acting *Charles I*, underwent a change: "However often I played that scene with him, I knew that when he first came on he was not aware of my presence or of any *earthly* presence: he seemed to be already in Heaven" (Cited in Salter 170).

Referring to theatre in a different geographic and temporal context, American painter and publisher William Segal (1904–2000) discusses masked noh performance in terms of "vibration" and "levels of being" in a way that helps us understand Irving:

> I remember seeing my first Noh play in Kyoto almost fifty years ago. I was absolutely struck by the initial appearance of the main player. It was the moment when he was crossing the bridge that separates the back of the stage from the stage itself. His was not the walk of an ordinary man. It sprang, instead, from an inner relatedness. It gave rise to a tension that became almost unbearable bringing the audience to a high degree of attention. All its concentration was focused on the deliberate movement of the slightly bent, robe-clad figure.
>
> His voice, too, in the few words he spoke, carried a weight. This slowly moving figure produced a vibration that seemed to speak to each one in the audience. One could not escape the fact of being present to something different from our ordinary existence, a change in the

The face in corporeal mime   107

conditions that were a result of the being of the player. Time was surely being examined in front of our eyes. One felt that something new was about to unfold. One passed a threshold in oneself from one part to another, to a different level of being.

It was a transformation. It was as if he was in between a world he had left and an entirely new world. In that moment he embodied a kind of stillness that is difficult to achieve in our everyday lives.

(Segal 225)

In this passage, written toward the end of the twentieth century, Segal describes an ancient genre—noh (entirely different from England's nineteenth-century melodrama). Nonetheless, Segal's words (concerning a mid-twentieth century noh performance) could apply just as well to Henry Irving's other worldly interpretation of *The Bells*. Irving had, on stage, turned his face into a timeless death mask like the one he saw as a child in Cornwall, like the ones used in what Jacques Copeau would call the Golden Ages of Theatre—the Greeks, the noh and commedia.

Jacques Copeau (1879–1949)

Once, impatient with an actor's tense demeanor, French stage director Jacques Copeau improvised a surprising experiment with far-reaching consequences. His nephew and assistant, Michel Saint-Denis describes the pivotal event:

Tired of having to wait for her to relax [he] . . . threw a handkerchief over her face and made her repeat the scene. She at once relaxed and her body was able to express what she had been asked to do. This inspired incident led to our exploring the possibilities of mask work in the training of actors. We found that by covering his face with a mask, the actor was often able to forget his inhibitions and go beyond his usual limits. While it increased the power of his physical expression, it at the same time taught him economy of gesture.

(Saint-Denis 1982, 169–70)

Saint-Denis highlights here two essential elements of Copeau's pedagogy: economy of gesture and the inexpressive mask. Later, in founding acting schools in the United Kingdom, Canada, France and the USA, Saint-Denis always included mask training in the curricula, reflecting Copeau's teaching at the Ecole du Vieux Colombier:

In getting the student to wear masks [in silent improvisations], we were not aiming at aesthetic results nor was it our intention to revive the art of mime. To us, a mask was a temporary instrument . . . offered to the curiosity of the young actor, in the hope that it might help his concentration, strengthen his inner feelings, diminish his self-consciousness and

108   *The face in corporeal mime*

lead him to develop his powers of outward expression. A mask is a concrete object. When you put it on your face you receive from it a strong impulse which you have got to obey. But the mask is also an inanimate object [that] . . . the personality of the actor will bring to life. As his inner feelings accumulate behind the mask, so the actor's face relaxes. His body . . . made more expressive by the very immobility of the mask, will be brought to action by the strength of inner feeling. Once the actor has acquired the elementary technique that is demanded by wearing a mask, he will begin to realize that masks dislike agitation, that they can only be animated by controlled, strong and utterly simple actions which depend upon the richness of the inner life within the calm and balanced body of the performer. The mask absorbs the actor's personality from which it feeds. It warms his feelings and cools his head. It enables the actor to experience, in its most virulent form, the chemistry of acting: at the very moment when the actor's feelings are at their height, beneath the mask, the urgent necessity of controlling his physical actions compels him to detachment and lucidity.

(Saint-Denis 1976, 103–4)

Copeau, who used masks to cultivate in the actor's performance this calm and simplicity, also found these same qualities in the honest and truthful gestures of experienced manual laborers. Copeau, who himself had never done physical work for a living, observed:

I'm interested in the work of the laborer who pushes a birch-wood broom from right to left and from left to right on the tile floor of the station platform. He sweeps as one would mow hay, curved in two and throwing a large half-circle in front of himself. The man is old and his élan sometimes makes him stumble. For sweeping, this gives a rather good result, but not a perfect one.

(Copeau 1991, vol. 1, 716)

While the sweeper engaged whole-heartedly in truthful gesture, Copeau notes the poignant details of the old worker's efficiency. We see Copeau's preference for the risky "right" energy that has the worker constantly negotiating between the safety of equilibrium and the danger of falling. As Copeau wrote elsewhere: "Beauty is absolute honesty" (Copeau 2000, 289); he wanted to train actors to

use an economy of gesture so that everything seems in its rightful place. That comes from their really doing something, that they do what they do and they do it well, knowing the reason, absorbing themselves in it. The movements of their actions are sincere, they observe real time and correspond to a useful end toward which they are perfectly appropriate.

(Copeau cited in Rudlin 45)

The face in corporeal mime   109

The words "really doing something" sum up Copeau's approach: *doing*, not *pretending* to do. While Copeau devised mask experiments for students in the school, he found it difficult to reform senior actors in the company, as even his more experienced collaborators had a tendency to pretend by relying on the face:

> I understand, in looking [in the cinema] at those close-ups of faces of ham actors, how [Charles] Dullin could be confused by them, and not be able to think of anything but that [the face], that lie.
>
> (Copeau 1991, vol. 2, 118)

We don't have a date for Copeau's consequential gesture of covering the actor's face with his handkerchief, but his visit to Edward Gordon Craig in Florence in 1915 might have inspired such an action. There, in Craig's workspace, the Arena Goldoni, Copeau saw masks on display and listened to Craig's pronouncements: "One can do nothing artistic with the human face" (Copeau 1991, vol. 1, 718–9). During this 1915 visit to Florence, Copeau reflected on the skill required for an actor's artistic use of the face and wrote the following eloquent paragraph upon seeing for the first time prominent Italian actor Ermete Novelli:

> I have never seen [an actor] more certain, stronger in his effects. His method is to make emptiness around himself, or rather to fill the whole stage. The other actors watch him perform. One would say that they [the other actors] don't have faces, so powerful and mobile, so skillfully maneuvered is Novelli's. These are not impressions, feelings, played on a human face, more or less deeply altered. The actor, to make each of his successive gestures, sculpts a new face, hardening his traits, hollowing out here, making prominent there, like a sculptor using each muscle advisedly. Successively, [different] masks appear.
>
> (Copeau 1991, vol. 1, 748–9)

If Novelli's face could transform into a kind of mask, Copeau reasoned, the actor then became a sculptor whose habitual facial gestures no longer served as an easy fallback, but instead opened a new field for careful observation, study and practice. These observations intertwined with his projects for a school to "renormalize" professional actors, on the one hand and, on the other, to begin training young apprentices before they became deformed by the commercial theatre of the day.

Ever sensitive to the tyranny of the face, Copeau wrote:

> I have already noticed, notably with Dalcroze, that the student, from the moment one calls on a sentiment in him (fatigue, joy, sadness, etc.) to provoke a movement, determine a mime, straightaway and perhaps unconsciously, from necessity, he allows the intellectual element to

110   *The face in corporeal mime*

predominate in his action, the play of facial expressions. This is an open door to literature and ham acting.

(Copeau 2000, 101)

In working tirelessly to close this open door, Copeau often had initial, brilliant inspirations, leaving their realization to his long-time collaborator Suzanne Bing, his daughter Marie-Hélène, and senior students including Jean Dorcy. Bing and Maïène (as Copeau's daughter was known) taught the material that Copeau envisioned: in a class entitled *mime corporel* or "the mask," students, as unclothed as decency would allow, improvised with covered faces, discovering expressivity in their newly liberated bodies.[4]

From 1921 until 1924, Copeau and Bing developed their mask pedagogy. "They began in December (1921) using handkerchiefs, stockings, cardboard, papier-maché, shellac and flour, and linen and glue" (Leigh 1979, 30). The sculptor Albert Marque helped the students achieve a more neutral mask that Madame Dasté referred to, in conversation with me in the 1980s, as "the noble mask." Jean Dorcy remembered that "Without Albert Marque, we should have continued to make masks 'small and pretty.' A good mask must always be neutral; its expression depends on your movements," (Dorcy cited in Rudlin 240):

For Copeau and colleagues, the mask became a temporary tool, a weapon in their warfare against affectation and ham acting, as noted above. However, Copeau's larger vision entailed nothing less than reforming human beings:

All the vulgarities, all the lies of the contemporary theatre, are reflected and, as if combined, in the person of the actor.

And yet, it's not at all a question of perfecting his technique. The problem is transforming his state of mind. Not teaching him to act, [but] teaching him to live, inviting him to feel and appreciate beauty—in short, placing him in a new and healthy atmosphere, natural, good in fostering his individual development at the same time as his work as a collective creator.[5]

(Copeau 2000, 202–3)

Eleanora Duse (1858–1924)

Copeau agreed wholeheartedly with legendary Italian actress Eleanora Duse's often-quoted, deliberately hyperbolic statement:

To save the theatre, the theatre must be destroyed, the actors and actresses must all die of the plague. They poison the air, they make art impossible. It is not drama that they play, but pieces for the theatre. We should return to the Greeks, play in the open air; the drama dies of stalls and boxes and evening dress, and people who come to digest their dinner.

(Duse cited in Symons 220)

The face in corporeal mime 111

Duse, who followed Copeau's activities from afar, wanted to adopt some of Copeau's methods for achieving a healthier theatre in her native Italy. She intuitively knew when to communicate with him:

> During the war, at precise moments when my strength waned, it happened that Duse wrote me a letter or sent me a telegram to give me courage, reestablish my confidence, renew her attachment to our theatre, which she called "This living and noble thing."
>
> (Copeau 1931, 48)

When, in June 1922, in the last years of her life, Duse visited the Vieux Colombier, Copeau and his students had the "unforgettable honor" of receiving her on their stage:

> On the softly lighted stage I had assembled all the actors, all the staff, and a few special friends. Duse entered. She was leaning on the arm of my dear friend Croiza, who resembles her, and who, like, her has a big heart. All the assistants had stood up, without saying anything. Our little students in white dresses came forward a bit awkwardly. My daughter, leading them, carried a spray of roses that she placed on Duse's arm. Then, in bending down to kiss her, she knocked off Duse's large old-fashioned hat. Gina Barbieri said some words in Italian, and I said a few in French. Duse stammered two or three sentences that her emotion made barely understandable. But it mattered little. We had her to ourselves, among us: her eyes, her hands, her voice. On the stage or in life, she was one of those beings whose simple presence touches you like a blessing. Our little ceremony didn't last much longer than fifteen minutes. Back in her car, Duse said to Croiza "This will be my best memory of Paris."
>
> (Copeau 1931, 49–50)

Many contemporaries, like critic and translator Arthur Symons cited below, praise Duse's acting, mentioning her face as a mask:

> The face of Duse is a mask for the tragic passions, a mask which changes from moment to moment, as the soul models the clay of the body after its own changing image. Imagine Rodin at work on a lump of clay. The shapeless thing awakens under his fingers, a vague life creeps into it, hesitating among the forms of life; it is desire, waiting to be born, and it may be born as pity or anguish, love or pride; so fluid is it to the touch, so humbly does it await the accident of choice. The face of Duse is like the clay under the fingers of Rodin. But with her there can be no choice, no arresting moment of repose; but an endless flowing outward of emotion, like tide flowing after tide, moulding and effacing continually. . . . The outline of the face is motionless, set hard, clenched into immobility; but within that motionless outline, every nerve seems awake, expression

112   *The face in corporeal mime*

after expression sweeps over it, each complete for its instant, each distinct, each like the finished expression of the sculptor, rather than the uncertain forms of life, as they appear to us in passing. . . . At such moments, as at the supreme moment of death, all the nobility of which a soul is capable comes transformingly into the body; which is then, indeed, neither the handmaid, nor the accomplice, nor the impediment of the soul, but the soul's visible identity. The art of Duse is to do over again, consciously, this sculpture of the soul upon the body.

(Symons 223–24)

Symons's description here of Duse as a sculptor of her own ever-changing face and body (or of her facilitating the soul's modeling of the body "after its own changing image"), echoes testimony obtained from other witnesses we have summoned in this chapter: Irving, Craig, Copeau and Decroux. We might see Duse's transcendent face as an extension of her same thought that, for hours before a performance, kept her praying: "One must forget self . . . forget self . . . it is the only way" (Duse cited in Le Gallienne 166). Similarly, Copeau wrote and spoke lines in a play of his own devising: "Your appearance, your thoughts and your memory should have been eaten up by the memory, thoughts and appearance of a stranger who is trying to become more present in you than you are yourself. You are not ready unless you have been completely replaced" (Copeau cited in Rudlin 106). Although separated by miles and years, both Copeau and Duse seem to have learned some of the same lessons about the living mask and the "possession" known to Irving: "*You are not ready unless you have been completely replaced.*"

Charlie Chaplin, master of silent acting, wrote of Duse's performance in Los Angeles, weeks before she died in Pittsburgh:

When Duse came to Los Angeles, even her age and approaching end could not dim the brilliance of her genius. She was supported by an excellent Italian cast. One handsome young actor gave a superb performance before she came on, holding the centre of the stage magnificently. How could Duse excel this young man's remarkable performance? I wondered.

Then from extreme left up-stage Duse unobtrusively entered through an archway. She paused behind a basket of white chrysanthemums that stood on a grand piano, and began quietly rearranging them. A murmur went through the house, and my attention immediately left the young actor and centered on Duse. She looked neither at the young actor nor at any of the other characters, but continued quietly arranging the flowers and adding others which she had brought with her. When she had finished, she slowly walked diagonally down-stage and sat in an armchair by the fireplace and looked into the fire. Once, and only once, did she look at the young man, and all the wisdom and hurt of humanity was in that look. Then she continued listening and warming her hands—such beautiful, sensitive hands.

After his impassioned address, she spoke calmly as she looked into the fire. Her delivery had not the usual histrionics; her voice came from the embers of tragic passion. I did not understand a word, but I realized I was in the presence of the greatest actress I had ever seen.

(Chaplin 194–95)

From Chaplin's description of Duse's silent acting with mask-like face, I recognize elements of his own performance. Chaplin comments only on the quality of her presence which touched him.

Critics inevitably drew comparisons between Duse and her contemporaries; we rely on Symons again for a clear-eyed estimation:

To act as Duse acts, with an art which is properly the antithesis of what we call acting, is, no doubt, to fail at a lesser thing in order to triumph in a greater. Her greatest moments are the moment of most intense quietness. . . . Contrast her art with the art of Irving, [for whom] acting is all that the word literally means; it is an art of sharp, detached, yet always delicate movement; he crosses the stage with intention, as he intentionally adopts a fine, crabbed, personal, highly conventional elocution of his own; he is an actor, and he acts, keeping nature, or the too close semblance of nature, carefully out of his compositions. . . . His emotion moves to slow music, crystallises into an attitude, dies upon a long-drawn-out-word. . . . [By contrast Duse's art is] always suggestion, never statement, always a renunciation. . . . [It turns acting] into an art wholly subtle, almost spiritual, a suggestion, an evasion, a secrecy.

(Symons 225–26)

Symons could have easily described myriad qualities that Irving and Duse shared. The primary difference seems to be the way they willingly played their memorable silences: he with cubistic or pointillistic precision, she with a more diffused impressionistic palate.

Etienne Decroux (1898–1991)

As we have learned from other essays in this collection, Decroux had seen, as a child, the last vestiges of nineteenth-century pantomime, and reacted strongly against it as he began to develop corporeal mime in the late 1920s and early 1930s. If the pantomime performer crouched forward to catch reflections from the footlights onto his white makeup, the corporeal mime, according to a new paradigm, would stand upright, illumined by overhead lights. If a voluminous white costume obscured the pantomime's body, the modern performer would affect nudity. If the *mime ancien* used hands to tell his story, Decroux would eschew storytelling altogether, relegating hands

114 *The face in corporeal mime*

and arms to a secondary position. And most importantly, if the pantomime made exaggerated facial expressions, the corporeal mime would either cover the face with a mask or a cloth, or make his uncovered face the site of subtle and almost imperceptible changes. Decroux said:

> [Old-style pantomime] to exist was condemned to do certain unpleasant things, but I couldn't see why it wanted to exist. For example, the lighting was weak, provided by candles so one couldn't see their facial expressions and that explains in part why they had white face makeup with black lines for emphasis. That explains above all why they had to make exaggerated facial expressions. . . . They didn't need to treat comic subjects, they were already comic.
>
> (Decroux cited in Pezin 59)

Decroux often rhetorically asked which of the fine arts was first of all comic: "When is the last time you saw a funny painting, or heard a funny orchestral concert?"[6] He elaborated:

> I detested this form [pantomime] that seemed comic before you knew what it was about. I thought we should do a serious thing first, that art should first of all be serious. Art is first of all an expression of suffering. Someone who is happy with things has no business being on the stage. . . . What is certain for me is I don't see how one can practice an art if not to present our suffering, our displeasure.
>
> (Decroux cited in Pezin 61)

Decroux's early years

Between the ages of 15 and 25, Decroux held mundane jobs that didn't require advanced academic education, but that augmented his diverse embodied knowledge; he drew from this source for the remainder of his life. Decroux describes his early observations:

> These things seen and experienced first hand, gradually moved into the back of my mind, down the back of my arms, and finally down to my fingertips where they modified the fingerprints.
>
> (Decroux cited in Veinstein ii)

While working as an orderly at Paris' Beaujon Hospital, Decroux encountered an impatient elderly man whose lined and hardened face softened in death to become noble, sublime, mask-like, the contrary of his living visage. Decroux eventually created a hyper-alive, minutely articulated marionettized body to transport the corporeal mime's mask, borrowed from that dead man's noble, translucent face, echoing the death mask Henry Irving saw, and that incited our story some pages back.

Decroux came upon this concept of the face through his own work but also through Craig whose preference for the mask over the face influenced him twice: Decroux first received indirect homeopathic doses of Craig's mask theory from his teacher Copeau and later, more generously elaborated ones directly from Craig himself. Craig was helpful in other ways: he writes warmly and appreciatively of Decroux's performance in 1931 ("At Last, A Creator in the Theatre"); he lent his name as President to Decroux's school the following year; he actively undertook a search for an impresario to help book tours for Decroux's troupe; and sent his daughter Daphne and his apprentice Harvey Grossman to study with Decroux—all signs of admiration and selfless affection perhaps unmatched in Craig's somewhat egocentric life.

Decroux *chez* Copeau

Etienne Decroux differed significantly from his fellow students at the Vieux Colombier in age (five to ten years older), in class (a working class butcher's assistant), and in origin (called "The Foreigner," because his parents were from the distant French province of Savoy) (Fournier 92). He auditioned for Copeau on 15 October 1923 and soon after began his studies as an auditor (observer). Decroux remembered:

> One day, during a diction class, the teacher told us: "Do you know that in the other class (he meant the more advanced class) they do interesting exercises with masks?" I asked myself "If their faces are covered, how can they express anything?" You can see how limited my ideas were. In these classes, then, students wore masks. But, let me emphasize this, *inexpressive* masks: *inexpressive*, to be sure that they didn't express with the face. They wore shorts—that's to say they were almost naked and after a quick consultation during which they invented a scenario, they tried to play small scenes back-to-back. Since, furthermore, they studied ballet and gymnastics, they had a pleasant way of moving. We didn't wonder why they were nude; it was obvious that they needed to be and it wasn't indecent since they were moving.
>
> This is how I realized the importance of the mime that I designated as "corporeal." I'm the one who gave it that name—whereas *they* said strangely: "We're doing mask work."
>
> (Decroux cited in Pezin 62)

In the lecture cited above (probably from the 1970s). Decroux remembers students calling the class "the mask"; in his 1939 article ". . . Originates in the Vieux Colombier" in *Words on Mime*, Decroux lists "corporeal mime" among the subjects offered to students. Then, for one section of the article entitled "Corporeal Mime at the Vieux Colombier (School)," in referring to the course, he begins with "We called it the mask." Confirming Decroux's conflation of the terms "mime," "corporeal mime" and "mask," Jean Dorcy

116 *The face in corporeal mime*

wrote: "After the material side [mask making] came the exercises. The themes required months of constant research. We baptized our mask efforts: mime" (Dorcy cited in Rudlin 241).

What exactly comprises a neutral or noble mask and how could it lead to corporeal mime? Decroux thought that

> a neutral or inexpressive mask . . . is sublime. Sublime does not mean that it's good. . . . . Sublime in this case means that one does not have before one a man, but mankind in general—a man who has left his tomb to tell the story of his life. Not only man in general, but Man from all times, from creation until the end of time. That's what I call sublime: beyond limits.
>
> (Decroux cited in Pezin 134)

Decroux's unusual terminology, comparing the actor to "a man who has left his tomb to tell the story of his life," echoes the noh actor's impersonating ghosts, Henry Irving's childhood experience in Cornwall, and Decroux's own admiration for the sublime death mask. Just as he had admired his deceased patient's transformed face at the Beaujon Hospital, so later his own father's plaster death mask held a prominent place on the wall of Decroux's study in Boulogne-Billancourt.

This sublime face "beyond limits" allows the audience to project desires, hopes, fears and despair onto the actor-as-screen in the way that visitors to the Jardin des Plantes in Paris project their emotions onto the faces of orangutans living there [See Chapter 3]. Early in his research, Decroux, in using masks that lacked subtle features, created an unintended consequence. While wanting the audience to ignore the play of expression on the actor's face, focusing instead on the articulated trunk, the audience sometimes watched only the mask, as its strangeness drew their attention. Then Decroux intuited a compromise: he realized that corporeal mime required a human face *like* a subtly inexpressive mask or the heads from Angkor at the Musée Guimet. Mime required a mask-like face (rather than a mask)—a transformed *human* face constantly and subtly changing, resembling clouds moving slowly in the sky (Pezin 134).

Thus, at the Ecole du Vieux Colombier, Decroux's exposure to the mask, this extraordinarily useful tool in Copeau's and Bing's arsenal of pedagogical tools, gave rise to Decroux's life's work called corporeal mime. Following Copeau's emphasis on training actors physically (some critics believed at the expense of adequate vocal training), Decroux quickly realized that not just the face but the whole body might become "noble" and "articulate." Decroux said:

> I oppose old-fashioned pantomime that foregrounded the face and hands. Obviously, the old-fashioned mime had a body and he used it, but, incredibly, when we see drawings of pantomimes, they are represented

by their face and hands. It is just as obvious that we [corporeal mimes] have face and hands and arms, but that we emphasize the body, the mass of the body. That's a big difference.

(Decroux cited in Pezin 104)

Whereas Decroux opined that nineteenth-century audiences strove to decode the pantomime's gestures (as substitutions for words), Decroux's work in the twentieth century signals a paradigm shift. The actor's movements do not supplant words. Decroux explores the dramatic (rather than dancing) moving body in its encounter with gravity: in portraying manual work; in love duets; in physical combat; in bodies imitating (in modernist fashion) the mechanized movement of the Industrial Revolution; in the movement of trees through the changing seasons, and even the body's portrayal of meditation, among other subjects. He amplifies for us the many and significant pre-, post- and non-verbal moments of human life, with situation but without plot. Decroux intended to locate the drama within the actor's body—this body that, in movement and in stillness, suffices.

We call together people who like this [corporeal mime]. There are people who like to see the body in motion without knowing what it means. Then, there are others who are not interested. On this point we should not make concessions.

(Decroux cited in Pezin 92)

As nineteenth-century pantomime, music and painting tended toward the programmatic, Decroux's twentieth-century corporeal mime mostly avoided story-telling, selecting titles that might offer a context for the composition in the way cubist painters did; a title such as "Still Life with Oranges" offers the audience a toehold while not encouraging a guessing game.

Lev Kuleshov (1899–1970): an imaginary meeting

During the same decades, but in different countries and in dissimilar circumstances, Russian film giant Lev Kuleshov and Etienne Decroux each happened upon many complementary principles in actor training. "Multiple independent discovery" or "simultaneous invention" explain innovations which emerge concurrently in different parts of the world with no direct communication between researchers (such as the invention of television, the formulation of calculus or the discovery of oxygen). I surmise a similar principle at work in the overlapping experiments of Decroux and Kuleshov.

Comparing Kuleshov's work, primarily in the cinema, and Decroux's efforts, principally in the classroom, moves our understanding of Irving's and Craig's notions forward. These observations bring us closer to the mask-like face and the marionettized body as seen by this Russian whom Decroux certainly never met. However, as Decroux frequented the Paris Cinémathèque,

118   *The face in corporeal mime*

he may well have seen films by Kuleshov or his students in the Montage movement in which actors used "biomechanical" and "eccentric" acting techniques.

Decroux's conception of the human face, inexpressive or veiled, resembled Kuleshov's research through a groundbreaking and now famous experiment in film montage: using existing footage of a well-known actor looking into the camera with an unchanging but lively expression, Kuleshov intercut three disparate scenes: a bowl of soup, a dead child in an open coffin and a beautiful woman reclining on a divan. A test audience imagined the actor's neutral (lively, not frozen) face had changed from hunger to sorrow to attraction. "The discovery stunned me," Kuleshov wrote (200). This experiment defined what is now known as "The Kuleshov Effect" and suggests that actors might achieve impressive results by providing a living, screen-like mask upon which audience members project their own imaginings.

The expressively inexpressive (present-yet-absent) face of silent film actors inspired both Kuleshov's and Decroux's research, leading them to favor corporeal articulations over facial expression. Kuleshov wrote of Chaplin that in *Woman of Paris* he "virtually obliterated the elementary portrayal of emotion communicated facially. He demonstrated the deportment of a person in various aspects of his life by means of his relationship to things, to objects" (Kuleshov, 145).

In order to communicate without words (in silent films), Kuleshov preferred the power of economic gestures; he developed his own performance methods including "somersaults, tricks, leaps, battles, and chases" (Kuleshov, 13). While perhaps more overtly acrobatic than Decroux's usual approach, these techniques would have worked well in Decroux's *Little Soldiers*.

Concerning psychological subjects in film work, Kuleshov felt that reliance on the actor's facial expressions in order to reveal a character's changing states of being constituted a "fundamental error." Indeed, he argued that "[o]n the screen the most seemingly unnoticeable changes of the face become too crude—the viewer will not believe in such acting" (Kuleshov 107). Rather than from facial play, Kuleshov preferred instead that tensions emerge from the troubling arrangement of elements: "People calmly sit on barrels of gunpowder and wait. And only the viewer knows that the barrels are about to explode" (Kuleshov 93).

Decroux, who dedicated his only book, *Words on Mime,* to Chaplin, does not mention an "inexpressive" face in Chaplin's work, but does comment on Chaplin's use of immobility:

> Let's remember Chaplin's [definition] "Mime is immobility." Thus, the mime will be alive like the sun. For us the sun does not move in a visible way. We don't see it dance, we don't see its oscillations and yet it shines and warms us. It is alive without displacing itself, that's marvelous. It's the impression one often has in seeing certain photographs. I remember a photograph of Einstein. When he died, I was in Oslo and newspaper vendors printed a small poster with the face of Einstein. It didn't have

The face in corporeal mime 119

to move to send us spiritual rays. It is, by the way, the case of a speaking actor when he performs intensely, he does not displace himself, he speaks and he peoples the space with words. But we, mimes, don't. So, when one wants to allow oneself to be completely immobile, one must have a sufficiently interested, and therefore interesting, face. As Victor Hugo said: there is "[n]o dazzling person who is not [himself] first dazzled." An immobility can be longer or shorter depending on the more or less interested face one has. The Bible tells us God said to man, "You will earn your bread with the sweat of your brow." About us, one could say that we earn our faces with the sweat of our thought.

(Decroux cited in Pezin 126–27)

Here Decroux argues that in fact the "inexpressive" face communicates a great deal through invisible "oscillations" like the sun, or "spiritual rays" and that the better the actor, the longer he can do "nothing" (more difficult than it may seem) and remain interesting.[7]

Kuleshov simultaneously developed his own solution to the actor's problems. He wrote:

If the actor is well trained, he can perform the most minute, the slightest movements to perfection, and, most importantly, will be able to move from one position to another with perfection. . . . [The actor works] unconsciously, precisely and clearly, so that he can move differently. Dilettantes will give the impression of jerking marionettes, who are categorically unacceptable for the screen, which requires foremost of all— reality and simplicity.

(Kuleshov 113)

Kuleshov's "jerking marionettes" recall Craig's "spasmodic and ridiculous expression of the human face" cited at the beginning of this chapter.

In 1932, Decroux had his first cinema role in *L'Affaire est dans le sac*. He subsequently performed in at least 21 films, including the legendary *Les Enfants du Paradis* in 1945. If we consider Decroux and Barrault's collaboration at the Atelier Theatre in 1931 as the beginning of his work on corporeal mime, we see the cinema's influence on Decroux almost from the start. He said once in class, holding up a stick: "This is our art. On one end: the cinema actor, on the other: the acrobat. Our work, corporeal mime, happens between the two, and joins them." In 1974 Decroux wrote in a statement for his students:

Imagine that Raimu [French film and stage actor, 1883-1946] were skilled in gymnastics, and that thanks to that, he translated through the body what before only his face and his voice had expressed. We would thereby have an image of our mime. We would have the wrong image if we thought of [the ballet dancer] Serge Lifar [1905–1986].

(Decroux 1974, 11)

120   *The face in corporeal mime*

Decroux encountered this reality anew with each film he made, while at the same time looking for the links that connected subtle shifts of the face to larger but no less sincere movements of the acrobat's body. Decroux's artistic life played out between, on the one hand, commercial theatres, film and radio studios (where he earned his living) and, on the other hand, the mime classroom where he conducted his research, constantly moving his discoveries from one domain into the other.

Kuleshov discovered in his somewhat similar research that "Imitating, pretending, playing are unprofitable, since this comes out very poorly on the screen. . . . Film needs real material and not a pretense of reality." (Kuleshov 63). Decroux also wanted his students to fully appreciate how weight affected the body, to experience authentic pushing and pulling of matter as well as struggling with ideas and emotions (See Chapter 7).

Kuleshov described the special abilities of what he named the actor-mannequin:

> The "actor-mannequin" is not an obedient mannequin in the hands of the film director, as even some contemporary film scholars interpret this term. The actor mannequin is a natural, real person, as in life, but one who is able to do anything. He is higher and more complete than the theatrical actor.
>
> (Kuleshov 209)

Kuleshov's use of the word "mannequin" brings us closer to Irving's articulated body, Craig's Übermarionette, and Decroux's corporeal mime.

The face in corporeal mime

Decroux once wondered aloud why an actor on a cubistically designed stage set would move in the same way he did in his own living room, a mismatch Craig never could have tolerated. In fact, Craig's scenography called for, evoked and demanded an abstracted way of moving (and, of course, speaking). While Craig's scenery complemented actors as diverse as those in the Moscow Art Theatre and Duse, any reasonable actor would find it impossible to "mumble, stumble and scratch"[8] on one of Craig's sublime platforms, before one of his astonishing arches. Copeau's whole experience of returning to the Golden Ages of Theatre (Greeks, commedia, noh, the Wooden O) achieved by eliminating clutter, reached its logical conclusion with Decroux's nearly nude actor on a bare stage. The corporeal mime's marionettized body complemented a mask-like face; each required the other. We might ask if Decroux agreed with Craig's assessment of Irving: "A great believer in puppets, Irving's regret was that in his theatre they had to be made of flesh and blood" (Craig 1930, 107). Decroux certainly did, as Craig wrote of Irving, rehearse his "actors unceasingly and tried to make good marionettes of them" (Craig 1930, 107).

The face in corporeal mime 121

Decroux often spoke of the Cambodian heads at the Musée Guimet, mentioned earlier in this chapter. He said, substantially (I paraphrase, drawing from memory): "Look how gravity operates in reverse on these sublime faces. They fall upward! They are thinking, but of something else. They are present yet absent. Something fine, subtle and invisible oscillates within. They vibrate!" Or, as Craig wrote:

> A perfect theatre would neither tighten nor loosen the muscles of the face, and would neither contract the cells of the brain nor the heartstrings. All would be set at ease and to produce this state of mental and physical ease in the people is the duty of the Theatre and its Art.
>
> (Ibid.)

In an unpublished 1956 manuscript[9] on Indian art and philosophy, Decroux wrote "Art is a vibration." The serenely untroubled surface of the corporeal mime's face stretches over and reflects a sea of micro-movements, of pulsing vibrations recalling Irving's face, or at least Craig's loving recollection of it. Likewise, the corporeal mime's marionettized body, looking backward in time, finds a forebear in Irving's magnetized (and magnetizing) elaborately phrased movement scores.

Irving, Craig, Copeau and Decroux; Grotowski, Barba and Bogart; Duse, Chaplin and Kuleshov—these and other twentieth-century workers have left us a bounteous repository of evidence documenting their research into theatre-making. Phrasing silence as well as speech, these wooden actors, in all their various approaches, found organicity in *kata* and theatrical life in scores—in the conscious musical articulations of time and space.

Notes

1. Nineteenth-century plaster casts of the deceased's face, called death masks, preserved likenesses in the period before photography's easy availability. Later, the common usage of photographic portraits obviated the need for the death mask and the also popular death-bed photographic portrait.
2. Jane Goodall observes that "mesmerism in dramatic acting begins with the transformative self-hypnosis of the player" (Goodall 102).
3. In subsequent decades, as Etienne Decroux elaborated corporeal mime, he would adopt a motto and clarion call: "One thing at a time!"
4. In Paris of the 1920s, Isadora Duncan and others made dress reform and liberation from corsets and shoes an important issue.
5. Copeau and company coined the phrase "collective creation" and encouraged "devising."
6. My recollection, from Decroux's classes, 1968–1972.
7. Decroux once said in class "We study movement for years so that we can stand still on stage, doing nothing, and remain interesting."
8. These taunting words critiqued naturalistic acting in American theatre circles in the 1950s.
9. Fonds Decroux, Bibliothèque nationale de France, Richelieu–Louvois, arts du spectacle, Paris.

122 *The face in corporeal mime*

Works Cited

Bentley, Eric (1964) *The Life of the Drama*, New York, NY: Atheneum.

Batchelder, John Davis (1883) *Henry Irving: A Short Account of his Public Life*, New York, NY: William S. Gottsberger.

Booth, Michael R. (2015) *Victorian Spectacular Theatre 1850-1910*, Routledge.

Copeau, Jacques (1931) *Souvenirs du Vieux Colombier*, Paris: Nouvelles Éditions Latines.

——— (1991) *Journal 1901-1948*, ed. Claude Sicard, Paris: Seghers.

——— 2000. *L'Ecole du Vieux-Colombier (Registres VI)*, Paris: Gallimard.

Craig, Edward Gordon (1930) *Henry Irving*, New York, NY: Longmans, Green & Co, 52–4.

——— (2009) "The Actor and the Über-Marionette," *On the Art of the Theatre*, ed. Franc Chamberlain, New York, NY: Routledge.

Chaplin, Charlie (2012) *My Autobiography*, Brooklyn, NY: Melville House.

Decroux, Etienne (1974) "A Concise Explanation of the Nature of Corporeal Mime," *An Etienne Decroux Album, Mime Journal 2000-2001*, Claremont, CA: Mime Journal.

——— (2003) "L'interview Imaginaire," ed. Patrick Pezin, *Etienne Decroux, Mime Corporel*, Saint-Jean-de-Védas: L'Entretemps éditions.

Fournier, Christiane (2001) "For Love of Human Statuary, A Man Decides to be Silent," in *An Etienne Decroux Album*, Claremont, CA: Mime Journal.

Frackers, William (n.d.) srjarchives.tripod.com/1998-09/FRACKERS.HTM

Goodall, Jane (2008) *Stage Presence*, New York, NY: Routledge.

Holroyd, Michael (2008) *A Strange Eventful History: The Dramatic Lives of Ellen Terry, Henry Irving, and Their Remarkable Families*, New York, NY: Farrar, Straus and Giroux.

Kuleshov, Lev (1974) *Kuleshov on Film*, ed. and trans. Ronald Levaco, Los Angeles, CA: University of California Press.

Kusler, Barbara (1974) "Jacques Copeau's School for Actors, L'Ecole du Vieux-Colombier" Diss., University of Wisconsin.

Le Boeuf, Patrick (2010) "On the Nature of Edward Gordon Craig's Über-Marionette," *New Theatre Quarterly (2010)* DOI: 10.1017/S0266464X10000242

Leigh, Barbara Kusler (1979) *Jacques Copeau's School for Actors*, Allendale, MI: Mime Journal.

Le Gallienne, Eva (1966) *The Mystic in the Theatre*, Carbondale, IL: Southern Illinois University Press.

Macready, William C. (1912) *The Diaries of William Charles Macready*, Vol. 1 and 2, ed. William Toynbee, New York, NY: G. P. Putman's Sons.

Noakes, Richard. ore.exeter.ac.uk/repository/bitstream/handle/10871/15940/Noakes_Harrison_Dictionary_19th_C_Scientists.pdf?sequence=2

Pezin, Patrick, ed. (2003) *Etienne Decroux, mime corporel*, Saint-Jean-de-Védas: L'Entretemps éditions

Read, Michael (2008) "The Chief and His Champion: Irving and J.L. Toole" *Henry Irving: A Re-Evaluation of the Pre-Eminent Victorian Actor-Manager*, ed. Richard Foulkes, New York, NY: Routledge.

Riskin, Jessica (2009) "The Mesmerism Investigation," pdfs.semanticscholar.org/2f67/bf77c713330c5b27f89648337aafe6e321a0.pdf

Rudlin, John (1986) *Jacques Copeau*, Cambridge: Cambridge University. Press.

Saint-Denis, Michel (1976) *Theatre: The Rediscovery of Style*, New York, NY: Theatre Arts Books.

Saint-Denis, Michel (1982) *Training for the Theatre*, New York, NY: Theatre Arts Books.

The face in corporeal mime 123

Salter, Denis (1992) "Henry Irving, the 'Dr. Freud' of Melodrama," *Melodrama*, Cambridge: Cambridge University Press.

Segal, William (2003) *A Voice at the Borders of Silence: An Intimate View of the Gurdjieff Work, Zen Buddhism, and Art*, Woodstock: Overlook Press.

Stoker, Bram (1906) *Personal Reminiscences of Henry Irving, Volume I and 2*, London: The Macmillan Company.

Symons, Arthur (1907) *Studies in Seven Arts*. New York, NY: EP Dutton and Co.

Veinstein, André (1985) "Preface," *Words on Mime*, trans. Mark Piper, Claremont, CA: Mime Journal.

10 L'Homme de sport

Sport and statuary in Etienne Decroux's corporeal mime

> Decroux, in a book dedication (in Leabhart 2019, 43), points out that sport (unlike mime) was not a fine art but rather a competitive event. And yet, he admired the aesthetic aspect in sport, just as he did in sculpture. His always lively response either to sport or to sculpture never seemed academic or purely theoretical. Decroux spontaneously shared discoveries, often with the glee of a much younger enthusiast, thereby winning over all but the most cynical student. We catch a glimpse in this essay of intermingling ideas related to sport and statuary. They, in turn, open the door to Decroux's least-understood concept: the "circulation of energy" in the actor, which may also produce a visceral response in the audience member. Along the way, we identify references to this phenomenon in certain European as well as Asian theatre practices. Let's start with Ionesco's contention that "the sporting match gives us the most exact idea of what the theatre is in its purest state: live antagonism, dynamic conflict, the motiveless clash of opposing wills" (Ionesco 232). Decroux, like certain of his contemporaries, recognized and celebrated this circulation of energy in sport, in statuary, and in performance.

The theatre/sport connection

Although the successful execution of a sport is often beautiful to behold, the goal is competitive—one seeks to defeat others. In the theatre, however, as in the other fine arts, competition is replaced by the aesthetic aspect. There is no one or nothing to "beat." Decroux claims, in fact, that Georges Carpentier's unique boxing *style* played an essential role in the formulation of corporeal mime. Decroux even named one of the pillars of his research Man of Sport. And Carpentier, whose manner so inspired Decroux, went on to become—surprisingly—a popular film actor.

Outside Decroux's hermetic world, analogies abound comparing competitive sports with text-based theatre. In Stanislavsky-derived actor training since the Second World War, for example, one can identify their shared vocabulary: *goals*, *obstacles* and *tactics*. Acting textbooks, such as Robert Benedetti's *The Actor at Work*, feature exercises, like Push/Pull, derived from sport (11). Robert Barton's *Acting Onstage and Off* describes states of "relaxed

DOI: 10.4324/9781003205852-10

L'Homme de sport 125

readiness," consisting of varied physical and mental warm-ups (24), many of which find corollaries in sports activities.

The further we range from that mainstream paradigm and venture toward experimental or laboratory theatre, the more apt the comparison with ever more athletic activity. However, theatre and sport merge not only on the economic and artistic edges of commercial theatre, in the laboratories housing "pure research," but also at the other end of the artistic spectrum. Here, soaring, tumbling acrobatic actors in the $75 million Broadway production of *Spiderman* (2010) gave new meaning to the term "physical acting."

Actors, like athletes, try to enter into an extra-quotidian state of successful effort. As described by contemporary psychologist Mihaly Csikszentmihalyi (1934–2021) in *Flow: The Psychology of Optimal Experience*, both sport and theatre

> provided a sense of discovery, a creative feeling of transporting the person into a new reality. [They] pushed the person to higher levels of performance and led to previously undreamed of states of consciousness. In short, they transformed the self by making it more complex.
>
> (Csikszentmihalyi 74)

Actors typically access this "new reality," also referred to elsewhere in this volume as "the zone," through relaxation as well as warming up before going on stage. Sweating during performances comes not just from the heat of theatrical lighting but also from the considerable psycho-physical effort required. Performances, often impassioned, almost sport-like, encounters among actors, depict conflicting extremes of human behavior, including armed and unarmed combat. But unlike a real sporting event, they never change the play's predetermined outcome. Though intensely physical, the theatrical event remains artistic, not competitive, and although Hamlet will always die at the end, actors must move, speak and think as if they didn't know it.

This chapter will explore links between sport and corporeal mime, especially Decroux's category of *homme de sport*; the use of counterweights; and the acting techniques these engendered (Sections 1–3 of this chapter). I then associate Decroux's performance discoveries with three nineteenth-century French sculptors, with French singing teacher and theoretician François Delsarte, and with Paul Bellugue, professor of anatomy at the Ecole des Beaux-Arts, who collaborated with Decroux in the formulation of theoretical aspects of the corporeal mime technique (Sections 4–8).

The sculptors, along with Delsarte, Decroux *et al* lived in a world impacted by the Dress Reform Movement of the late nineteenth and early twentieth centuries. Then, "a growing number of people including feminists, health advocates, physicians, artists, and educators" (Schoeny) rejected restrictive clothing, laced corsets, rigid collars, clenched neck ties, tightly-buttoned

126 *L'Homme de sport*

shoes, vests, suspenders and belts worn by many middle-class people. In 1923–1924, Decroux observed the masked improvisations at Copeau's Ecole du Vieux Colombier. These explorations featured partial nudity not for health reasons but rather to reclaim the expressive potential of the trunk. In 1931–1932, when teaching at the Atelier Theatre, Decroux advocated partial nudity in actor training and in performance (see Decroux's "Ancient Combat" and "The Statue," among others).

Like Dress Reform adherents, Decroux found that most contemporary garments limited his optimal movements on or off stage; he therefore based his own sartorial choices entirely upon comfort. Indoors, even while teaching, he preferred pajamas and slippers or boxing shorts and a long-sleeved shirt. For his rare ventures outdoors, he disregarded fashion by wearing outsized tuxedo trousers, a voluminous long-sleeved sky blue shirt, untucked at the waist, and white running shoes. Thus, in Decroux's daily life and in his research, he attempted to extend the physical and psychic range of the human form to liberate himself not only from confining clothing but also from mental constraints—from the mental binding of his time that advocated covering the human form when he championed its near-nudity. Eschewing traditional ways of imagining and moving the human body, he placed his own and his students' bodies into precarious positions, following the energetic lines of classical sculpture and contemporary sport. Thus, in their effort to create "new" arts, Decroux, as well as modern dancers (Figures 10.21, 10.29, 10.30), engendered arts that resembled ancient ones just as Dress Reform garments recalled the less constricting togas, tunics and capes from earlier times.

And finally, I suggest that Decroux, through the category *homme de sport*, helped actors realize an "alchemical" way of acting by performing what Artaud identified in Barrault's performance as "disciplined movements and stylized mathematical gestures" (145) (Sections 9 and 10).

The goal keeper/C-curve/fulcrum

How Decroux's corporeal mime resembles sport and vice versa

Decroux gave the title Man of Sport to one of the primary categories in the pedagogy that he evolved over a period of more than 50 years. He often spoke of the actor as a vigilant goalkeeper and quoted the Bible's warning, "No one knows when the thief is coming," to underscore his belief that the effective actor performs on the alert, on guard. Eugenio Barba uses the term *sats* to designate this ideal state of readiness in acting as well as sports:

> When Occidental performers want to be energetic . . . they often begin to move in space with tremendous vitality . . . [using] large movements, with great speed and muscular strength. And this effort is associated

L'Homme de sport   127

with fatigue, hard work. Oriental actors (or great Occidental actors) can become even more tired almost without moving. Their tiredness is not caused by an excess of vitality, by the use of large movements, but by the play of oppositions. The body becomes charged with energy because within it is established a series of differences of potential which render the body alive, strongly present, even with slow movements or in apparent immobility.

(Barba 13)

The seemingly immobile goalie, not knowing whence the ball (the thief) might come, watches and listens expectantly, alert for an attack. His readiness focuses, in "apparent immobility," not only his own body but the audience's bodies as well.

Barba's "play of oppositions" requires that the actor "not know" what will happen next. Of course, he does know *in his mind*, but he must not *in his body*. When the actor "knows," the audience relaxes and the drama ends—the "differences of potential" have ceased to exist both within and outside the actor's body. This "play of oppositions" and these "differences of potential" comprise the core of Decroux's idea of drama in all its varied forms. For example, in performing for the camera, a play of oppositions manifests itself in minute movements in the muscles of the face, with tensions ebbing and flowing. In mime, however, the actor's micro-movements originate in areas other than the face—the trunk, the limbs or perhaps, interestingly, with a tightening of the scalp which will affect the face, but indirectly.

Decroux describes mime as

mobile immobility, the pressure of water on the dike, the hovering of a fly stopped by the window pane, the delayed fall of the leaning tower which remains standing. Then similar to the way we stretch a bow before taking aim, man implodes yet again.

(1985, 51)

These strenuous *im*plosions (with low center of gravity and weighted movements) of actors, of mimes and of athletes—as contrasted to the *ex*plosion (with airborne movements) that Decroux assigned primarily to dance—often place the body naturally into a configuration often referred to, in various movement modalities, as a "C-curve." American voice teacher Arthur Lessac (1909–2011) returned to this figure and this term again and again in his teaching. His books provide, through numerous drawings, examples of this forward curve of the body in sports activities (fencing, cycling, running, pitching a baseball, playing golf, basketball and ping-pong), as well as singing, floating in a bathtub, carrying packages, jumping rope, climbing stairs, squatting naturally as babies do, conducting an orchestra, yawning

128 *L'Homme de sport*

and pushing a refrigerator. These activities create the C-curve, the inside of which Lessac named a "Crescent" (Lessac 1996).

Figure 10.1 depicts a forward inclination of the chord in an effort to displace (pushing or pulling) a weight along a horizontal line. Figure 10.2 shows a backward inclination of the chord as the trunk descends along a hook-shaped line in order to release an extensor. Decroux taught that, in order to work efficiently, the chord must incline to the extent that lifting, pushing or pulling requires (counterweight against weight). The chord of

Figure 10.1 Thomas Leabhart performing the planing section of "The Carpenter," c. 1970. Chord of the arc (dotted line) tilting forward around a fulcrum (just below the navel).

Source: Unattributed photograph from the author's collection, edited by Eric Culhane..

L'Homme de sport 129

Figure 10.2 Thomas Leabhart, c. 1985, performing The Extensor. Chord of the Arc (dotted line) tilting backward around a fulcrum.

Source: Photograph by Craig Arteaga-Johnson, edited by Eric Culhane.

the arc remains mostly vertical for walking or accomplishing light counterweights. As the weight to be displaced increases, so does the degree of inclination around a vital fulcrum—the energetic hub of the body. In Figure 10.3, we see this hub, just below the navel, at the intersection of the diagonal lines. In Figure 10.4, one can follow the trajectories of the diagonal limbs to locate the hub. In Figures 10.5 and 10.6, we see inclinations and translations of the chord of the arc in photos taken of the actor in a costume imagined by Decroux and realized by Michèle Renaud-Molnar.

130 *L'Homme de sport*

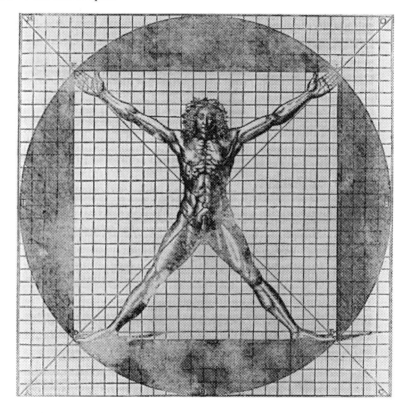

Figure 10.3 Vitruvian Man.
Source: Drawing by Cesare Cesariano (1475–1543).

A "motivating image"/face vs. body

Covering the face and uncovering the body in Decroux's work

In Figure 10.7, which depicts the French boxer Georges Carpentier,[1] we recognize the forward C-curve of the trunk; the dotted line represents the chord of the body's arc. Across from the chord's midpoint—about an inch below the navel—we find the fulcrum (the hub). Decroux described Carpentier's: "Vigor and grace; strength, elegance; dazzle and thought; a taste for danger and a smile. . . . We would never suspect that he was the motivating image for our study of physical mime (tragedy section)" (1985, 14).

The performer/boxer's partially nude body resists indecency, Decroux asserted, by maintaining effortful postures. Decroux considered the nude body in relaxation suggestive—glandular rather than muscular. Decroux and his students originally practiced in the briefest garments in order to simulate the nudity of athletes and classical statues. In later years he took the advice

L'Homme de sport 131

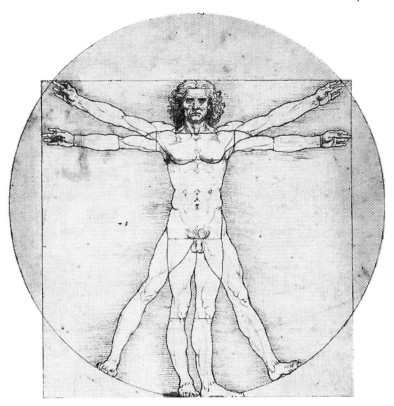

Figure 10.4 Vitruvian Man.
Source: Drawing by Leonardo da Vinci (1452–1519).

of French actress Madeleine Renaud who believed that tights, paradoxically, made a performer appear more naked but without the distractions presented by an unclothed body (Leabhart 1978, 39). Since Decroux considered the uncovered face—but not the unclothed body—obscene, he concealed the face but not the body. He finally dispensed with the covered face, having determined that masks and veils distracted from the actor's movement. Instead, his uncovered face would emulate the "neutral" and beatific ones in the statues at Angkor in Cambodia. Decroux said, as quoted in a 1962 French newspaper interview:

> I affirm that nothing is more beautiful than a corpse. Take a man who was all his life envious, unctuous, calculating, a liar. His face is unbearable to you. Dead, he has all the nobility of a pharaoh. . . . The body is never indecent. When the body plays [acts]—as does a sportsman, a worker—it can go to the extreme without indecency. [However] it only takes a little to make a face perfectly obscene.
>
> (Caviglioli)

132 L'Homme de sport

Figure 10.5 Thomas Leabhart improvises in "The Carpenter" costume. Costume conceived by Decroux and realized by Michèle Renaud–Molnar.

Source: Photograph by Andrew Kilgore, c. 1975.

The above citation encapsulates Decroux's worldview: In order to energize the body and foster in actors the expressive animation demonstrated by athletes and workers, actors ought to obscure the face or otherwise limit its expression. Most people live, Decroux contended, in the periphery of their bodies, with emphasis on face and hands, body parts he described as "instruments of falsehood, henchmen of gossip" (1985, 94). Decroux reversed that hierarchy and, like an athlete, relocated the corporeal mime's energetic and expressive initiator in the sub-navel center of the trunk. Decroux doubtless took this cue from his mentor Jacques Copeau who included many athletic elements in his comprehensive approach and who, as we see in other chapters in this book, experimented with masks on student actors (Leabhart 1995). Thus, an appreciation of sports and participation in masked improvisations helped Copeau's actor and Decroux's corporeal mime discover energetic wellsprings within the body, replacing the "falsehood" of face and hands.

Artists, from medieval cathedral sculptors to Picasso, saw the body as a face and the face as a body, one example of which we see represented in Magritte's *The Rape* in Figure 10.8. In corporeal mime, Decroux contended, "the entire body . . . becomes a face" (1985, 130) and, "once the face was obliterated, the body needed all of its parts to replace it" (1985, 4). Decroux's paradigm, then, exchanged the low slung spine of the actor in nineteenth-century pantomime

Figure 10.6 Thomas Leabhart performing the last moment in Decroux's "The Carpenter." Costume conceived by Decroux and realized by Michèle Renaud–Molnar.

Source: Photograph by Andrew Kilgore, c.1975.

for the strenuously and athletically engaged trunk of the corporeal mime, at the same time trading the pantomime's animated face for a sublime one. Decroux, the man who "preferred to stand," often disparaged the culture built around a sedentary lifestyle.

Counterweights, physical and mental

Transitioning from sport and manual labor to theatre

Decroux, the militant socialist-anarchist, son of a left-leaning manual laborer, spent his youth as a mason and a dock-worker, among other trades. During our rehearsals (1968–1972, Paris) for "The Carpenter" and "The Washerwoman," (see Figure 10.31) two pieces that reveal his first-hand rapport with labor, Decroux expressed regret that machines accomplished so much of the work in the modern world. It wasn't that he wished workers would suffer physically in order to earn a living. It was rather that he saw the value and the beauty in craft, in efficient functional movement, honed over time. He broke into

134 *L'Homme de sport*

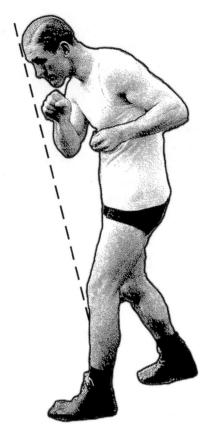

Figure 10.7 Georges Carpentier, with chord of the arc (dotted line) added.
Source: Image created by Eric Culhane based on an unattributed photograph.

hearty laughter imagining the impossibility of making mime pieces from the activities of a modern day carpenter or washerwoman, considering that power tools now obviate the need for most counterweights. He predicted that audiences would one day go to the theatre to see real physical work—counterweights in action—since they would have mostly disappeared from real life. I fully realized this in 1995, when I performed in Sweden with ISTA (International School of Theatre Anthropology). Before the performance, a member of the cleaning crew moved effortlessly across the stage, gently guiding a machine that washed and dried the floor. I smiled inwardly noticing that her work required not the smallest counterweight (inclination of the chord of the arc) and produced not a bead of sweat; an hour later, I was performing exhausting and exhilarating—but imaginary—counterweights, perspiring abundantly onto that clean floor.

L'Homme de sport 135

Figure 10.8 The Rape.
Source: René Magritte, 1934.

While the manual laborer and the boxer struggle against external weights and adversaries, the psychological actor (not necessarily trained in Decroux's mime) portrays her character's internal conflicts, or wages a mental or verbal—but not a physical—assault against an external adversary. Then the counterweight becomes what Decroux calls a "metaphysical" or "phantom" one: the actor, negotiates energy fluctuations through the body, experiencing Barba's "play of opposites" and "differences of potential." A person wrestling with a burdensome idea or extreme emotion (Figure 10.9) might resemble a person lifting a heavy weight (Figure 10.10), resulting in many of the same attitudes and using the same force to mediate energy and weight change (see Chapter 7).

Figure 10.9 Metaphysical Counterweight.

Source: Eric Culhane photographed and redrawn by Eric Culhane.

New or old?

Going forward by going backward

I sometimes accompany my students to the Getty Villa Museum in Malibu, inviting them to discover the vast collection of ancient artifacts housed there. Representations of moving figures, whether in sculpture, on painted vases or in mosaics, exemplify certain characteristics also appearing in corporeal mime: body parts rotating, inclining and translating; lunges onto one leg, enabling the trunk to push or pull; and inclinations of the body into what art historian Sir Kenneth Clark called "heroic diagonals."

At the Getty, millennia-old terra cotta figures dance merrily through the centuries. In them, students can identify a multitude of C-curve: forward, backward, sideways and in rotation. Students can also trace, as they develop a keener eye, invisible plumb lines dropped from a figure's *entrejambe* [crotch] and intersecting a sometimes chipped or broken ankle (Figure 10.11). These various lines in space—so many design elements—often represent counterweights and fall easily into Decroux's *homme de sport* category. As such, these lines (as components of a counterweighted figure) deliver more than merely aesthetically pleasing shapes: An understanding of counterweights proves essential to actors as well as visual artists in depicting physical or

L'Homme de sport 137

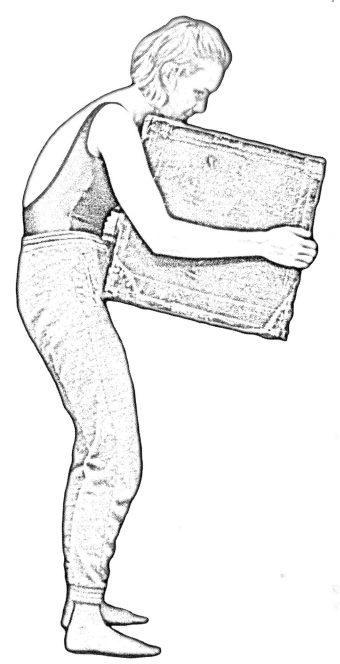

Figure 10.10 Physical Counterweight.
Source: Megan Marshall photographed and redrawn by Eric Culhane.

Figure 10.11 Roman Mime (First Century C.E.).

Source: Terra-cotta statuette in the British Museum, from Allardyce Nicoll's *Masks, Mimes & Miracles* (1963).

metaphysical heaviness. Counterweights demonstrate a dynamic internal logic that testifies to the truth of the movement or the image. Morevoer, these carefully positioned lines in space generate the dramatic tension to which the viewer (well schooled in gravity's inexorable pull) responds. After one museum visit, a student wondered aloud whether Decroux had truly invented corporeal mime or had instead rediscovered ancient principles that artists have always known. Decroux himself contended that he was not an inventor, but simply a furniture mover [*déménageur*], as he took what his perceptive eye observed, whether in other arts or on the street, and transposed them for the stage.

In Figures 10.11, 10.12 and 10.13, we glimpse three actors from three different centuries depicting three various weight displacements, two of which Decroux applauded for their risky forward gravity and one, the

L'Homme de sport 139

Figure 10.12 Séverin Cafferra (1863–1930).
Source: Unattributed photograph.

pantomime, against which he rebelled because of Pierrot's comfortable backward stance (plumb line over the back foot).

Decroux frequently expressed his aversion to what he called "*pantomime ancienne*" (Figure 10.12), including in his descriptions (in *Words on Mime* and in "The Imaginary Interview") of the pantomime he saw as a young boy at the

140   *L'Homme de sport*

turn of the twentieth century. Of course, Decroux did not witness everything called "nineteenth-century pantomime," but only certain strands of it to which he reacted negatively. Later, as a theatre practitioner, he explained his distaste for this form:

> If I've been impressed by all the arts, even if not equally impressed by all of them, there is one that frankly displeased me. And that is pantomime. Pantomime: that play of face and hands which seemed to try to explain things but lacked the needed words. I detested this form. But that's rather strange because pantomime was always supposed to amuse people. Art should be serious first of all. Painting is, first of all, serious. It is serious before we see amusing things like the work of Dufy, statues of Daumier. First we have something serious. Music is, first of all, serious. Poetry is almost always serious, and what isn't? An art is first of all serious and adds the comic aspect later. And this pantomime seemed to me to be systematically comic, even before one knew what the subject was.
>
> (Decroux 1978, 9)

In the iconic images by French photographer Nadar (1820–1910), we can observe the ample costume of the nineteenth-century pantomime Charles Deburau, son of the illustrious performer Jean-Gaspard Deburau (1796–1846). Likewise, in photo postcards of the day, we find the pantomime Séverin (1863–1930), whose costume—a voluminous white sack—concealed his trunk (Figure 10.12), as the costumes of his forebears had done. Marcel Carné's classic film *Children of Paradise* (discussed elsewhere in these pages) celebrated this genre's silent storytelling that used expressive face and hands during the government's proscription of the spoken word in certain theatres. While those full costumes shrouded the trunk, effacing its potential expressivity, Decroux, in his modernist experiments in the early twentieth century, revealed the trunk (Figure 10.13), restoring in some way the visible spines of ancient performers (Figures 10.11 and 10.14).

In those visits to the Getty, my students and I try out for ourselves some of the weight displacements and configurations we observe in the works of art, often to the bemusement of puzzled museum guards. In the glass cases, we discover small clay Greek and Roman statues whose attitudes—whose spines—suggest unfettered movement (Figures 10.11, 10.14 and 10.17). If that liberated trunk was apparent both in Decroux's work and in the representations of movement from the museum's ancient artifacts, it was decidedly less so in the generation of theatre performers just previous to Decroux's experiments (Deburau, Séverin *et al*). For example, though the Hellenistic dancer's costume depicted in Figure 10.14 reveals only her eyes and forehead, the fluidity of her clinging veiled garment mirrors and amplifies the slightest shift of weight or spinal rotation in a way that Pierrot's "flour sack"

Figure 10.13 Thomas Leabhart in Etienne Decroux's "The Carpenter," costume conceived by Decroux and realized by Michèle Renaud–Molnar.

Source: Photograph by Andrew Kilgore, c. 1974.

did not (Figure 10.12). The nineteenth-century ballet dancer (Figure 10.15), following the fashion of her time, did not shroud the trunk but did corset it, subjecting her to a constraining support through the midriff. There, too, the focus lay not on the spine or trunk's full range of motion but rather on the dancer's airborne quality. By contrast, early twentieth-century modern dancers, like Ruth St. Denis, (Figure 10.16), freed from both corsets and toe shoes, found the lower center of gravity of their ancient forebears.

Although Decroux's project distanced itself fundamentally from dance, including the modern dance of his contemporaries, both corporeal mimes and modern dancers reclaimed their ancestors' liberated bodies. They did, nonetheless, embrace artistic constraints but not those of the ballet dancers of their day, whose spines (as mentioned above) remained partially supported, cinched. Beyond theatrical performance, a newly freed body emerged with

142 *L'Homme de sport*

Figure 10.14 Dancing woman.

Source: Bronze statuette in the Metropolitian Museum of Art, New York, 3rd–2nd century BCE.

L'Homme de sport 143

Figure 10.15 Nineteenth-century ballerina.
Source: Drawing by Craig Arteaga-Johnson based on an unattributed print from the period.

144 *L'Homme de sport*

Figure 10.16 Ruth St. Denis (1879–1968).

Source: Unattributed photograph, c. 1915, Jerome Robbins Dance Division, New York Public Library.

the rediscovery of sport in the early twentieth century, both for the average person and as a tool in actor training. (The Olympic Games revived in 1896 after centuries of inactivity.)

Throughout history, sculptors often selected athletes and dancers as models since they so skillfully embodied dynamic visual text. In turn, dancers, mimes and actors have used statues as inspiration for their activities. The sculptors "froze" movement, while actors and dancers "thawed" it, restoring its fluid state, perhaps hundreds or even thousands of years afterward, as if trying to reanimate prehistoric insects caught in ancient amber or attempting to regenerate, from frozen DNA, a now-extinct wolf. We might ask ourselves, as did my student during the Getty visit, if modern dancers and modern mimes truly discovered new ways of moving or if they rediscovered old ones through statuary. Isadora Duncan, for example, thought she had unearthed the heart of Greek performance, with ancient statuary as the primary source for her rediscovery.

L'Homme de sport 145

Figure 10.17 Dancing woman. Hellenistic terra-cotta statuette, 2nd century BCE.
Source: de Young Museum in San Francisco.

146 *L'Homme de sport*

François Delsarte

A theoretician who unwittingly paved the way for modern dance and corporeal mime

François Delsarte (1811–1871), French theoretician and teacher of music, oratory and acting, gained renown for his brilliant lectures and innovative training techniques that included explorations of vocal as well as physical expression. In 1826, after a troubled and poverty-stricken childhood, he entered the Ecole royale de musique et de déclamation (precursor to today's Conservatoire National Supérieur de Musique et de Danse de Paris). Two years later, he received the school's second prize for vocalization. His teachers, however, expelled him the following year, deeming further study useless after Delsarte damaged his voice. From that time, Delsarte's passion lay in discovering rules that governed voice production and performance, resulting in the publication of his *Méthode philosophique du chant* in 1833. Despite his impaired voice, he gave vocal recitals, warmly praised and enthusiastically attended by the glitterati of his day, and maintained a successful career as teacher of voice and gesture (Porte 265–76). One of his students, observing through the lens of Dress Reform, describes Delsarte's attire for his open evening classes,

> where he was seen to the utmost advantage. There, dressed in the vast shapeless coat, which drapes itself about him as he gesticulates, his neck free from the cravat which puts modern Europeans in the pillory, and allowing himself greater space than at his concerts—there, and there alone, is Delsarte wholly himself.
>
> (Arnaud cited in Delaumosne, 348)

Following Delsarte's death, his teaching, by then largely ignored in France, traveled to the United States primarily via the American actor and director James Steele MacKaye (1842–1894) who had studied with Delsarte in Paris for six months during the last years of Delsarte's life. Some scholars argue that MacKaye, rather than Delsarte, created Harmonic Gymnastics, the physical exercises taught in Delsarte's name. Others maintain that Delsarte himself never taught movement exercises *per se* (see Leabhart, 2004/2005). In any case, MacKaye introduced Harmonic Gymnastics to Genevieve Stebbins who in turn, instructed numerous students, some of whom came to influence Isadora Duncan, Ted Shawn and Ruth St. Denis, to name but three modern dance pioneers for whom this study proved transformative.

Discernible similarities exist between some of the corporeal attitudes illustrated in books on American Delsartism and classroom figures evolved by Decroux. Delsarte and Decroux, autodidacts, each evolved a complex, Cartesian system of expression for articulating the body, rendering it, in practice, quite fluid. And for each of them, but in different ways, a strongly spiritual, if not traditionally religious, component informed life and work.

For Delsarte this study manifested as devout Catholicism and for Decroux as a mystic atheism, described in other chapters.

Nancy Lee Chalfa Ruyter extensively documents the Delsarte strand in American dance (*Reformers and Visionaries: The Americanization of the Art of Dance* and in *The Cultivation of the Body and Mind in Nineteenth-Century American Delsartism*). Beyond that link with dance, the Delsarte component in contemporary theatre can be traced to Jerzy Grotowski, who acknowledged Delsarte in *Towards a Poor Theatre* (16). Grotowski, as a young theatre student in Poland, studied two texts by Prince Sergei Mikhailovitch Volkonsky on Delsarte. Grotowski writes of "one absolute rule. Bodily activity comes first, and then vocal expression" (183). Compare that with Delsarte's "Gesture must always precede speech" (Delaumosne 51) and Decroux's desire to ban language from the theatre for a period of 25 years (Decroux 1985, 27). Delsarte, Grotowski and Decroux each arrived at strongly held beliefs in the primacy of the body over "talking heads," in opposition to the prevailing practices of their times.

Decroux, Delsarte and sculpture

An informing metaphor for a career

Decroux's early experience sensitized him to sculpture: his parents provided him with modeling clay as his first toy, and his father often took him to visit an Italian sculptor and stonemason. Decroux subsequently called one of his most important categories of research *statuaire mobile*. He spoke reverently of public statues representing struggling and marching figures; he extolled their influence on public morality. At the same time he greatly admired Auguste Rodin's embracing figures and Aristide Maillol's reclining ones. Statuary, through immobility, often represents dynamism, movement. Decroux asserted that he created his corporeal mime movements from immobilities, in the same way that one makes flip books or pixilated films out of quick successions of still images.

Decroux wrote on sculpture in *Words on Mime*:

I should like to have been a sculptor.

The spirit becomes clear only when filtered through stone.

Statuary is an art carved out of reality, and whose creations are permanent.

The model of the sculptor is the transformer that touches and is touched and whose name is man. In transforming stone, the sculptor touches it, and once his work is finished, we can touch it.

(1985, 12)

And later Decroux added:

148 *L'Homme de sport*

> It is my desire that the actor accept the artifice and sculpt the air, making us feel where the line of poetry begins and where it ends. . . . Our thought pushes our gestures in the same way that the thumb of the sculptor pushes forms; our body sculpted from inside, stretches. . . . Mime is, at the same time, both sculptor and statue.

(Ibid.)

As French custom often placed statues of great persons and allegorical figures in prominent places for the admiration and edification of the population, Decroux naturally saw sculpture as a teaching tool. Three nineteenth-century statues on permanent public display in Paris shed light on Decroux's project: The *Dancing Faun*, by Eugène-Louis Lequesne, in the Luxembourg Gardens; *The Dance*, by Jean-Baptiste Carpeaux, on the front portico of the Opéra Garnier; and the *Genius of Liberty*, by Auguste Dumont, atop the Column of the Bastille. And while, to my knowledge, Decroux did not comment upon Lequesne, he often spoke in class about Carpeaux and Dumont. Thus, Decroux's reflections on those two sculptors have informed my way of looking at Lequesne.

Despite remarkable differences among them, each statue depicts a nude male figure in heroic and vigorous movement. They stand at three of Georges-Eugène Haussmann's most important intersections of a newly configured Paris. Having remained in place for more than 100 years, albeit more invisibly each year, they have increasingly blended into the cluttered visual cityscape: more people, traffic, noise and distraction equals less visibility. Most passersby seem to take them for granted, not worthy of a second glance.

As Albert Boime (1933–2008) wrote in his book on nineteenth-century French sculpture,

> Sculpture not only represents something outside itself, but presents itself as an object in the universe of things. It simultaneously produces narrative while occupying space like a piece of furniture or natural or sacred object which has to be surmounted or gotten around somehow. This ambiguity in its physical presence and signifying function allows it through time to generate fresh meaning within its public context.

(Boime 14)

For Decroux, this "fresh meaning" had everything to do with modern mime and the rediscovery of the fluidly moving body that he uncovered while working on precise, geometric articulations of the trunk and limbs. Through careful analysis, he created sequential studies of human movement, like time-lapse films of blossoming flowers and burgeoning trees, documentaries he so admired on his visits to the Paris Cinémathèque. The "unfreezing" and decoding of classical statues, mentioned above, indelibly marked both Delsarte's and Decroux's projects. Stebbins, quoting from Angélique Arnaud, writes that Delsarte studied statues from antiquity for 15 years;

Stebbins herself carefully studied the collections of ancient statues "in the galleries of the Louvre, making notes, checking off every law and principle of Delsarte's opposition, sequence and poise, and trying for one whole year to find a really artistic contradiction to his general formulation, but in vain" (Stebbins 445–46).

Three nineteenth-century French sculptors

The Recovery of a fluidly articulated spine

Eugène-Louis Lequesne (1814–1887), born in Paris of working class parents, became a lawyer in 1839. In 1841, he began studies with the well-known sculptor Pradier at the Ecole des Beaux Arts and, in 1842, traveled to Rome, where he made works that were later shown in Paris at the Salons of 1842 and 1843. In 1844, after winning the Prix de Rome, he moved to Italy where he produced large athletic figures. After living in the Villa Medicis for five years, he returned to Paris with his most famous work, the *Faune dansant*, exhibited in the Salon of 1852 and subsequently placed in the Luxenbourg Gardens, where it remains. The faun's gaze now rests somewhere just beyond the metal grill which separates the leafy manicured garden from the frantically busy city street. In the *Dancing Faun* (Figure 10.18) created before Decroux's birth, and perhaps unknown to him, I find an example of what became a key element in Decroux's project: the precariousness of the faun's stance, balanced on one foot on the greased surface of an inflated (or wine-filled) goatskin. When Decroux implored his students to "settle into the unsettled" or to "move to the edge of the precipice" or to "place the pyramid on its point," he unknowingly urged us to imitate that insouciant faun by moving with abandon to greater and greater imbalance in our own bodies.

We might see Lequesne's faun—balanced on his left foot, the right leg raised—as a complement to another dancer with a different disposition of limbs, origin, date of creation and raison d'être: the Hindu god Shiva Nataraja. He inhabits (Figure 10.19) a two-dimensional ring of fire, while the faun breaks the frontal plane and inhabits an invisible yet discernible three-dimensional sphere of circulating, dynamic power. Despite their differences, either faun or Shiva could awaken, in any attentive passerby, kinesthetic empathy, perceived as an energetic movement along the spine.

Augustin-Alexandre Dumont (1801–1884) studied with his father, Jacques-Edme Dumont, and later with Cartellier. Although his many works figure prominently in France and abroad, the *Genius of Liberty* on the July Column in the Place de la Bastille in Paris (Figure 10.20) has become his most celebrated sculpture. First exhibited in the Salon of 1836, this precariously balanced figure was placed atop the column in 1840. Some contemporary critics saw only "one of those banal mythological allegories" (Fusco and Janson 63) while most twentieth-century Parisians overlooked it entirely. It blended, for the most part, with the generic Parisian ambience, too high in the air to

150 *L'Homme de sport*

Figure 10.18 Dancing Faun by Eugène-Louis Lequesne (1851).
Source: Image edited by Eric Culhane from a photograph by Selbymay, 2012.

be really seen. The rare curious observer risked, at best, a stiff neck and, at worst, an unwanted encounter with a passing vehicle. Decroux, however, saw a man (perhaps a sportsman or a corporeal mime) dangerously perched on one foot, on half-point, on a polished sphere, on a high column in the middle of a teeming city square. Thus, despite Decroux's own poor sense of balance, he identified with the statue's representation of a daring position: as a life-long student of the body, Decroux's kinesthetic empathy told him that

L'Homme de sport 151

Figure 10.19 Shiva Nataraja, *Lord of the Cosmic Dance.*

Source: Photograph of a sculpture in the Metropolitan Museum of Art, c. 11th century.

only a subtle but constant micro-shifting would prevent an animate, rather than a bronze, *génie* from falling to the swarming street below.[2]

Jean-Baptiste Carpeaux (1827–1875), the best-known of these sculptors, studied with François Rude and soon afterward, in 1844, enrolled in the Ecole des Beaux Arts. He became a pupil of Francisque Duret and won the coveted Prix du Rome in 1854. His controversial work elicited praise from the Goncourt brothers and disdain from many others.

Carpeaux's *La Danse* (Figure 10.22), commissioned for Garnier's Opéra, was unveiled in 1869, prior to the opening of the Opéra itself in 1875. Instead

L'Homme de sport

Figure 10.20 The Genius of Liberty by Augustin-Alexandre Dumont.
Source: Marie-Lan Nguyen/Wikimedia Commons.

of nude allegorical figures, some outraged citizens saw cavorting, offensively naked bodies. Although, at the time, plans existed to replace the controversial work, it has outlived temporary infamy to become a popular Parisian landmark.

Thus, these three prominent allegorical figures inhabited the world into which Decroux was born; though Decroux mentioned only two of them in

Figure 10.21 Anna Duncan (1894–1982).

Source: Photograph by Arnold Genthe, 1916–18.

his lectures, the third (*Dancing Faun*) would just as easily have served as an example of his *homme de sport*.

Paul Bellugue

Decroux's collaborator and friend

Paul Bellugue (1892–1955), a professor of anatomy at the Ecole des Beaux-Arts in Paris, so firmly believed that artists should study the living and moving human figure (as opposed to the plaster casts so commonly used at the time) that he invited athletes, dancers, music hall performers and mimes into his classroom. To contemplate the moving human figure, he also took students to sports stadiums or the circus. In the late 1960s and early 1970s, Decroux identified Bellugue as a significant influence on his work, a colleague with whom he presented lecture demonstrations in the 1940s and

154　*L'Homme de sport*

Figure 10.22 Jean-Baptiste Carpeaux's *La Danse*.

Source: Image edited by Eric Culhane from a photograph by Sailko.

1950s. A polymath, Bellugue, through his study of sport, ballet, gymnastics, posture through the ages, Cambodian dance and sculpture, antique statuary and classicism, helped Decroux define an aesthetic well grounded in art history and in anatomy. A brilliant theorist and great friend of Decroux's, we know Bellugue today only through a posthumously published book of essays entitled *A propos d'art, de forme et de movement,* where he asked:

> How, then, can the statue which is inert matter manage to give us the sensation of the movement that it does not make? By bearing the traces of this movement, or rather, the trace left in matter by the gesture of the sculptor who carries out the movement. When we see these traces, we recreate the actions of the sculptor and consequently his sensations.
>
> (108)

Bellugue explains the magic of kinesthetic empathy and, in his mention of mime, reminds us of what he might have learned from his colleague Decroux (Leabhart 1978, 45).

The circulation of energy

Common threads

What do these individuals—three sculptors, a teacher/theoretician of voice and movement, and a teacher of anatomy—have in common? Each in his way closely examined the living, unimpeded, moving human body in order to produce or better understand a work of art. The work of four of these artists, Delsarte and the three sculptors, opened a path that Decroux would follow. And Decroux's friend Paul Bellugue served as a sounding board, thus providing encouragement during corporeal mime's formative years, especially for the category *homme de sport.*

The delirious bacchanalian nude figures of Carpeaux's sculpture, *La Danse,* on the façade of the Paris Opera's 1875 Palais Garnier provoked a scandal at its unveiling. The utterly unrestricted movement portrayed in those nude figures stood in stark contrast to the modesty assured by the constricted garments that were the fashion of the day for female audience members (Figure 10.23). And as we've mentioned, even the ballerinas on stage, although more exposed, bore the restrictions of tightly corseted costumes (Figure 10.15). The limitless movement possibilities inherent in Carpeaux's sculptural figures shocked, at the time, by their immodesty but also adumbrated, from our twenty-first century perspective, Dress Reform, the liberated dance of Isadora Duncan, and the full body articulations of corporeal mime.

Although the audience members and dancers seemed elegantly attired, their corsets and tightly laced shoes, high starched collars and layer upon layer of fabric, surely caused discomfort to varying degrees. This illustration (Figure 10.24) of a woman's constrained body gives us some idea of how much these corseted vestments compressed organs and skeleton, preventing harmonious breathing, successive movement along the spine, and other normal quotidian movements.

156 *L'Homme de sport*

Figure 10.23 Nineteenth-century woman.

Source: Drawing by Craig Arteaga-Johnson based on an unattributed photograph of the period.

While Lequesne, Dumont and Carpeaux based their nineteenth-century projects on the study of ancient statuary, examples of the nude human form in movement had already infiltrated the European consciousness by other routes. As early as the 1790s, Emma Lyons [Lady Hamilton] used newly uncovered marbles and bronzes from Pompeii as a source for her unique statue posing performances (Schachenmayr), anticipating the modern dancers

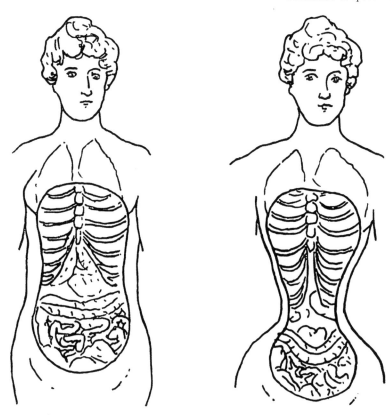

Figure 10.24 Effects of the corset on the body.

Source: Drawings by Craig Arteaga-Johnson from Bernard Rudofsky's *The Unfashionable Human Body*.

(Figures 10.21, 10.29 and 10.30). And, to decorate their already elaborately cluttered residences, wealthy travelers visiting the recently uncovered ruins of Pompeii took home small bronze souvenir replicas of a dancing faun (Figure 10.25), excavated in 1830 (Museum of Classical Archaeology, Cambridge). These immobile figures hinted at vigorous and harmonious movement, bearing witness to the unrealized potential fitfully sleeping along the spines of the bourgeois who collected them.

When Lequesne, Carpeaux and others won the Prix de Rome, the terms of the award required them to sculpt replicas of classical works for export to France. Lequesne, like many before him, fulfilled this requirement to his own educational benefit, as well as for the edification of French citizens who appreciated the commissioned work. This gradual, subterranean influence moved above ground (out of galleries and private homes and onto the streets) when Lequesne's *Faune dansant* found its place in the Luxembourg Gardens, at the edge of one of Paris' major intersections in 1852; when the *Genie of the Bastille* first balanced on his column in 1840; and when Carpeaux's *La Danse*

158 *L'Homme de sport*

Figure 10.25 The Dancing Faun.

Source: An illustration of the statue in the Naples Museum from *Pompeii: Its History, Buildings, and Antiquities* by Thomas H. Dyer (1887).

enlivened one of Paris' most centrally placed, significant new buildings in 1869.

The sculptors, along with Decroux, Bellugue and the American modern dancers influenced by Delsarte, were all concerned with the unimpeded movements of the human body, and naturally adopted the unrestricting garments of the Dress Reform Movement. For example, one scholar believed that Ruth St. Denis'

> greatest debt was to the Delsarte exercises that had developed her naturally flexible spine and taught her such "successive movements" as a jointless arm ripple that she added as a fillip to her routines. She specialized in twists of the torso and the swirl of draperies that became her stock-in-trade.
>
> (Shelton 29)

St. Denis herself wrote, in her article for the first issue of *Denishawn Magazine:*

> Dancing is the natural rhythmic movements of the body that have long been suppressed or distorted, and the desire to dance would be as natural as to eat, or to run, or swim, if our civilization had not in countless ways and for diverse reasons put its ban upon this instinctive and joyous action of the harmonious being. Our formal religions, our crowded cities, our clothes, and our transportation, are largely responsible for the inert mass of humanity that until very lately was encased in collars and corsets. But we are beginning to emerge, to throw off, to demand space to think in and to dance in.
>
> (St. Denis 3)

Not unusually, these "movers," each one, despite the real differences among them, needed space "to think in and to dance in" and free limbs with which to discover and express. They found natural allies along the artistic edges of an increasingly commercial and industrial world. Compare St. Denis' remarks above with Isadora Duncan's praise of Delsarte: "He should receive universal thanks for the bonds he has removed from our constrained members" (Cited in Blair 17). Decroux, too, in a Parisian newspaper article of the 1960s, was credited with tearing the body "loose from the prison of clothes" (Fournier).

Alchemical acting

An image to facilitate the circulation of energy

I studied Delsarte's system with Ted Shawn at Jacob's Pillow in the mid 1960s and corporeal mime with Decroux (1968–1972). Arthur Lessac, in the late 1980s and early 1990s, introduced me to "wheels spinning within wheels"

160 *L'Homme de sport*

(Figure 10.27). In reading (especially Jean-Louis Barrault, who wrote "the human being has always made me think of a tree . . . for man as for the tree, life is: Exchange" [73]) and in my own practice of teaching and performing, I began to imagine "energy" moving through and around the performer. These teachings and influences spontaneously merged in my thinking into a Theory of Alchemical Acting in Copenhagen at the 1996 meeting of ISTA (Eugenio Barba's International School of Theatre Anthropology). There, during Barba's introduction to a lecture demonstration, he spontaneously asked several of us—the invited performers (including some members of ISTA's artistic staff)—to represent, one by one and in whatever way we chose, the word "energy."

On this occasion, I understood more fully Artaud who wrote, "All true alchemists know that the alchemical symbol is a mirage as the theatre is a mirage" (49). Through the imagination, the ordinary human body, with its mundane human experience, transforms base matter into the pure gold of dramatic presence; the actor facilitates a kind of flow, what Barba calls a "play of oppositions" that negotiates "differences of potential."

In reponse to Barba's request, an image suddenly came to me that I was able to describe while performing it: a drawing up of "energy" (something rising—like sap, electricity, steam, water, thought) from a reservoir deep within the earth, that then travels up through the legs. These lines of force wrap around to the sacrum, then trace a return to the front, reaching a point below the navel. From there, the two—now central—rising parallel lines of force continue up along the sternum, lifting the spine. At the top of the sternum, the lines diverge right and left toward each shoulder. At the collarbones (near the base of the neck), the tracing hands turn, palms now facing outward, pulling the lines of force up the sides of the neck. At the base of the skull the hands turn again inward, palms caressing the back of the head as they rise toward the crown. From there, the hands skim forward across the top of the head, at which point they spring abruptly beyond the head to trace the generous front of the circle that now begins its descent. The size of the circle might increase or decrease in order to encompass the audience (Figure 10.26). We could say that this acting stuff or substance (presence), ascends like steam in a high arc above the audience, and falls in an enveloping rain behind them, only to be drawn up once more through the roots of the actor's feet and toward the abdominal furnace. This circulating sphere of movement englobes actor and audience in a synergetic whole, changing the actor's inner and outer movement while communicating directly to the spines of the audience. The energy flows/dances/spirals on and around the sphere created by the body's channeling force and produces a weather system complete with air currents, thunderstorms, lightning, perhaps even tornadoes and hurricanes, buffeting actor and audience alike. This metaphoric meteorology differs from, but links with, the poetic descriptions ("a sunburst between the shoulders") that Decroux chose to

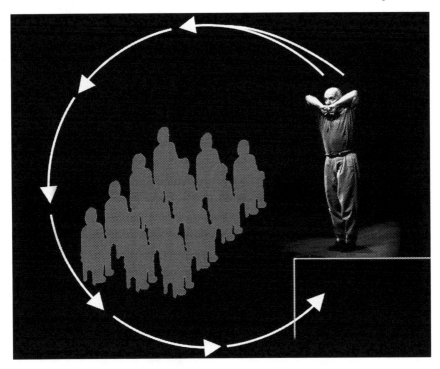

Figure 10.26 The Alchemical Actor.

Source: Eric Culhane's redrawing of a photograph of Thomas Leabhart.

induce the required inner work resulting in the outward form of his exercises as well as his students' improvisations. The "up" and "down"—the inner eruptions or bubbling up as well as the drag or pull in the opposite direction—constituted the embodiment of changing levels of consciousness that formed the essence of Decroux's pedagogy. His dazzling technical "scales" and figures appear mechanical, robotic, without this ever-varying inner song.

Arthur Lessac, in his *Body Wisdom: Use and Training of the Human Body*, discusses "The Body's Personal Space Spheres," which he defines as "the body's 'follow-through energies' and its configured physicality . . . dimensionally controlled body spheres, arcs, wheels, and curves naturally extending into outside, physical living spaces" (Lessac 226–27). This reminds me of the Hebrew prophet Ezekiel's vision, as translated by jazz great Louis Armstrong, "a wheel within a wheel a-rollin' way in the middle of the air" (Figure 10.27). Lessac named the "non-derived, primitive energy states": Radiant, Buoyant,

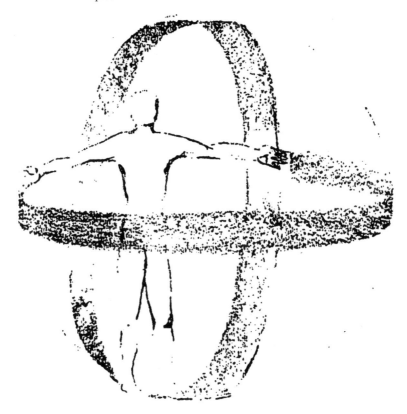

Figure 10.27 "Auditory Space Sphere."

Source: Unattributed drawing from Arthur Lessac's *Body Wisdom*, Second Edition 1990.

Potent and Inter-Involvement (Lessac 34). Similarly, Barba writes of *kerns* and *manis*, *tandava* and *lasya*, Animus and Anima (Barba 64).

Transforming the wheel into a globe, Decroux writes, in *Words on Mime*, that

> we can see the picture of the speaking actor slowly forming, showing him as he should be from the mime point of view: a Greek statue changing shape under a globe. Statuary, which often uses an athlete in action for its model—the discobolus, the antique boxer, the "génie de la Bastille"— has produced a vast number of trunks which differ from each other only by nuance, indiscernible to the undiscerning. So many trunks! . . . The actor must change his statue under his transparent glass globe as a sky changes shape and color.
>
> (1985, 38)

How did Decroux's statue change form? Comparing our work to that of plumbers fitting pipes, Decroux promised that this "tiresome work" would later allow hot steam to circulate, creating actor presence. Decroux, not content to wait for the steam to rise in the cold actor, constructed exercises specifically to achieve this end.

One of them, an arm study named Sea Horse Tail, demonstrates on a practical level how the statue under the glass globe forms and reforms. The trunk inclines to the side so that one arm hangs freely. The biceps relaxes and, from the inside, the actor "plucks the string" of the muscle, making the whole arm quiver. The single pluck multiplies into a series, the slices of relaxation/tension become thinner and thinner, closer together, until the biceps vibrates with an unceasing alternation between tension and relaxation. This vibration raises and lowers the elbow (since the engagement of the biceps bends that joint), even as the lower arm, hanging softly, repeatedly billows away from the body and floats back down. This alternation of rapid and minute impulses, contractions, then generates a steady pulsation through the entire arm. The actor can produce this vibratory movement in the buttocks as well as in the biceps. The variability of the timing of these slices of tension/relaxation produces a different effect: allowing greater space (more time) between a tension/relaxation cycle results not in vibration but in "punctuation" (a single "toc" followed by relaxation) that lifts the sternum (through a contraction in the upper back). Students who try to imitate the external shape fail, looking to effect instead of cause. These keys to energy circulation in corporeal mime provide contrast, color and dynamism to otherwise mechanical movements.

Eugenio Barba's chapter entitled "Energy, or rather, the Thought" in *The Paper Canoe* addresses molding energy (Barba 51) as a sculptor models clay or as Decroux's thought shapes his body from the inside:

> In order to re-shape her/his own energy artificially, the performer must think of it in tangible, visible, audible forms, must picture it, divide it into a scale, withhold it, suspend it in an immobility which acts, guide it, with varying intensities and velocities, through the design of movements, as if through a slalom course.
>
> (Barba 71)

The Theory of Alchemical Acting, yet another way of thinking of energy in a "tangible, visible, audible" form, unearths principles and techniques that dancers, athletes, sculptors and vase painters knew thousands of years ago. In certain periods, people forget and then must rediscover or remember the flow of energy from sacrum to occiput. When they forget, the Delsartes, Decrouxs, Lequesnes and Bellugues remind them. When they remember, they regain what Copeau identified as a golden age of theatre.

Grotowski's "acting that glows" (121) manifests itself in some of the strands we investigated above: in Decroux's *homme de sport* and in Barba's "play of oppositions" and "differences of potential" with which we started this chapter and which we also see in the early days of American modern dance (see Figures 10.28 and 10.29).

164 *L'Homme de sport*

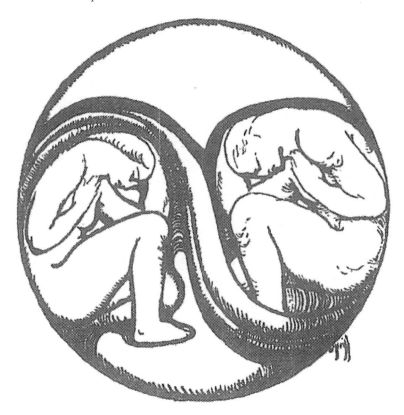

Figure 10.28 Unattributed drawing from the cover of the first issue of *Denishawn Magazine*, 1924.

Source: New York Public Library, Jerome Robbins Dance Division.

Postscript

Artaud brings us back to Decroux and sport

And now taste these words of Antonin Artaud, who knew about bodies and gestures that glow:

> The Actor is an athlete of the heart. . . . All the tricks of wrestling, boxing, the hundred-yard dash, high-jumping, etc., find analogous organic bases in the movement of the passions; they have the same physical points of support. . . . The gifted actor finds by instinct how to tap and radiate certain powers; but he would be astonished indeed if it were revealed to him that these powers, which have their material trajectory by and in the organs, actually exist, for he has never realized they could actually exist.

L'Homme de sport 165

Figure 10.29 Doris Humphrey.
Source: Unattributed photograph, 1924.

To make use of his emotions as a wrestler makes use of his muscles, he has to see the human being as a Double, like the Ka of the Egyptian mummies, like a perpetual specter from which the affective powers radiate.... The belief in a fluid materiality of the soul is indispensable to the actor's craft. To know that a passion is material, that it is subject to the plastic fluctuations of material, makes accessible an empire of passions that extends our sovereignty.... To know that the soul has a corporeal expression permits the actor to unite with this soul from the other side, and to rediscover its being by mathematical analogies.

(Artaud 133–35)

166 *L'Homme de sport*

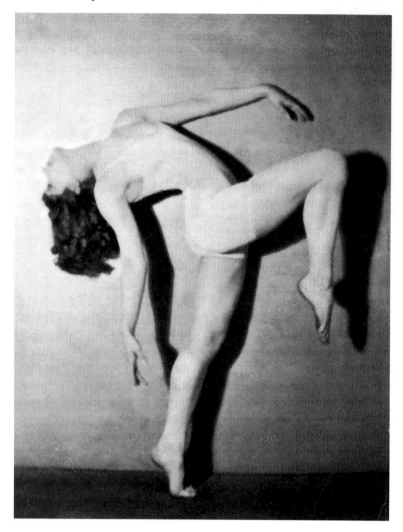

Figure 10.30 Denishawn dancer Jane Sherman (1908–2010).
Source: Photograph by Edwin F. Townsend.

Here Artaud points out the truth he witnessed in Decroux's rigorous, scientific approach to the study of the body, which paradoxically enabled him "to unite with this soul from the other side, and to rediscover its being by mathematical analogies." Artaud recognized the soul's corporeal expression in Decroux's corporeal mime, in particular the Man of Sport that he saw when Barrault performed *Autour d'une mère* in June of 1935 at Charles Dullin's Montmartre Theatre (later the Atelier) in Paris. Artaud writes of

Figure 10.31 As per Decroux's direction, the Washerwoman pauses, then turns toward a sound she thinks she hears. Costume conceived by Decroux and realized by Michèle Renaud–Molnar.

Source: Photo of Thomas Leabhart, copyright Béatrice Helg.

Barrault's acting in this devised performance, but which Barrault identified as Total Theatre (1972, 84):

> A great, young love, a youthful vigor, a spontaneous and lively effervescence flows through the disciplined movements and stylized mathematical

168 *L'Homme de sport*

gestures like the twittering of birds through colonnades of trees in a magically arranged forest. . . . His spectacle demonstrates the irresistible expressiveness of gesture; it victoriously proves the importance of gesture and of movement in space. He restores to theatrical perspective the importance it should never have lost. He fills the stage with emotion and life.

(Artaud 145)

In mentioning "disciplined movements and stylized mathematical gestures," Artaud again recognizes the geometric pathway that Decroux and Barrault followed to rediscover "flow" through their vertebrae, the "thawing" of the statue, restoring "to theatrical perspective the importance it should never have lost."

Acknowledgment

An early version of this article appeared in the 1996 issue of *Mime Journal, Theatre and Sport*, a French translation of which appeared in Patrick Pezin's *Etienne Decroux: Mime Corporel* in 2003. In 2013, 2018 and 2021, the article underwent significant revision.

Notes

1. Franco Ruffini treats the Decroux-Carpentier connection thoroughly in his article in *Incorporated Knowledge, Mime Journal*, 1995.
2. Decroux often lamented in his daily teaching, as he failed repeatedly to hold his balance, that he had invented an art form that required an excellent equilibrium, that he himself did not possess.

Works Cited

Artaud, Antonin (1958) *The Theatre and Its Double*, New York, NY: Grove Press.

Barba, Eugenio, Savarese, Nicola eds. (1991) *A Dictionary of Theatre Anthropology*, New York, NY: Routledge.

Barton, Robert (1989) *Acting Onstage and Off*, Fort Worth, TX: Holt, Rinehart and Winston, Inc.

Barrault, Jean-Louis (1972) *Souvenirs pour demain*, Paris: Editions du Seuil.

——— (1979) "Le corps magnétique" en *Cahiers Renaud Barrault*, Vol. 99. Paris: Gallimard.

Bellugue, Paul (1967) *A propos d' art, de forme et de mouvement*, Paris: Maloine.

Blair, Fredrika (1986) *Isadora*, New York, NY: William Morrow.

Benedetti, Robert (1981) *The Actor at Work*, Englewood Cliffs, NJ: Prentice-Hall.

Boime, Albert (1987) *Hollow Icons: The Politics of Sculpture in Nineteenth- Century France*, Kent, OH: The Kent State University Press.

Caviglioli, François (1962) "Le Mime Decroux part en guerre contre la Pantomime," *Combat*, December 22.

Csikszentmihalyi, Mihaly. (1990). *Flow: The Psychology of Optimal Experience*. New York, NY: Harper & Row, Publishers.

L'Homme de sport 169

Decroux, Etienne (1978) "The Origin of Corporeal Mime" in *Etienne Decroux 80*th *Birthday Issue*. Claremont, CA: Mime Journal.

———— (1985) *Words on Mime*, trans. Mark Piper. Claremont, CA: Mime Journal.

Delaumosne, M. L'Abbé and Arnaud, Angélique (1893) *The Delsarte System of Oratory*, New York, NY: Edgar S. Werner.

Fournier, C. (2001) "For Love of Human Statuary, A Man Decides to be Silent" in *An Etienne Decroux Album*, Claremont, CA: Mime Journal.

Fusco, Peter and Janson, H.W. (1980) *The Romantics to Rodin*, Los Angeles, CA: The Los Angeles County Museum of Art.

Grotowski, Jerzy (2002) *Towards a Poor Theatre*, New York, NY: Routledge.

Ionesco, Eugene (1964) *Notes and Counter Notes: Writings on the Theatre*, New York, NY: Grove Press.

Leabhart, Thomas, ed (1978) *Etienne Decroux Eightieth Birthday Issue, Mime Journal*, Allendale, MI: Grand Valley State Colleges.

———— (1995) "The Mask as Shamanic Tool in the Theatre Training of Jacques Copeau," *Incorporated Knowledge*, Claremont, CA: Mime Journal.

———— (2005) "Misunderstanding Delsarte (and Preserving the Cherries)," *Essays on François Delsarte*, Claremont, CA: Mime Journal.

———— (2019) *Etienne Decroux*, 2nd Ed, Oxon: Routledge.

Lessac, Arthur (1990) *Body Wisdom: The Use and Training of the Human Body*, 2nd Ed, San Bernardino, CA: L.I.P. Co.

———— (1996) Leabhart conversation with Arthur Lessac in Los Angeles, March.

Porte, Alain (1992) *François Delsarte: Une Anthologie*, Paris: Editions IPMC.

St. Denis, Ruth and Shawn, Ted eds. (1924–25). *The Denishawn Magazine*, vol. I, no. 1, New York, NY: Denishawn, Ruth St. Denis and Ted Shawn School of Dancing and its Related Arts.

Schachenmayr, V. (1997) *Emma Lyon, the Attitude, and Goethean Performance*. New Theatre Quarterly, Vol. 13 (49). doi: 10.1017/S0266464X00010757, Cambridge: University Press.

Schoeny, M. (2000, April 14). *Reforming Fashion, 1850-1914: Politics, Health, and Art*. Historic Costume & Textiles Collection. https://costume.osu.edu/2000/04/14/reforming-fashion-1850-1914-politics-health-and-art/.

Shelton, Suzanne (1981) *Divine Dancer*, Garden City, CA: Doubleday & Company, Inc.

Stebbins, Genevieve (1977) *Delsarte System of Expression*, 6th ed, New York, NY: Dance Horizons. (reprint of 1902 edition published NY: Edgar S. Werner Publishing and Supply Company, Inc.)

Museum of Classical Archaeology, Cambridge. (n.d.). *Dancing Faun*. Museum of Classical Archaeology Databases. http://museum.classics.cam.ac.uk/collections/casts/dancing-faun.

Index

Note: Page numbers in *italics* denote figures. Page numbers of the form XnY denote footnote Y on page X.

absence/presence 12, 24, 26–7, 44–7, 81–4, 118, 121; *dédoublement* [dual personality] 91
Acocella, Joan 55
actor-mannequin 120; *see also* Kuleshov, Lev
Alaniz, Leela 50n2
Alchemical acting 126, 159–63
Alessi, Rino 93
Alvin Ailey Dance Company 96
anarchism vii, 7, 16, 33, 39, 133
"Ancient Combat" 11, 126
Angkor Wat Buddha Statues 3, 81, 96, 116, 131
animal observation 20–7
Appia, Adolphe 84
Armstrong, Louis 161
Arnaud, Angélique 146, 148
Artaud, Antonin 3, 5, 13, 84, 126, 160, 164–8
Astier, Marie-Bénédicte 53
Atmos actor 76
Atmos clock 76
Autour d'une mére 166; *see also* Barrault, Jean-Louis
axis mundi 64, 78n3, 87–8

ballet 7–9, 63, 67, 70–1, 115, 119, 124, 141, 154
Barba, Eugenio 4, 16, 22, 69, 95, 126–7, 136, 160–4; "pre-expressivity" 65, 69
bare stage 8, 97, 120
Barrault, Jean-Louis ix, 3–4, 8, 12, 24–6, 59–60, 119, 126, 160, 166–8
Barton, Robert 124
Batchelder, John Davis 101
Baudelaire, Charles 33, 82

Beckett, Samuel 7
Beckford, Jaqui 40
The Bells 102–5, 107
Bellugue, Paul 125, 153–5, 159, 163
Benedetti, Robert 124
Bentley, Eric viii, ix, 9–10, 102
Bing-Copeau School *see* l'Ecole du Vieux Colombier
Bing, Suzanne x, 3, 5, 8, 17, 20–2, 26–7, 67, 80, 85, 91–2, 95–7, 110, 116
Blair, Fredrika 159
Blake, William 43–4
Bogart, Anne 3–4
Boime, Albert 148
Booth, Michael R. 103
Boulogne-Billancourt 37, 39, 52, 81, 94–5, 116
Brecht, Bertold 33
Broadway 63, 125
Brodribb, John Henry *see* Irving, Henry
Brook, Peter 19, 22, 77–8, 96
The Brothers Karamazov see Les Frères Karamazov
Bull Tamer see Mignon, Leon
Bunier, Luis-Otavio 96
Bunraku viii, 42–3, 49

C-curve 58, 71–4, 126–30, 136, 161; *see also* counterweights; Lessac, Arthur; Turtle Man
Cafferra, Séverin 139–40
Carné, Marcel *see Les Enfants du Paradis*
Carpeaux, Jean-Baptiste 148, 151, *154*, 154–7
"The Carpenter" 11, 13, 59–60, *128*, *132*, 133, *141*, 135

Index 171

Carpentier, Georges 124, 130, *134*, 168n1
Cartellier 149
Cathedral of Notre Dame 77
Caviglioli, François 131
Cesariano, Cesare *130*
Cézan, Claude 90
Chakras 52, 77
Champoiseau, Charles 52
Chaplin, Charlie 112–13, 118, 121
Charles I 102, 106
Charcot, Jean-Martin 105
Children of Paradise see Les enfants du paradis
Clark, Kenneth 53, 136
Cole, David 80, 84–91, 93
commedia dell'arte 2, 58, 69, 83, 86, 93, 107, 120
Copeau, Jacques x, 3, 5, 8–9, 33, 58, 81–97, 107–12, 115–16, 120, 134, 164; animal observation 19–27; journals 23–7; *La Maison Natale* 92; *Le Miracle du pain doré* 93; *Le Petit Pauvre* 94; Marie-Hélène (daughter) 110; *Santa Uliva* 93
counterweights 13, 25, 31, 58, 68–73, 74, 78, 125, 128–9, 134–8; jumping to fall on the head 69, 71–2; re-establishment of two elements on the oblique 69–70; removing the support 69, 73–4; wool carding machine 69, 72–3
Craig, Edward Gordon vii, viii, 3–5, 15, 33, 40–50, 62, 84–5, 99–101, 103–4, 106, 109, 112, 115, 117, 119–21; Arena Goldoni 85, 109; Daphne (daughter) 40, 45, 115; *see also* Übermarionette
Csikszentmihalyi, Mihaly 81, 125
Cubism 12, 113, 117, 120
Cullberg, Birgit 7

da Vinci, Leonardo 131
Dada 44
Dasté, Jean 21, 83, 85–6, 88–91, 93
Dasté, Marie-Hélène 89, 93, 110
Davenport Brothers 100
de Billy, Madame 37–8
death masks 101, 107, 114, 116, 121n1
Deburau, Charles 140
Deburau, Jean-Gaspard 140
Decroux, Maximilien 13, 33, 40, 61, 92–3
Decroux, Suzanne 16, 29–31, 33, 37–8, 61–2
Degrees of Inclination for the Pelvis *57–8*
Delaumosne 146–7
Delsarte, François 33, 64–5, 125, 146–9, 155, 159, 163
Dench, Judi 80

Denishawn Magazine 159, *164*; Sherman, Jane *166*
départ brusque 70
dervish 12, 44, 49, 52, 63, 67
Descartes, Rene 83
Dickens, Charles 102
Diderot, Denis 89
"Direct Descent" 14; *see also* "Indirect Descent"
Dorcy, Jean 24, 60, 76, 83, 86–8, 91, 110, 115–16
Dress Reform Movement 121n4, 125–6, 146, 155, 159
Dullin, Charles 5, 12, 33, 40, 59, 83, 89–90, 109, 166; Atelier Theatre 59, 119, 126, 166
Dumont, Auguste: Dumont, Jacques-Edme (father) 149; *Genius of Liberty* 148–9, *152*, 156
Duncan, Isadora 121n4, 144, 146, 155, 159
Duras, Marguerite 13
Duse, Eleanora 110–3, 120, 121
dynamo-rhythm 19, 34, 42, 45, 47, 50, 104; *see also* muscular respiration; vibratory quality

Egypt, ancient 14, 41, 43, 165
Ek, Anders 7
Ek, Mats 7
Elizabethan Theatre 58, 83
enchaînements 9, 21, 58, 104
Epstein, Alvin 61
Epstein, Mark 61
Études 9, 56, 57–8, 68, 75, 95; The Extensor 128, 129; Sea Horse Tail 9, 21, 163

the face 2–3, 34, 53, 55, 71, 73, 75, 85–6, 87, 99, 109, 111, 114–16, 118, 120, 121, 127, 131–2
"The Factory" 13, 16n1
Faraday, Michael 102
Faulkner, William 13
Faust 101–2
Fields, W.C. 19
First World War 84, 68
Fitzgerald, F. Scott 44
flamenco 12, 49, 63
Fournier, Christiane 115, 159
Frackers, William 102
Fratellini Brothers 23–4
Freemasonry 101–2
Freud, Sigmund 105
Frondon, Jean-Michel 17

172 *Index*

Fuller, Loie 55–6
Fusco, Peter 149

Gabin, Jean 12
Galli, Yvonne 88
German Occupation 55
Getty Villa Museum 136, 140, 144
Giacometti, Alberto 63
Gide, André 87, 92
Golden Ages of Theatre 58, 83, 107,
  120, 164
Gontard, Denis 8
Goodall, Jane 100, 102, 121n2
Graham, Martha 52
Granville-Barker, Harley 92
Greek, ancient 2, 14, 41, 45, 52–3, 55, 58,
  83, 86, 107, 110, 120, 142–3, 162
Grossman, Harvey 45, 115
Grotowski, Jerzy 1, 12–13, 27n1, 48,
  50, 51n7, 52, 64, 67, 76, 78n3, 80, 90,
  96, 97n1, 121, 147, 164; Principle of
  Induction 48, 76
Guyon, Eliane 13, 40

ham acting 85, 109–10; *cabotinage* 21, 27, 95
the hands 11, 41, 53, 55, 86, 113–14,
  116–17, 132, 140
Handspring Puppet Company 43
Harmonic Gymnastics 146
Harrison, William H. 105
Haussmann, Georges-Eugène 148
Hiturelde, Madame 38
Homme de Salon 35
Homme de Sport (Man of Sport) 35, 124–6,
  136, 153, 155, 163, 166
Hood, Thomas 101
Hugo, Victor 33, 82, 119
Humphrey, Doris 64, *165*
Hybner, Boris 1

illud tempus 84, 87, 89–90, 93
improvisation (corporeal mime) viii, 6,
  11, 18–21, 24, 26–7, 32–6, 38, 51n8, 67,
  77, 80–1, 83–4, 87, 91–2, 95, 107, 161
"Indirect Descent" 14; *see also* "Direct
  Descent"
inter-spatial displacement 64, 68, 76, 77
intra-corporeal movement 64, 68, 75
Ionesco, Eugène 124
Irving, Henry 5, 45–6, 48, 51, 99–107,
  112–14, 116–17, 120–1
International School of Theatre
  Anthropology (ISTA) 4, 44, 134, 160;
  see also Barba, Eugenio

Jabloňová panna (The Apple Maiden)
  see Pojar, Břetislav
Jacob (biblical) 76, 78–9
Jacob's Ladder 64
Jacob's Pillow 159
Jaeger-LeCoultre 76
Janson, H.W. 149
Jaques-Dalcroze, Emile 84, 109
Jarry, Alfred 84
Johnstone, Keith 96
Jones, Basil *see* Handspring Puppet
  Company
Jouvet, Louis 3, 5, 12, 33, 41
Joyce, James 13

kantan 8, 17, 92–3; *see also* Bing, Suzanne
kata 3–5, 64, 121
King, Eleanor 7
King Kong 62–3
Kohler, Adrian *see* Handspring Puppet
  Company
Komparu, Kunio 2–5
Kuleshov, Lev 19, 117–21; The Kuleshov
  Effect 118

La Danse see Carpeaux, Jean-Baptiste
Laban, Rudolf 13
L'Affaire est dans le sac 119
Lange, Jessica *see King Kong*
Le Boeuf, Patrick 42
le diable au corps see Voltaire
Le Gallienne, Eva 112
Lebreton, Yves 61
l'Ecole du Vieux Colombier 8, 17, 19, 21,
  23, 24, 26, 32, 40, 45, 68, 84, 87, 88,
  91, 92, 97, 107, 111, 115–16, 126
Lecoq, Jacques 13, 21, 69
"The Legend of Three Ducats" 82
Leigh, Barbara Kusler 8–9, 91–2, 110
Lequesne, Eugène-Louis: *The Dancing
  Faun* 148–50, 157
Les Frères Karamazov 83, 89, 90
Les enfants du paradis ix, 12, 57, 119, 140
Lessac, Arthur 127–8, 159, 161–2
Lifar, Serge 119; *see also* ballet
Little Soldiers 11, 118
Loui, Annie 61
Louvre Museum 14, 52, 149
"Love Duet" 11, 35–6, 117
Lyons, Emma (Lady Hamilton) 156

ma 4–5; *see also* Salz, Jonah
MacKaye, James Steele 65, 146
Macready, William C. 102

Magritte, René 132, *135*
Maillol, Aristide 14, 147
Mallarmé 62–3
Marceau, Marcel 40, 61
Marey, Etienne-Jules 27n2
marionette 4, 15–16, 19, 21, 23–6, 32, 40, 42, 44–50, 63, 67, 75, 78, 99, 103, 114, 117, 119–21
Marque, Albert 110
Martinez, Ariane ix
mask 1–3, 6, 8, 10, 15, 17, 19, 21, 23, 26, 47, 51n6, 76, 81, 83–91, 94–7, 99–101, 106, 107–18, 121n1, 131–2
masked improvisation 8, 91, 97, 126, 132; *see also* improvisation (corporeal mime); mask
"Meditation" 11
Mesmer, Franz Anton 105
mesmerism 100–6, 121n2
Meyerhold, Vsevolod 15
Michelangelo 49, 53
Mignon, Leon 62
mime corporel 97, 110
"The Mischievous Spirit" 13; *see also* Decroux, Maximilien
Mobile Statuary *see statuaire mobile*
Morgan, Michèle 12
Mori, Masahiro 45
movement phrases *see enchaînements*
Munroe, Jan 35–6
muscular respiration 12, 34, 45, 47, 49, 51n5, 100
Musée Guimet 81, 96, 97n2, 116, 121; *see also* Angkor Wat Buddha Statues
Muybridge, Eadweard 27n2

Nadar 140
Nénette 17–20, 26–7
Noakes, Richard 105
noh 1–3, 5, 8, 12, 17, 49, 58, 63, 67, 70, 81, 83, 91–3, 106–7, 116, 120
Novelli, Ermete 109
Noyes, Zoe 10

"Offering the First Grapefruit of the Season to the God" 14
Olympic Games 55, 144
Opéra Garnier 148, 151, 155
organicity 4–5, 26, 68–9, 79, 121; *see also* International School of Theatre Anthropology (ISTA)

pantomime ix, 1, 13, 15, 25, 41, 53–5, 57, 73–5, 97, 113–14, 116–17, 132–3, 139–40
the pearl metaphor *see* de Billy, Madame

Péguy, Charles 82
Pezin, Patrick 32, 114–19
Philibert, Nicolas *see Nénette*
Pierrot 139–40
Pinok and Matho ix
Piper, Mark 32, 38
Pitt, Leonard 37
play of oppositions 127, 160, 163
Pointillism 48–9, 113
Pojar, Břetislav 1–2
Polívka, Bolislav 1
Pompeii 55, 156–7, *158*
Ponge, Francis 12–13
Porte, Alain 146
Prague Puppet Museum 1, 2, 5
Prénat, Jacques 85–6
Principle of Induction *see* Grotowski, Jerzy
"promontory" 58–9
puppet viii, ix, 1–3, 5, 15, 40, 41–7, 50, 51n3, 67–8, 101, 120

Raimu 12, 119
The Rape see Magritte, René
Read, Michael 100–1
Renaud, Madeleine 131
Renaud-Molnar, Michèle 129, 132–3, 141
Richards, Thomas 64
Rimbaud, Arthur 84
Riskin, Jessica 105
"The River" *see* Maillol, Aristide
Rodin, Auguste 14, 55, 111, 147; Musée Rodin 26–7
Roman, ancient 14, 58, 138, 140
Rudlin, John 94, 108, 110, 112, 116
Ruffini, Franco 168
Ruyter, Nancy Lee Chalfa 147

Saint Francis 94
Saint-Denis, Michel 18, 21, 83, 96, 107–8
Saint-Exupéry, Antoine de 44
Salter, Denis 103, 106
Salz, Jonah 4
Sampson, Joseph 82–3, 94
sats 122, 126; *see also* Barba, Eugenio
Savonarola see Alessi, Rino
Saül 87
scales 25, 49–50
Schachenmayr, Volker 156
Schechner, Richard 91
Schoeny, Marlise 125
"The Sculptor" 11
Segal, William 106–7
Shakers 52, 63
Shamanism 8, 49, 91, 93–6, 104
Shawn, Ted 146, 159

174 *Index*

Shelton, Suzanne 159
Shiva Nataraja 149, 151
Sklar, Deidre 87, 96
Smith, Anna Deavere 71
socialism 7, 33, 133
The Spiritualist 105
Spoor, Will 51n6
St. Denis, Ruth 141, 144, 146, 159
Stages of Consciousness 75
Stanislavsky 33–4, 78n3, 91, 124
statuaire mobile 14, 55–6, 147
"The Statue" 13, 126
Stebbins, Genevieve 146, 148–9
Stoker, Bram 102–6
Symbolist movement 5, 41, 55
Symons, Arthur 110–3

"Taharqa offering to Falcon-god
  Hemen" 14
taiko 2; *see also* Komparu, Kunio
Taylor, Nel 13
Terry, Ellen 122
The Theatrical Event see Cole, David
The Thinker 35–6, 80–1; Pure Thought
  35, 81
Théâtre du Vieux Colombier 17, 92; *see
  also* l'Ecole du Vieux Colombier
Théâtre Renauld-Barrault 95
Tomaszewski, Henryk 1
Toole, J.L. 100–1
Total Theatre 167; *see also* Barrault,
  Jean-Louis
Touchard, Pierre-Aimé 94
tréteau nu 8; *see also* bare stage
Trnka, Jiří 2
the trunk ix, 25, 34, 49, 53–9, 65, 68–70,
  72–3, 116, 126–8, 132–3, 136, 140–1,
  148, 162
Turba, Ctibor 1
Turtle Man 74, 78

Übermarionette viii, 4, 40–50, 99, 120;
  see also Craig, Edward Gordon
Udaka, Michishige 81; *see also* noh
"uncanny valley" *see* Mori, Masahiro

Veinstein, André 114
Verry, Pierre 40
vertical pelvis 57–8
vibratory quality 12, 19, 21–2, 34, 42,
  47–9, 52, 64, 68, 76–7, 106, 121, 163;
  micro-movement 19, 21, 34, 56, 121,
  127; pre-movement 34, 64, 68, 75
Viollet-Le-Duc 78n6
Volkonsky, Prince Sergei Mikhailovitch 147
Voltaire 101

Walks 33, 50, 58, 68; Nazism 56; Walk of
  the Poet 56
"The Washerwoman" 11, 133–4, 167
"wet drapery" 53
William the Silent 29, 63
Winged Victory of Samothrace 37, 52–4,
  56, 58
Wolfe, Matt 80
Wolliaston, Elsa 96
Woman of Paris 118
Wooden Actor ix, 1, 4–5, 43–5, 49–50,
  67, 99; *see also* marionette; puppet;
  Übermarionette
Woolf, Virginia 13
Words on Mime (Paroles sur le mime) 40, 61,
  95, 97n4, 115, 118, 139, 147, 162
Wroclaw Pantomime Theatre *see*
  Tomaszewski, Henryk
Wylie-Marques, Katherine 93

Zarilli, Phillip 91
Zeami 2; *see also* noh
"the zone" 75, 81, 125; *see also*
  Csikszentmihalyi, Mihaly

Printed in the United States
by Baker & Taylor Publisher Services